THE HISTORY OF
ESPIONAGE

THE SECRET WORLD OF SPYCRAFT, SABOTAGE AND POST-TRUTH PROPAGANDA

ERNEST VOLKMAN

THIS IS A CARLTON BOOK

This edition published by Carlton Books Limited 2019
20 Mortimer Street
London W1T 3JW

ISBN 978-1-78739-257-1

Project Editor: Ross Hamilton
Project Art Direction: Natasha Le Coultre
Design: Emma Wicks
Picture Research: Steve Behan
Production: Peter Hinton

Printed in Dubai

THE HISTORY OF
ESPIONAGE

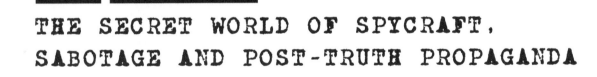

THE SECRET WORLD OF SPYCRAFT, SABOTAGE AND POST-TRUTH PROPAGANDA

ERNEST VOLKMAN

CARLTON
BOOKS

CONTENTS

INTRODUCTION

The Duke of
Wellington was once asked what he
did during the long, lonely hours
of the night before a major battle
was to due take place.

THE OTHER SIDE OF THE HILL

He could not sleep, the Duke replied, because his mind was obsessed with one question. A question he asked himself over and over: "What's on the other side of the hill?"

No one has ever come up with a better summation of the intelligence process, the formal name for what is more popularly known as espionage or spying (or the modern euphemism, 'intelligence collection'). Whatever the name, the process has been an integral part of human existence since early Homo sapiens first became concerned about the strength and intentions of neighboring clans and tribes. Espionage was born at the same time as another vital component in the history of humankind emerged, armed struggle.

As long as humans make war against each other, espionage is vital, for it involves fundamental questions. What are enemies or potential enemies planning to do? What are their capabilities? What are the dangers? How imminent are those dangers? Espionage, often called 'the world's second oldest profession', became the process by which those questions are answered.

Defined legally, espionage is the act of obtaining the military, political, economic and other secret information of a nation-state by the use of spies, theft, monitoring or other means. It is regarded as a serious crime in every nation, almost universally punishable by death. The Geneva Convention, which regulates the conduct of war, specifically exempts spies from the definition of 'lawful combatant'. Any combatant who 'acts in disguise' can be 'punished with trial', traditionally interpreted to mean a captured spy can be shot out of hand. However, a combatant in uniform who is spying is regarded as conducting reconnaissance, a legitimate military objective, and thus must be treated as a prisoner of war if captured.

Espionage is the process of gathering intelligence, which should be distinguished from information. Basically, intelligence can be broadly defined as processed information. The process is roughly similar to the one that goes on each day inside a newspaper office. A large amount of information of varying reliability flows in there to be checked, digested, analyzed and processed into a package that the editors believe represents a reasonably complete report on the important

or entertaining events of the day. In intelligence agencies, the same process is often called 'intellection', by which is meant the processing of collected information – called 'raw intelligence' – into conclusions called 'finished intelligence'. These conclusions are then given to policymakers – known as 'users' or 'customers' in intelligence jargon – who are supposed to make important decisions based on them.

Traditionally, intelligence functions on three levels:

Strategic: The capabilities and intentions of foreign countries, for example, whether a nation is covertly developing nuclear weapons and what it intends to do with such weapons once developed.

Tactical: Operational intelligence, such as how many tanks another nation has or how many men it has under arms.

Counterintelligence: Protection of a nation's secrets from the espionage operations of other nations.

Like all human activity, the intelligence process is subject to the vagaries of human beings. How intelligence judgments are received rests largely on the confidence of the customers in the spies providing the judgments and often, more significantly, on the quality and reliability of the intelligence itself. It is this intellection process, involving important questions of confidence and reliability, which is the tricky part. The process is constantly affected by the biases of the people who make the judgments, the predilections of the customers and more often than not a sheer inability to make solid deductions because of a lack of complete information. In that case, intelligence judgments tend to become hedged and indefinite. Witness this super-cautionary conclusion in a report by American military intelligence in 1965: "These basic characteristics of uncertainty will almost certainly continue to be operationally significant for the foreseeable future."

Even apparently infallible intelligence is seldom actually

infallible. In World War II, the British code-breaking operation known as ULTRA allowed the Allies to read virtually all of the German High Command's secret radio traffic. By late 1944, having provided a priceless advantage in anticipating and defeating German plans, ULTRA was regarded as an intelligence paragon, an unfailing source of intelligence on the next German moves. In other words, it was the perfect spy.

However, the Allied commanders who came to rely on ULTRA forgot that it read only the decisions and orders dispatched via encrypted radio signals using the Enigma code machine. It could not detect verbal orders, nor could it read any information sent by telephone over secure land lines. Therefore, when Adolf Hitler in the winter of 1944 decided on an all-out offensive in the West and used only land lines to dispatch his attack orders, ULTRA could provide no warning. The result was the Battle of the Bulge, a near-disaster for the Allies.

The Battle of the Bulge incident is just one of many such intelligence failures throughout history. It underscores the fact that so long as espionage is conducted by humans, it is subject to human foibles: preconceptions, biases, bureaucratic politics and often simple blindness. In the winter of 1950, American intelligence concluded that

if General Douglas MacArthur's forces moved toward the Yalu River in North Korea, the Chinese would certainly intervene militarily. It was not an especially difficult conclusion to reach since the Chinese had used every diplomatic channel in existence to convey a warning of intervention. However, MacArthur was convinced that the Chinese would not invade North Korea for fear of superior American military power. "It would be the greatest slaughter," he confidently told President Truman and refused to believe the intelligence. His own spies could find no indication of a Chinese military presence in North Korea – no supply dumps, no radio signals ordering unit movements, no troop concentrations and no fires to keep soldiers warm in the subzero Korean cold.

However, what MacArthur did not know was that the Chinese, aware of which telltale clues MacArthur's spies looked for, had taken elaborate efforts to make their army invisible. The Chinese troops were subject to rigid march discipline, ordered to march only at night and

ABOVE: CIA headquarters in Langley, Virginia. For many years a sign on a highway marking the exit to the building read, "Department of Roads" – a clumsy attempt to hide the sprawling complex.

hide in buildings during the day, out of sight of American reconnaissance planes. There were no radios below regimental level, thus defeating the standard espionage technique of determining the locations of units by their radio signals. Troops were strictly forbidden to light any fires, another way to defeat aerial reconnaissance. Troops were also only given two weeks' rations, with no recourse to supply dumps. As a result, more than 200,000 Chinese troops took up attack positions in North Korea, detected only when they fell upon MacArthur's unprepared forces and inflicted a terrible defeat.

In the popular conception, such myopia is assumed to be a feature of totalitarian societies, where rigidly-enforced belief systems tend to spawn narrow thinking imposed from above or no thinking at all. The classic example of such a totalitarian mindset is Joseph Stalin's incredible blindness in 1941, when his spies – undeniably the best in the world – sent detailed, unequivocal intelligence that Nazi Germany was about to invade the Soviet Union. Stalin simply refused to believe any of it, contemptuously scrawling across one report that gave the precise date and time of the invasion, "British provocation". He was convinced that Hitler would not invade and no amount of intelligence was about to change his mind. Predictably, the heads of his intelligence apparatus dutifully fell into line, telling their supreme leader he was undoubtedly right and the spies passing on such 'provocations' would be suitably punished. We can also consider the case of the junior officer on the German General Staff in 1914 who had the temerity to send a memo to General Helmuth von Moltke, supreme commander of the German armies. He advocated the creation of an economic intelligence unit, arguing that it would be a long war in which economics would play a vital role; the nation with the best economic resources would win. Von Moltke returned the memo unread with the waspish comment, "Don't bother me with economics. I am busy conducting a war." Three years later, the German war economy collapsed.

Democracies, with their systems of checks and balances and reputation for open-mindedness, would appear at first glance to be less subject to this kind of narrow thinking imposed from above. However, democratic leaders are humans too and make very human mistakes. Often, their blindness is related to politics. In 1960, Senator John F. Kennedy, the Democratic candidate for President of the United States, was effectively using the 'missile gap' issue to bludgeon the Republicans. The so-called gap stemmed from the shock of the 1957 launch of Sputnik by a Soviet rocket with intercontinental range and public boasts by Soviet Premier Nikita Khrushchev of a huge arsenal of such rockets so accurate, they could "hit a fly in space". Kennedy sought to take political advantage of a widespread public perception that the U.S. was badly lagging behind the Soviet Union in ICBMs by harping on about the missile gap, despite claims by then-President Eisenhower that the USA was comfortably ahead in the arms race.

Concerned that talk of a missile gap would undermine public confidence in American military superiority over the Soviets, Eisenhower ordered the CIA to give candidate Kennedy a top-secret briefing. At that briefing, Kennedy was ushered into America's greatest intelligence secret – U-2 spy planes overflying the Soviet Union had photographed every important Soviet military installation. It was an operation which proved the Russians had deployed only a small number of missiles, far fewer than the American arsenal. Kennedy expressed his admiration for this espionage feat, then delivered a speech two days later berating the Eisenhower-Nixon administration for allowing a missile gap that endangered American national security. As Kennedy conceded privately, the missile gap was a myth, but it was also too good to pass up as a campaign issue in a tight race.

With the dawning of the Information Age, there was no end of experts who predicted that advanced technology, most of it born from the microchip, would revolutionize intelligence. They believed spies in the traditional sense

ABOVE: A Native American scout carrying out the most basic function of all intelligence – reconnaissance.

ABOVE: James Bond as portrayed by Sean Connery. The popular perception of what a spy looks like.

would largely become obsolete as increasingly sophisticated machines would take over most of the work of intelligence collection. The idea was that espionage would become largely scientific and thus invulnerable to human error. Satellites capable of reading a license plate from 25,000 miles up, 'ferret' technology that could vacuum millions of electronic communications in the blink of an eye and supercomputers that could perform billions of computations a second would provide objective, incontrovertible intelligence. This mountain of raw data would be processed by vast, sprawling organizations staffed with highly-trained minds that would produce detailed, irrefutable, on-time intelligence.

However, it hasn't worked out that way. The theorists forgot that no amount of science can remove human bias, self-deception and the very human tendency to disbelieve uncomfortable truths. Moreover, there are limits to the processing abilities of the human mind. Like every other field of human endeavor, intelligence is drowning in oceans of information that are beyond human capacity to absorb and interpret. Each day, the data flowing into the average

government agency is greater than all documents produced during the first one hundred years of printing. Many intelligence professionals like to call it the 'Astor Syndrome', after Lady Astor, who reputedly quipped while aboard the Titanic: "I asked for a glass of ice water, but this is ridiculous."

Despite all the expensive technology, modern espionage is still marked with colossal error, usually attributable to human faults. This explains why American intelligence, despite its dazzling technology and a budget of billions of dollars, somehow came to believe that there was a vast arsenal of weapons of mass destruction in Iraq, when in fact none existed. It also explains why the Soviet Union's KGB, the world's largest spy agency, somehow missed the obvious fact that an invasion of Afghanistan would ignite a revolt by Muslims.

All of which means that espionage, however flawed, will remain a part of human existence for as long as there are humans. Some 200 years after the Duke of Wellington spent sleepless nights in his tent, they will still be obsessed with finding out what's on the other side of the hill.

LEFT: A Wehrmacht soldier peers across the English Channel in 1941, toward Germany's deadliest enemy — an impenetrable mystery to German intelligence.

EYELESS
IN GAZA

From their watchtowers atop the fortress of Masada, the sentries gazed out into the clear desert air of the Judean wilderness that allowed them to see for miles.

ABOVE: The ruins of Masada. Believed by its Zealot defenders to be impregnable, it was destroyed in a Roman siege in 72 CE that utilized superior intelligence.

LEFT: A Sumerian tablet of 1500 BCE. The first known secret communication in history, it details the formula for making porcelain, a Sumerian monopoly, in one of the earliest ciphers.

Just after dawn that spring day in 73 CE, they spotted in the distance a large cloud of dust heading directly toward them, signaling the approach of a large body of men. They cried out the alarm: "Romans!"

The nearly 1,000 Israelites in the fortress near the Dead Sea were expecting this event ever since they had fled from Jerusalem and holed up in Masada some weeks before. They were people of a sect called Zealots, the most fanatical among the Judean revolutionaries who seven years before had begun an armed revolt against the Roman occupiers of their ancient land. One by one, the revolutionary bands had been hunted down and slaughtered. Now, all that remained of the revolutionary movement was this last group of Zealots. They knew the Romans would inevitably come after them, for they had been using the fortress as a base for raids against Roman occupying forces. They had no illusions about what would happen if the Romans were to succeed in capturing the fortress – death or enslavement.

However, the leaders of the Zealots were convinced they could actually defeat the Romans, a conviction that had much to do with Masada itself. Constructed decades before by Herod, it represented the state of the art in Middle East fortifications. Sited atop a plateau of sheer cliffs 1,700 feet high, with a 20-foot-high wall several feet thick, it had deep cisterns that provided a near-infinite supply of water, along with huge food storehouses. It also had armories for the manufacture of swords, arrows and spears. There was no doubt among the Zealots – Masada could not be taken.

In that moment, they were doomed, for the Romans had no intention of fighting the way the Zealots assumed they would. They would not attack with soldiers, some with scaling ladders, clawing their way up the cliffs toward the wall, there to be picked off by spears, arrows and the Zealots' most feared weapon, the stone sling made famous by the biblical account of David's slaying of Goliath. Tragically for the Zealots, their assumptions were just that – assumptions. They had not bothered to send any spies to find out anything about their enemies – how many of them there were, what kind of weapons they had and, above all, how they planned to besiege Masada. Convinced that Masada was impregnable and that their great god Yaweh would make them invincible, they saw no need for spies.

On the other side, General Flavius Silva, commander of the Tenth Legion, did not make that mistake. For months, a battalion of his spies had given him reports on every aspect of the Zealots, most importantly exactly how many of them were holed up in Masada and their armaments. They also provided detailed intelligence on Masada itself, from which Silva derived an in-depth understanding of the fortress' defenses and how he would defeat them.

What happened next unfolded precisely as Silva planned. His Tenth Legion, 5,000 men, set up camp on the valley floor below Masada. For months, the legionnaires made no move against the fortress. Instead, the defenders saw several men walking around the cliffs, making careful measurements. Poor farmers and peasants, the Zealots could not have guessed that the men were Greek mathematicians on Silva's staff determining the best spot to build a ramp up the plateau cliff. Then several thousand Jewish slaves, captured by Silva during his destruction of Jerusalem, were set to work under whip and cudgel building a 265-foot-long earthen ramp up the cliffs. Meanwhile, Roman engineers assembled a two-storey-high siege machine with a projecting battering ram several feet thick. The engineers also began assembling several strange contraptions the Zealots had never seen – torsion-engine artillery, called ballistae, that fired iron bolts or round stones.

Finally, the Romans went on the attack. Foot by foot, as the ramp was constructed, the siege machine was wheeled upward toward the fortress. When it came within range, the Zealots fired their arrows, but discovered that the machine had been encased in tin, deflecting all missiles. Atop the machine, the Romans had positioned several ballistae that fired volleys of stones, sweeping defenders off the wall. The siege engine eventually reached the wall, which crumbled under repeated blows of the battering ram. Roman assault teams raced through the gaps and within minutes, the Zealots' position was hopeless. With a last, anguished lamentation, they committed mass suicide, drawing lots to determine in what order they would murder each other.

The senior commander was the last, impaling himself on his sword after slaying the other remaining survivor as the Roman soldiers closed in.

EARLY LESSON LEARNED

The tragic events at Masada provided one of the more dramatic lessons that ancient civilizations had to learn the hard way – in a dangerous world, espionage was absolutely vital. It was a world in which the first 3,000 years of human history were marked by constant conflict among tribes that coveted the land, riches or food supplies of other tribes. In that time of inevitable conflict, the tribe which failed to gather information on the threats that surrounded them was doomed, destined to be overwhelmed by competitors with superior information. It was a truth established long before the Romans emerged from their tribal huts on a mission to conquer the world.

Early great civilizations – Egyptian, Hittite, Assyrian, Babylonian and Persian – were the inheritors of the tribal tradition of covetousness and conquest. Each of those civilizations was obsessed with the idea of a universal empire that controlled the entire known world, a concept that meant a premium on information about competing universal empires. Thus was espionage born.

No one is quite certain precisely when espionage as we now know it began. Early archaeological evidence from the dawn of civilization contains traces of early spying. Surviving clay tablets inscribed more than 4,000 years ago mention espionage operations, including a Sumerian tablet that discusses a spying operation which used fire signals from spies working inside the city of Babylon to convey intelligence about the city's defenses. Another surviving tablet, from Mesopotamia, uses one of the world's first known ciphers to transmit information about ancient Sumeria's greatest secret, the formula for enamel that had given the Sumerian potting industry a great advantage. The tablet goes on to warn that spies from other civilizations were actively seeking the formula, which was to be guarded at all costs.

The earliest detailed evidence of ancient espionage comes from the surviving artifacts of one of the first powerful civilizations, Assyria. The Assyrians embarked on an ambitious plan of conquest that involved nothing less than taking control of the entire Near East and beyond. To achieve it, the Assyrians created the world's first military dictatorship, a fascist-like state devoted exclusively to war and conquest. Its cutting edge was a powerful military machine, including a standing army of 50,000 men, unusually large by ancient standards.

The Assyrian war machine had a vital cog – the world's first government intelligence service. It was a corps of spies assigned the task of preparing in-depth intelligence reports on future targets for conquest, ranging from the state of that target's armed forces to the exact quantity of grain in storage (an indicator of how long a city could hold out against a protracted siege). Known as 'The King's Eye', the Assyrian intelligence service also sought to maintain control of conquered areas with another innovation, the world's first secret police force. Agents assigned to the secret police unit were called 'King's Messengers' and ostensibly worked as couriers for the king's written communications system along a network of roads. However, the Messengers had another role – reporting even the mildest expression of dissent in conquered lands against the Assyrian king. Surviving cuneiform tablets demonstrate the thoroughness of this secret police snooping. One reports restiveness among a tribe in occupied Armenia, with a recommendation that it be nipped in the bud as soon as possible before it flared into full-fledged revolt. Another tablet contains orders to a secret police agent to deal harshly with a critic of the king: "If there is a ditch in the countryside or the city, make this man disappear."

Egypt, another great ancient civilization, also had a flourishing espionage service, although it was much more decentralized than Assyria's. The Egyptian system relied on a network of governors in the empire's far-flung territory reporting to the pharaoh about what was going on in each governor's jurisdiction, especially any hint of incipient revolt. For intelligence outside the empire, the pharaoh relied on intelligence provided by a network of friendly merchants who ran the caravan trading routes to Babylonia, Assyria, and Palestine.

However, in 1379 BCE, Ikhnaton became the new pharaoh of the Egyptian empire, a reign that marked a precipitate decline in Egyptian espionage. Concerned almost exclusively with religious reform (he was the first pharaoh to believe in monotheism), Ikhnaton had no interest in maintaining an empire, much less expanding it. The regional governors were told to stop providing intelligence reports and merchants were no longer asked to collect intelligence along their caravan routes. As a result, Egypt became virtually blind, beginning a long decline as competing empires began to nibble at its edges.

The extent of that blindness was demonstrated by the first fully-documented battle in human history. The encounter took place in 1285 BCE between the Egyptians and their chief rivals – the Hittites – at Kadesh in what is now northern Lebanon. The Egyptian army was led personally by Pharaoh Ramses II. He had decided to balk Hittite ambitions with a preemptive attack on the Hittite army, which was besieging Kadesh. Ramses moved northward at the head of a mighty army that was almost totally blind. He had no idea where the Hittite army was located, no idea of what the Hittite king planned and no idea of the military capabilities of the Hittite

RIGHT: Part of a relief carved on Ramesses II's Temple at Karnak. It shows his 'victory' at the battle of Kadesh, including captured spies begging him for their lives.

forces. A supreme egotist, Ramses believed his military genius could overcome any threat, however unanticipated.

As the Egyptian forces neared Kadesh, two Bedouin tribesmen, claiming to be deserters from the Hittite army, approached Ramses and told him that only one Hittite division was investing Kadesh, with another three divisions lagging well behind. Ramses immediately decided to attack Kadesh with his superior numbers. However, just as the assault was about to get underway, several of his soldiers rushed to Ramses with ominous news. They had captured several Hittite spies who, after torture, confessed that the two Bedouins were spies sent by the Hittite king to mislead the Egyptians. In fact, the bulk of the Hittite army was concealed just behind Kadesh, waiting to close a trap on the attacking Egyptians. Armed with this vital intelligence, Ramses maneuvered around Kadesh to engage the Hittite army in the open. The maneuver set off a huge, swirling battle involving 5,000 Egyptian chariots and 3,500 Hittite chariots, along with tens of thousands of infantry. The battle ended in a draw, a fact that didn't prevent Ramses from describing Kadesh as a magnificent victory, a victory he modestly attributed to his brilliant generalship on wall carvings in the temple he built as a tribute to his reign.

The decline of the once-mighty Egyptian empire coincided with the ascent of two other empires whose rival ambitions in Asia Minor presaged inevitable conflict. One, the Persian empire, borrowed many components of the Assyrian, including an intelligence service, also known as 'The King's Eye'. However, unlike the Assyrians, Persian kings used their spies only rarely for foreign intelligence. Almost all their time was devoted to monitoring and crushing internal dissent within the empire. As a result, the Persians lacked much in the way of insight into an entity that was proving to be their chief rival, Greece. That deficiency was to prove very costly to Persia's ambitions.

Greece was actually a loose and often contentious collection of city-states, with Athens and Sparta the most powerful. The Greeks were great believers in the worth of espionage, an endeavor they strictly divided into two different functions – scout and spy. A scout, usually a soldier, was dispatched into a hostile area to collect strictly tactical intelligence, including the locations of enemy forces, terrain, conditions of roads, water depth in naval anchorages, etc. When he had collected a sufficient amount of intelligence, he returned home to report what he had seen. A spy, on the other hand, was a civilian who would live in enemy territory under cover (usually a merchant involved in foreign trade) for protracted periods of time. His mandate was strategic and political intelligence. This was dispatched via special spy couriers using a variety of ingenious methods, including messages etched on sheets of beaten tin sewn into sandals, messages concealed in a woman's large earring and messages written on the tree leaves used to cover the putrid ulcers of itinerant beggars.

NECESSITY OF KNOWLEDGE

As tensions with Persia began to increase in 490 BCE, the Greeks decided they needed some sort of key listening post where they could monitor the intentions of Persian King Xerxes, a megalomaniac who had made no secret of his goal of devouring all the Greek city-states for his empire. Some sort of early warning was imperative for the Greeks, who were badly overmatched by the mightier Persian empire. The chosen site was the city of Sardis, in modern-day Turkey. It was a key trading center that was a crossroads of the ancient world, directly athwart the boundaries of Persian and Greek areas of influence. Sardis was crowded with merchants from all over that world, a cosmopolitan stew usually abuzz with all kinds of interesting intelligence tidbits.

Three highly educated Athenians, enlisted as spies, were sent to Sardis in the guise of merchants to collect and make sense of all that intelligence. Aware that the Persian King's Eye had plenty of secret police agents in Sardis on the lookout for Greek spies, the Athenians were very careful, patiently working for months as merchants while making no attempt at espionage. When the King's Eye became convinced the three men were surely merchants and nothing more, the Athenians went to work.

In 490 BCE, the spies came up with an intelligence blockbuster. Xerxes had decided on an invasion of Greece by means of an amphibious landing on the country's east coast. Further, they learned of Xerxes' plan to land cavalry. This vital piece of information enabled the Greeks to deduce that there was only one spot on the coast whose flat plains were suitable for landing cavalry – Marathon. Accordingly, the Greeks moved their forces to that area, catching the Persians at their most vulnerable point, the actual landing. Nearly 7,000 Persians were killed and the invasion was turned back.

However, Xerxes wasn't finished yet. In 480 BCE, the three Sardis spies uncovered an even more ambitious Persian invasion plan – a bridge of boats lashed together across the Hellespont, over which an army of some 300,000 men would invade Greece and destroy the Greek city-states in a quick, overwhelming campaign. The spies consulted their maps and deduced that an army of such size would be able to traverse the mountainous terrain on Greece's coast only through one large pass, located in an area called Thermopylae. A force of 7,000 Greeks, including 300 Spartans, moved to block the pass. Xerxes, personally leading his army, had not bothered to dispatch any spies to report on the Greek strength or any other matter of significance. Convinced that his mighty host would easily sweep away all opposition, he concluded he did not need any intelligence. He soon learned the penalty for such arrogance.

Although he outnumbered the Greeks forty to one, only a limited number of Persian units could assault through the pass at any one time, so the Greeks were able to turn back attack after attack. By the second day of battle, some 30,000 Persian dead lay in heaps and Xerxes hadn't been able to advance a yard. He ordered his troops to press on. By the fourth day, the Persians finally prevailed, but at a cost of appalling casualties that bled the Persian army white. Fatally weakened, that army was finally defeated a year later, ending the Persian threat to Greece.

It is no exaggeration to say that the effectiveness of their spies, combined with the bravery of their soldiers, saved Greece from destruction. It was a lesson imperfectly learned by the greatest ancient empire of them all, Rome.

To a large extent, espionage was handled on something of an ad hoc basis in the Roman Empire. There never was a central intelligence agency similar to the King's Eye of Assyria and Persia. However, each Roman governor throughout the empire was responsible for collecting whatever intelligence he thought important for Rome to know. Intelligence collection was handled by officia. These were usually soldiers with combat experience who had been converted into civilian officials assigned the specific duty of keeping the governor informed about emerging threats, almost always defined as military. The preferred Roman method for collecting intelligence was bribery and lavish payments for information were made to tribal chieftains allied with Rome.

However, given the deadly dynastic and political struggles in Rome itself (75 per cent of Roman emperors were either assassinated or murdered by usurpers), the predominant interest in intelligence by Rome's rulers centered on domestic espionage. The empire's ruling elite hungered for any intelligence about their political enemies, along with anything they could learn about such perceived threats to their rule as the Christians. Emperors formed groups of speculatores. Officially special couriers entrusted with carrying confidential orders, they soon evolved into a secret police force assigned the job of keeping tabs on any developing political opposition. They also had another, more covert role – spying on officials the emperor didn't fully trust, often including members of his own family.

Other men involved in domestic spying were the vigiles, who began life as a fire brigade that patrolled the city, ready to douse any fire before it became a conflagration. However, given their extensive knowledge of the city and its people, it was inevitable Rome's rulers would tap into that knowledge for purposes other than firefighting. The vigiles became a secret police force, collecting every scrap of intelligence they could find, even neighborhood gossip. They grew into a force of 3,000 that divided the city into districts and stationed a force in each district, responsible for literally every scrap of intelligence within its jurisdiction.

Meanwhile, the Roman army, an important power center in Roman politics, maintained its own secret police force. These were the frumentari, who kept watch over the loyalty of soldiers and spied on the royal family. This was a key intelligence function, since the latest power shifts in the family could have important implications for the military. Aware of the frumentari, emperors formed a counterweight – agentes in rebus. These were the Roman equivalent of Soviet political commissars who kept tabs on the loyalties of men working in the various imperial bureaux, especially the military's Imperial General Staff.

This obsession with domestic spying at the expense of foreign intelligence was to cause a series of military disasters directly traceable to intelligence failure. In 90 BCE, the Gauls poured into Italy from France, determined to seize Rome and burn it to the ground.

The Romans only learned the Gauls' intention when the hysterical cackling of geese outside the walls alerted the city that a major invasion was underway.

Rome learned nothing from the experience. In 53 BCE, one of Rome's ruling triumvirate, Marcus Lucinius Crassus, decided he needed some sort of spectacular military triumph in order to gain the upper hand against his two co-rulers and bitter rivals – Julius Caesar and Gnaeus Pompeius (Pompey). In 73 BCE, Crassus had brutally suppressed a slave revolt led by Spartacus, but Romans sneered that triumph over ill-armed slaves hardly amounted to a glittering military victory. Crassus now decided he would take on the Parthians, a warrior tribe on the far edges of Rome's empire, in present-day Iran. The Romans had always regarded the Parthians with some nervousness, since they represented an incipient threat. However, extensive bribery had managed to keep them quiescent.

Obsessed with his vision of supreme power, Crassus decided that the vaunted Roman legions, the greatest military force the world had ever seen, would easily defeat the Parthians. He sent no spies into Parthian lands to determine their strength and military tactics, reasoning that the 50,000 Legionnaires he would lead into Parthia would so frighten the tribe's soldiers that they would be too terrified to fight. Therefore Crassus marched into Parthia with his eyes wide open, failing to realize he could not be more blind.

He did not know that the Parthians, assuming that at some point in the future they would take on the Roman army, had evolved new tactics and weapons designed to overcome Roman military advantages. Instead of battling toe to toe with the feared Roman infantry, much of the Parthian army had been converted into cavalry. This was a highly mobile force designed to attack the edges of Roman formations with a new composite bow that fired arrows at high speed into the ranks. Those cavalry forces were to be supplied by a constant stream of pack camels loaded with fresh batches of arrows, horse fodder and water.

Near the small town of Carrhae, the Parthians struck. The Roman formations were decimated by clouds of arrows fired by swarming cavalry operating just outside the range of Roman javelins and spears. Then the broken remnants were smashed by follow-on waves of Parthian infantry. The new Parthian tactics worked perfectly. In only a few hours, more than 20,000 Roman soldiers were killed, and another 10,000 were taken prisoner and later sold into slavery. Crassus himself was among the captives. Taken before the Parthian king, he was executed by means of molten gold poured down his throat.

Carrhae was among a series of military disasters in Roman history attributable to the Romans' arrogance in assuming all other peoples on Earth were inferior. Given that presumed inferiority, there was no necessity to gather any intelligence

about them. That raises the question: if Roman intelligence was so bad, then how did the empire last so long? Largely it was because Rome was always able to produce great military leaders who were not only firm believers in the necessity of intelligence, but also able to use it effectively in their own campaigns. This is best illustrated by the careers of Rome's two greatest military geniuses – Julius Caesar and Scipio Africanus.

Publius Cornelius, the man who became known as Scipio Africanus in honor of his defeat of Carthage, first came to notice in 206 BCE, when his legions in Spain defeated the Carthaginian forces under Hannibal – Rome's greatest enemy. One of the major reasons for Scipio's triumph was his decision to create a first-class intelligence organization. He selected the best and brightest among his officers and trained them rigorously in the espionage arts – how to operate under effective cover, how to gather intelligence with merely a glance at an enemy military formation and how to spot a critical defect in the enemy's military structure. His selection standards for spies centered to a large degree on how quick-witted they were, meaning their ability to think rapidly on their feet in times of acute crisis.

The most brilliant and quick-witted of Scipio's espionage recruits was Cornelius Lelius, who demonstrated an astonishing ability to learn what the Carthaginian commanders were planning. In one incident, he was sent into the Carthaginian camp under cover as a junior officer serving as Roman negotiator for the exchange of prisoners. He arrived with an entourage of slave assistants (actually Roman spies), who immediately began noting such items of interest as the numbers of weapons and troops, and the condition of the Carthaginian cavalry's horses. Suddenly, disaster loomed: a Carthaginian commander recognized one of the 'slaves' as a high-ranking Roman officer whom he had met years before while studying in Greece. As the commander began voicing his suspicions, Lelius instantly reacted. "Dog of a slave!" he screamed as he struck the slave with a whip. "How dare you array yourself so that you

might be taken for a Roman officer!" The 'slave', playing his part perfectly, cowered and beseeched forgiveness for his impertinence. The Carthaginians, aware that no Roman would ever dare strike a Roman officer, concluded that the commander was somehow mistaken.

Scipio's greatest espionage triumph came in 202 BCE, at the battle of Zama in present-day Tunisia, where he inflicted a decisive defeat on the Carthaginians that finally ended Hannibal's threat to Rome. Before the battle, Scipio was aware he had to come up with a solution to Hannibal's most powerful weapon – war elephants that inspired terror even among the most disciplined Roman formations. The Carthaginian leader used his elephants as the ancient version of tanks to rip gaping holes in the front ranks of enemy armies. Scipio ordered Lelius and his spies to find out if the elephants had a weakness he could exploit.

Lelius concentrated his efforts among Hannibal's auxiliary troops, which included the trainers and drivers of the war elephants. Liberal draughts of the finest Roman wine finally loosened some tongues. Lelius learned that the elephants tended to panic when confronted with any loud, sharp sound. Armed with that intelligence, Scipio rounded up every musician he could find in Rome, then distributed them among his infantry formations. On the day of the battle, Hannibal opened his assault on the Roman lines with an attack by an armada of 85 elephants. Just as the beasts were about to plow into the Roman formations, hundreds of musicians, on a signal from Scipio, let loose a mighty blast of sound from trumpets and horns. The elephants instantly panicked, turning back into Carthaginian lines, destroying the formations.

THE MIGHTY CAESAR

A century later, Gaius Julius Caesar, perhaps Rome's greatest military leader, began his own rise to power with a string of stunning military triumphs. Although history has concentrated on his talents as a military tactician and strategist, Caesar's most brilliant contributions to the art of war were his innovations in intelligence. Indeed, he is the father of military intelligence, for the espionage system he devised for his army would serve as the model for all military intelligence organizations for the next 2,000 years.

Caesar never made a move without a thorough understanding of exactly what his legions were facing, the extent of any given threat and precisely which enemy weaknesses he could exploit. The Caesarian intelligence organization included procursatores, trained scouts assigned the job of reconnoitering enemy forces immediately ahead of Roman forces, and exploratores, long-range scouts who operated deep behind enemy lines. It also

ABOVE: Julius Caesar. Rome's most famous soldier was the father of modern military intelligence.

included indices, enemy deserters and turncoats who were debriefed and emptied of whatever information they had by experts on Caesar's staff, and Caesar's supreme espionage weapon – speculatores. These were highly-trained spies working under various kinds of cover inside enemy territory, tasked with obtaining strategic intelligence.

During the Gallic wars, his greatest triumph, Caesar ordered his spies to pay particular attention to ethnic intelligence. He wanted to know what made the Gauls tick. He especially wanted to know whether their leaders were able to adapt rapidly to changing battlefield circumstances. The Roman spies were able to form a comprehensive picture of the Gallic psyche, including the priceless intelligence that the Gauls lacked resilience when confronted with unanticipated problems during battle. If an original battle plan was balked, the entire Gallic military structure was much too rigid and tended to unravel.

With that kind of insight, a brilliant tactician like Caesar had a very potent weapon as he sought to bring the Gauls under Roman heel. The overmatched Gauls were confused by Roman attacks that came from unanticipated directions, often using unorthodox tactics that ran counter to everything the Gauls thought they knew about how the Romans fought. In battle after battle, Caesar managed to unhinge the Gallic command structure by simply doing what no one expected him to do (such as recklessly moving out of range of his supply lines, unheard of in ancient military science). By 50 BCE, Caesar had achieved total victory, turning all of Gaul into a Roman province.

The conquest of Gaul, one of the greatest feats of arms in all history, made Caesar a titan in Rome. It gave him sufficient basis to seize total power by defeating his chief political rival, Pompey, in a civil war. Again, Caesar's military intelligence organization provided a huge advantage, giving him detailed information on the location, strength and fitness of the Pompeian forces.

Once Caesar achieved total power as emperor of Rome, his life would take a tragically ironic turn. Ever the military man, he saw no need to use his military intelligence organization in his political life. Although he was a military genius, Caesar had little political acumen, so it did not occur to him that he had made plenty of enemies in Rome – enemies who might be willing to kill the man they considered a dangerous dictator. As Caesar should have realized, murder was the chief method of solving political problems in ancient Rome. Blithely unconcerned, Caesar walked into the Roman senate one March morning in 44 BCE. He was stabbed to death by several senators – one of whom, Caesar had always thought, was his best friend. The master of intelligence in the ancient world had no clue that his killers had been plotting his death for months

WHISPERS IN THE WIND: CODES AND COMMUNICATION

ONE DAY IN THE SPRING OF 1917, A POSTAL CENSOR ASSIGNED TO THE MAIN POST OFFICE IN LONDON OPENED A LETTER FROM A DUTCH CITIZEN LIVING IN THE CITY. IT WAS ADDRESSED TO HIS BROTHER IN HOLLAND.

The letter seemed ordinary enough. It related some family gossip such as "Martha is trying desperately to become pregnant again," along with a few observations on current political matters.

However, despite the innocent-looking content, the letter aroused the censor's suspicions. For one thing, neutral Holland was notorious as the site of letterboxes for German intelligence. As a result, postal censors were instructed to pay special attention to any mail between England and Holland. For another, the letter-writer's political observations seemed oddly phrased: "Apparently neutral's protest is thoroughly discounted and ignored. Isman hard hit. Blockade issue affects for pretext one by-product, ejecting suets and vegetable oils." Even assuming that the letter-writer's grasp of English might have been less than perfect, there was nevertheless something very strange about the phrasing.

It took only a few minutes for the censor to realize that he was looking at one of espionage's oldest forms of secret communication, the letter system. It is a simple system with the message concealed in a prearranged sequence of letters. One letter in each word constitutes the body of the secret message. In this case, through simple trial and error, he deduced the key was the second letter in each word revealing the message: "Pershing sails for NY June 1."

The letter system is only one of the many ways human ingenuity has tried to overcome a spy's biggest hurdle – one that's been around for some 3,000 years: how to get whatever intelligence is collected to the people waiting to read it, without getting caught. It has proven to be a very difficult task. Every method ever devised, no matter how clever, always has defects, most dangerously self-incrimination.

In ancient China, mandarins who ran espionage operations devised what they believed was a foolproof secret communication system for spies. They shaved a spy's head, wrote a secret message on the bald skull, then waited until the spy's hair grew back, at which point he would be sent on his way. At his destination, his head would be shaved again, revealing the message.

The defect of such a system is immediately obvious – it takes time for a full head of human hair to grow back, meaning any intelligence on that skull cannot be very timely. In 480 BCE, Greek spies aware of that deficiency devised the scytale. This involved writing on the length of a sheet of papyrus wound around a staff, which, when removed and sent on, was intelligible only to a recipient who had a twin staff of precisely the same diameter and length.

By medieval times, the growing use of espionage meant longer messages, spurring the development of invisible writing, the art of concealing messages in invisible ink between the lines of ordinary-looking missives. Still in use today, the technique utilizes certain colourless liquids – most popularly lemon juice or copper sulphate – to write a message between the lines of an ordinary letter or document. The invisible writing is made visible by applying heat or chemicals. It is an easy technique to use, but counterintelligence has an entire battery of special chemicals designed to detect invisible writing in suspect documents and letters.

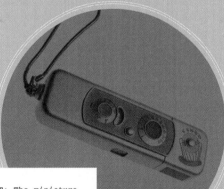

RIGHT: The miniature Minox camera. An essential tool of modern espionage, used to photograph secret documents on tiny pieces of film.

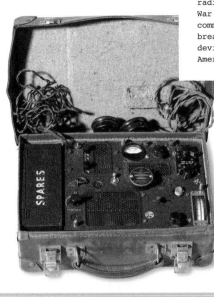

LEFT: The suitcase
radio. A World
War II espionage
communications
breakthrough,
devised by the
American OSS.

the ether is detectable. Consequently, counterintelligence agencies developed radio detection techniques which involved triangulating radio signals to pinpoint the location of spies' radio sets. American intelligence in World War II came up with an innovation, the 'suitcase radio', a radio miniaturized to fit into a small suitcase, making it mobile and thus very difficult to pinpoint.

At the same time, rapid advances in photographic technology provided new devices for spy messages. One was the Minox camera, a very small camera that uses high-resolution 8 x 11 mm film to photograph classified documents. The result is placed onto microfilm – tiny bits of film effortlessly concealed in the tiniest of spaces and easily transferred (a hollow coin remains a favorite means of transport). Even smaller is the microdot, a process invented by German intelligence in World War II that reduces photographs to the size of a tiny dot that can be hidden behind a postage stamp or in a period of a letter. The concealed message in the microdot is then read with a special microscope.

During the Cold War, the CIA devised what was then the ultimate solution to espionage communication problems, the burst transmitter. This wondrous technology, about the size of a small portable radio, electronically compresses even a very lengthy message into a tiny electronic blip. The blip is then transmitted in a seconds-long electronic burst – either to a satellite specifically designed to receive such transmissions or a ground station (usually concealed in an embassy). For spies, the burst transmitters were a godsend. Easily concealed inside a pocket, they made the dangerous task of sending messages quick and easy. However, newly-developed technology has caught up and even burst transmitters now can be located fairly quickly.

Despite such ingenuity, there is no foolproof method of spy communication, since even the most brilliant technology requires a spy to be in possession of it, which is therefore incriminating evidence of espionage. However, the world's intelligence agencies keep trying. The latest innovation is hiding messages in computer digital images. A computer's image in high resolution has over two million pixels, in which bits of information can be hidden -- much like the encrypted copyright protections hidden in some software programs and DVDs. However, given that hackers have already figured out ways of defeating those protections, it is only a matter of time before counterintelligence catches up and sets off still another round of innovation.

An alternative method, also still in use today, is the book system. This involves the spy and their control each using a copy of the same book. The spy writes a message by using words selected from the book, each of which is transmitted in numerical form – for example, 64-10-4, meaning page 64, tenth line, fourth word from the left. It is a simple enough method, but is very time-consuming.

Around the same time, another method of espionage communication was developed that remains the most popular system still used today – the dead drop. The spy and control select a pre-arranged site (the hollow of tree, a loose stone in a wall) in which the spy deposits a message (called a 'fill'). It is picked up later ('serviced') by a courier, who then delivers it. The spy signals a pickup is ready by making a chalk mark at a previously-arranged site, usually a utility pole. The Soviet KGB, which favoured the undersides of bridges for dead drops because of the unlikelihood of accidental discovery, developed a hollow bolt that blended in perfectly. It was reverse-threaded, reducing the possibility of someone accidentally unscrewing it.

A NEW DIRECTION

The development of radio at the turn of the last century promised a revolution in espionage communications, since spies could transmit their intelligence at long distances from deep within an enemy country. However, early radios were bulky and required aerials, wedding spies to fixed locations. Worse, any radio signal sent into

PANDORA'S BOX: POISON

UNDERSTANDABLY, THE DOCTORS WERE FEELING ACUTE ANXIETY. ROUSTED OUT OF THEIR BEDS IN THE MIDDLE OF THE NIGHT BY SS SOLDIERS, THEY WERE NOW BEING RUSHED BY PLANE TO PRAGUE, CAPITAL OF NAZI-OCCUPIED CZECHOSLOVAKIA.

They had orders to perform a medical miracle. Those orders, from Der Fuehrer himself, made no mention of what might happen in the event this group of Germany's best medical minds failed. However, no one familiar with the way things worked in Nazi Germany doubted disappointing Adolf Hitler was not a good option.

It was the evening of 27 May 1942. Some hours earlier, Reinhard Heydrich, the infamous Nazi overlord of Czechoslovakia, had been badly wounded in a bomb attack by Czech agents in an operation run by British MI6's Special Operations Executive (SOE). Taken to Prague's best hospital, his medical condition was listed as critical. Hitler was enraged by the attack on one of his favorites and had rounded up the best doctors in Germany with instructions to save the life of the Nazi he fondly called "the man with the iron heart".

The doctors were relieved to discover that they would not need a medical miracle. Heydrich's wounds, though serious, were not life-threatening and he would pull through. However, 24 hours later, Heydrich's condition began to deteriorate. Nothing seemed to work and, on the morning of 4 June, he suddenly died. The doctors were baffled. As one of them noted, their VIP patient in his last hours demonstrated all the classic symptoms of botulin poisoning. Forensic experts ordered in by Hitler were even more puzzled. Heydrich had died from some sort of "poison... carried by the splinters [of the bomb]." However, they had no idea what kind of poison, since the tiny traces they found resembled nothing they had ever seen.

There the mystery rested until some 50 years later, when declassification finally began to illuminate espionage's darkest corner – the development and use of deadly poisons to dispose of inconvenient humanity. Among the secrets revealed was the existence of British Intelligence's secret laboratory at Porton Down, which by 1941 had developed BTX, a deadly botulin toxin. It was BTX that was secretly put inside the specially-designed bombs SOE provided to the Czech assassins for the attack on Heydrich.

The Heydrich operation came to light during a wave of revelations following the end of the Cold War,

when it was learned that a number of nations, most prominently the United States and the Soviet Union, had built covert laboratories. Over the years these had been used to develop a wide range of horrors – advanced poisons to make assassinations look like natural deaths, instant-acting poisons for captured spies to avoid torture, deadly toxins to kill enemy agents in seconds and so-called 'truth drugs' to loosen the tongues of captured spies. No secrets were guarded more closely than this witch's brew of poison, deadly gases, toxins and mind-altering chemicals.

ANCIENT HISTORY

It had all started with the Romans, who were not great doctors, but were great poisoners. They learned how to extract poisons from certain plants and an entire class of professional poisoners was created. Covert agents in the endless dynastic and political struggles of Rome, they were adept at slipping poisons into ordinary food such as figs, apples and, most famously, the mushrooms that killed Emperor Claudius. Their successors in feudal Europe discovered what we now call T2 toxins, deadly poisons derived from grain molds, along with ricin, derived from the castor plant bean. Easily hidden in food and drink, such poisons were a convenient way for despots to get rid of competing despots without having to declare war.

That convenience was the chief reason for the resurgence in the use of poisons when a number of intelligence agencies began to get into the business of covertly killing people their governments wanted dead. An apex of sorts was reached in the 1950s and 1960s, when it seemed that espionage had largely become Murder Incorporated. Highly publicized incidents included an unsuccessful attempt by British Intelligence to murder Egyptian President Gamal Abdel Nasser with nerve gas and an equally unsuccessful attempt by the CIA to murder Cuban President Fidel Castro with a shellfish toxin. Soviet Intelligence was the most active. In 1921, it created a 'research institute'

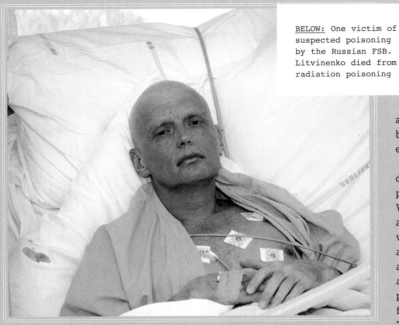

BELOW: One victim of suspected poisoning by the Russian FSB. Litvinenko died from radiation poisoning

with an apparent cardiac disorder. He died several days later. The Bulgarians and the KGB might have gotten away with it, except that an autopsy found the tiny ball, with traces of ricin, embedded in Markov's leg.

American Intelligence didn't get seriously into the poison business until World War II, when the OSS created a laboratory. Its initial focus was the development of a 'truth serum' to be used against captured enemy agents and instant-acting poisons for OSS agents facing capture and torture. The successor of the OSS, the CIA, later expanded the program to include the development of assassination poisons. Code-named MK/ULTRA, its arsenal included saxitoxins developed from contaminated shellfish. Even a pinprick from the poison causes death in ten seconds. U-2 pilot Francis Gary Powers, during his flights over the Soviet Union, carried a 'suicide pill' of saxitoxin concealed in a hollow silver dollar.

code-named Department Eleven, which was in fact a laboratory assigned the task of devising toxins and poisons. To that end it developed a frightening range of poisonous biological and chemical agents that would make a victim's death appear natural – from a poisonous gel placed on the door handle of a car to a cyanide gas that produced instant heart attacks. It even developed a plutonium dust to be placed on the drawers of a victim's desk, so when he opened the drawer, he inhaled the dust which produced virulent forms of cancer that caused death within a short period of time.

Department Eleven was responsible for one of the most sensational episodes in the history of covert war by poison – the 1978 murder in London of Georgi Markov, a prominent Bulgarian exile whose radio broadcasts irked Bulgaria's Communist rulers. They ordered Bulgarian Intelligence to get rid of him, but with the conditions that it must be accomplished without making it appear like an assassination and any trace of involvement by the Bulgarian government must be concealed. That mandated some sort of sophisticated poison, which moved Bulgarian Intelligence to seek help from their KGB friends who provided the means – a 1.52-millimeter watch bearing drilled with holes that contained ricin. The tiny ball was attached to the tip of an umbrella, with which an operative poked Markov in the leg as he waited for a bus. At first, Markov paid little attention to the tiny pinprick in his leg. However, within 24 hours he fell suddenly and mysteriously ill

CURRENT AFFAIRS

Although both the Russian and U.S. intelligence agencies claim they're out of the poison business, recent events are cause for wonder. In 2005, Ukraine President Viktor A. Yushchenko, an opponent of the Russian Federation regime, became violently ill after eating a bowl of soup. Doctors saved his life, but a subsequent CIA investigation revealed that Yushchenko had ingested a highly toxic dioxin. A year later, Alexander Litvinenko, a former agent of the FSB, the Russian Federation's foreign intelligence agency, fell seriously ill after drinking a cup of tea. Litvinenko, who had told friends he planned to reveal the 'crimes' of Russian Federation officials, died several days later. An autopsy revealed he had been poisoned by polonium-120, a deadly form of plutonium. Russian Intelligence insisted it had nothing to do with either case, arguing, with the kind of logic Stalin would have liked, that since the infamous Department Eleven no longer officially exists, then the FSB couldn't have poisoned anybody.

FIRE FROM THE EAST

It had rained heavily the night before. By dawn on 25 October 1415, the field near the small village of Agincourt in northern France, where the English army had camped, was a soggy mess.

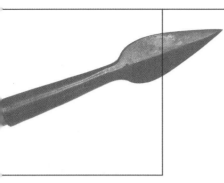

LEFT: The business end of longbow arrows designed to penetrate armor. The French intelligence failure to learn of the English 'superweapon' would result in the destruction of virtually all of France's knights.

The ragged force of 5,000 men and their king, Henry V, woke to a light mist and chilly air, worsening their misery. Most were sick with dysentery and bronchitis, diseases that had ravaged Henry's army since landing in Normandy six months before. Things looked bleak and they were about to become bleaker still. An attack by a French army three times their size was imminent.

Henry had spent months of exhausting maneuvers across the French countryside, seeking to gain an advantage over the French army in the long struggle known as the Hundred Years' War. Now, critically short of food and badly weakened by disease, the men later immortalized by Shakespeare as "we band of brothers" were pinned down in that soggy field by a vastly superior force.

As the morning mist cleared, the English soldiers saw what confronted them. A force of 10,000 French infantry had deployed in attack formation. Behind them, arrayed in battle order, was the real heart of French military power – 5,000 knights, the cream of the greatest military power in Europe. In the morning sun, the stars of France's aristocracy in polished armor – their flags of coats of arms and brightly coloured plumes atop their helmets fluttering in the breeze – were a magnificent and terrifying sight.

The knights looked down contemptuously at the English force of shabbily dressed peasants. All but 800 of them were archers. However, the French knights had no concern as they were outfitted in the latest triumph of German armorers, overlapping metal plates over chain mail, making them impervious to arrows fired by the standard short bows of the time.

Except for a few scouts the French had dispatched to determine the location of the English army, no attempt had been made to collect any kind of intelligence about Henry V and his troops. Why bother? The overwhelming French military superiority would easily destroy this rabble. Within a few hours, the French would pay a terrible price in blood for that arrogance.

ADVANCED WEAPONRY

What the French did not know was that the English archers were armed with the fifteenth-century version of a wonder weapon – the longbow. A foot taller than the man wielding it, the longbow originated in Wales sometime in the twelfth century. It was later adopted by Edward I and further developed into a killing machine as the main weapon for his army. It was quite a weapon – brilliantly designed to generate some 1,400 foot-pounds of power (the standard shorter bow generated about 150 foot-pounds of power). Its 37-inch-long arrows could skewer a man 250 yards away. A century later, Henry inherited an army of highly trained longbow archers capable of firing a high volume of arrows with tremendous accuracy. This was the weapon he brought to France.

Since the French had not bothered to collect any intelligence about English military developments, their infantry – confident of an easy victory – advanced toward a line of English archers without any idea of the terrible weapon that awaited them. The archers spiked arsenals of arrows in the ground beside them and then calmly waited for the attackers to come within range. When the French were two hundred yards away, the archers armed their longbows and fired. Thousands of arrows flew into the French formations with tremendous velocity. Entire ranks fell in heaps as the archers, firing 15 shots every minute, slaughtered the French infantry. Frightened by the constant swarm of arrows that sounded like angry bees headed at them, the French soldiers stopped advancing and milled around in terror. Quickly, the soggy field became soaked with blood.

The French knights now decided to go on the attack. Their progress hampered by the disorganized infantry, they made easy targets for the English archers, who cut them down. Amid the sounds of screaming men and horses, the cream of French nobility died – their armor penetrated like so much paper by longbow arrows at ranges of 200 yards. Finally, 90 minutes later, the battle ended. The French survivors of the slaughter fled the battlefield, leaving behind more than 10,000 dead and 1,000 prisoners. The dead included virtually every French knight in the battle. The English lost only 113 men.

ABOVE: The Knights Templar, the most famous of the orders of European knights among the Crusaders, found themselves balked by Arab spies.

The significance of events that morning on a muddy field in France cannot be overstated. In less than two hours, the old feudal order that had dominated Europe for centuries was dead. Ordinary men had slaughtered the feudal upper class and that class would never rise again. Those ordinary men for the first time realized they could be masters of their own destinies, a radical thought that was the seed of a political sea change.

Like a mighty earthquake, the repercussions of Agincourt spread shock waves in every direction. The rise of the modern state was born on that battlefield and with it the realization that the old ways of doing things would no longer work. As the French had proven, no political entity could conduct war under a system developed centuries before. No longer could armies afford to blunder into battle without any real idea of what kind of military threat they were facing. The modern European states which would eventually rise from the bloody ground of Agincourt would need some kind of

organized intelligence to prevent the kind of technological surprise that had destroyed France's nobility in only 90 minutes.

The Europeans should have learned that truth long before Agincourt because earlier in the millennium, two charismatic historical figures – a Mongolian chieftain and an Arab leader – had provided an object lesson.

In 1095, Europe was suddenly seized with a religious mania inspired by Pope Urban II, who decreed a holy war against Islam. The Pope's decree stemmed from a perception that the eastern wing of the church, based in Constantinople, was in grave danger from an Islamic tide that had already swept through most of the Middle East and Asia Minor. Further, Urban believed, the ultimate aim of Islam was to subsume all of western Europe and destroy the Catholic Church.

There is no evidence that the Arabs intended any such thing. However, the Pope's alarm was sufficient to inspire thousands of kings, lords and ordinary peasants to give away everything they owned and enlist in a mighty host to invade the Holy Land and seize all the lands occupied by Islam. In what would become known as the Crusades, these 'soldiers of Christ' were promised forgiveness of their sins and eternal salvation as spiritual rewards for their service.

The Crusader armies gathered all over Europe and marched to Constantinople, then embarked on ships that would take them to the Holy Land. They marched blindly to what they believed would be an apocalyptic struggle, with no real idea of what lay ahead of them. No one seemed to have considered the idea of conducting even a cursory reconnaissance of the territory. Nor was there any attempt to gather any intelligence on the size and capabilities of the Arab military forces.

As things turned out, the Crusaders were lucky. Though the Arabs were united religiously under the banner of Islam, they were badly divided politically. Individual satrapies rarely co-operated with each other – even in the face of invasion by the Crusaders. Only two years after invading the Holy Land, the Crusaders captured Jerusalem. Over the next 70 years, the Crusader armies established a string of captured cities and fortresses along the Mediterranean coast, withstanding unco-ordinated efforts by the divided Arabs to retake them.

However, the Crusader grip on its occupied chunk of the Holy Land was tenuous, since the resident Arab populations regarded the Crusaders only as unholy interlopers. They awaited their deliverance, which they understood would come only when the fractured Arab kingdoms would unite under one great leader. Finally, in 1171, that leader emerged. He was a man who would transform history. His name was Yusuf ibn Ayyub, known to his people as Salah-al-Din – 'rectifier of the faith' – and as Saladin to his Crusader enemies.

An officer with the army of one of the Arab warlords, Nur-al-Din of Syria, Saladin came to notice with a series of minor tactical victories over the Crusaders that soon propelled him to the front ranks of the Arab forces. Clearly, he was a military leader of the first order. Saladin tirelessly argued that the disparate Arab forces had to unite in order to expel the Crusaders. It was an assertion he proved by leading several Arab armies into victory against a powerful Frankish force that sought to expand Crusader territory into Palestine. Saladin's triumph electrified the Arab world and made him supreme leader of what now became a united Arab army.

The victory of Saladin owed much to superior espionage. As he recognized, the greatest Arab advantage was the sea of Arabs in which the Crusaders existed. This provided willing recruits for a cause they believed was a sacred mission of Allah. Saladin was a tireless spymaster and sought to take advantage of all those potential intelligence assets by creating an extensive intelligence operation. He melded the various espionage resources of individual Arab chieftains already at hand with an effort to penetrate the Crusader strongholds with battalions of new spies. His sprawling operation turned thousands of Arabs under Crusader occupation into his eyes and ears.

Saladin realized he could not rely exclusively on the espionage resources of individual caliphs, who tended to keep such assets strictly to themselves. Each caliph had a kharbar (roughly, head of information), most often a favored eunuch or emir responsible for providing intelligence. Although the purpose was supposed to be keeping the caliph aware of any emerging threats from the outside, in practice many caliphs directed their kharbar to concentrate their efforts on domestic enemies. These often included members of their own courts and families. The Caliph of Baghdad's kharbar had 1,700 old women on his payroll. They collected every piece of gossip, no matter how trivial, with special attention to any utterance of even the mildest disloyalty. In a preview of what would happen to the people of Baghdad some 700 years later, the caliph's subjects learned to be very careful about every word they said in public, since they never knew which listener might be a government spy.

Saladin provided an object lesson in how to use intelligence in his defeat of the Frankish army in Palestine. The 80,000 strong army marched into the arid lands, intending to engage the Arab forces and defeat them in an open battle, where the Frankish knights would have an advantage over the more lightly-armed Arab infantry. Thanks to the spies he recruited among the Arabs living under Crusader occupation, Saladin was well aware of that plan. He was further aware that the Franks could carry only so much water. At some point, they would need a water source to replenish their supply and continue operating. His spies told him exactly how much water the Franks packed with them, which allowed him to formulate a very precise battle plan.

NEW TYPE OF WARCRAFT

The plan's first phrase involved guerrilla warfare. Saladin avoided direct battle and instead harassed the Frankish flanks with hit and run raids. The Franks were unaware that those raids were shepherding their troops along a route that Saladin wanted them to move – away from known wells. Gradually, the Frankish water supply began to run dangerously low – at which point, Saladin knew the Franks would have to move toward the largest water supply within marching distance. These were the springs at a small town called Hattin. There, Saladin laid an elaborate trap, into which the desperately thirsty Franks stumbled. Saladin's force struck, slaughtering Franks by the thousand. Out of the 80,000 Franks who marched into Palestine, only 3,000 managed to escape.

The victory was aided in no small part by Frankish intelligence myopia. The Franks' commander, Guy of Lusignan, was a religious fanatic who believed that God would guide his army to certain victory. Therefore he saw no reason to recruit any spies to determine what threats he faced in Palestine. He did not know how many Arab troops were there, how they were armed, where they were located and how they intended to combat the Frankish invasion. Carrying the 'true cross', Guy of Lusignan was certain that God would miraculously save his army. It was a belief he held fervently right up to the last moment, when an Arab soldier severed his head with one blow of his sword.

Whatever God's intentions in the Holy Land, they apparently did not include intervening on behalf of the Crusaders. Strangers in a hostile land, they found themselves helpless against the continuing victories by Saladin that whittled away the Crusader footholds. Even infusions of fresh forces in the Second and Third Crusades failed to stop the bleeding. Nor did better military talent – notably Richard Lionheart and the Crusaders' greatest fighting force, the Knights Templar – turn the tide.

The central problem was that the Crusaders had no insight into their Arab enemies, while Saladin enmeshed the Crusaders in a huge web of espionage "so that nothing that passes shall remain unknown," as he phrased it. His intelligence web included a wide variety of assets who lived in cities occupied by the Crusaders. Most were ordinary citizens who had access to areas of intelligence interest – such as the seller of vegetables to Crusader soldiers, a job that allowed him to count exactly how many men the Crusaders had under arms.

Meanwhile, Richard and the Knights Templar generally disdained intelligence, believing that their military skills would be sufficient for an eventual triumph over the Arab forces. They failed to grasp the fact that so long as Saladin knew the precise strength of the Crusaders and what they were planning, they had no hope of defeating him. Richard learned that truth the hard way in 1192, when he decided to retake Jerusalem from Saladin, who had captured the holy city some years before. Saladin's spies discovered that Richard planned to support his attack with a seaborne logistics pipeline. Ships would deliver supplies to preselected accumulation points on land as Richard's army marched along the coast. The largest accumulation of supplies would be landed at the point where Richard planned to turn inland and then march toward Jerusalem.

Armed with intelligence from his spies on the precise amounts of supplies available to Richard, Saladin deduced that there was no way Richard would have sufficient supplies for the march to Jerusalem. At some point along the way, he would need to forage for food, fodder and water. Saladin ordered the countryside all around the route

ABOVE: Gengis Khan, leader of the Mongol Empire, whose appetite for intelligence was nearly insatiable.

of march devastated and the water wells poisoned. As he headed toward Jerusalem, Richard realized too late that he could not replenish his supplies. Checkmated, he and his army arrived at the city's gates desperately hungry and thirsty. Only 2,000 of his infantry and 50 of his knights were fit for battle. With no hope of victory, Richard worked out a deal with Saladin. The Crusaders would abandon any plan to take Jerusalem, in exchange for a guarantee that Christian pilgrims would be permitted to visit the city. With that, Richard left the Holy Land, never to return. Within a few years, what remained of the Crusader presence there was driven out for ever.

The defeat of the Crusaders represented a disaster of the first order for the Europeans. However, despite earlier fears, the Arab threat to Europe itself never extended beyond southern Spain. The same could not be said for what turned out to be a much greater danger, this one from the east – the terror of the Mongols. It was a threat that revealed still another grave intelligence gap, one that nearly proved fatal for Europe.

NEW ORDER

Like a thunderclap, a new great power suddenly appeared on the world stage early in the thirteenth century. From its beginning as an insignificant kingdom in north central Asia, tribes of Mongolian nomads were united into a huge empire under a great leader named Genghis Khan. He forged those tribes into a formidable military instrument dedicated solely to conquest. All Mongol males were enrolled in the army when they reached the age of 14, an army honed into a powerful instrument by constant training. Composed of 60 per cent cavalry and armed with a powerful composite bow capable of killing at ranges of up to 350 yards, it had unprecedented mobility. It was able to cover up to 1,500 miles in ten days.

Mongol military power was enhanced by the Khan's insistence that his army would never make a move without complete intelligence about its enemies. He created a two-tier espionage system. One level was highly-trained reconnaissance units that scouted enemy forces and routes of march. The other was formed from officers on his general staff assigned the task of combing every available source for intelligence. Given lavish funds to buy whatever they needed, Khan's intelligence experts got information from travelers, merchants and religious pilgrims. They formed this material into detailed intelligence reports that told field commanders everything they needed to know. If a Mongol force was about to cross a bridge, it was certain to have an intelligence report about how wide that bridge was, what maximum weight it could handle and whether the enemy intended to defend it.

The Mongol armies thundered westward, destroying

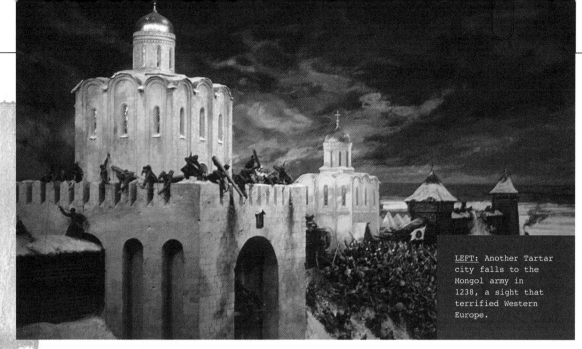

LEFT: Another Tartar city falls to the Mongol army in 1238, a sight that terrified Western Europe.

everything in their path. Using their superior mobility in great sweeping maneuvers to defeat every army that dared to challenge them, by 1241 the Mongols were knocking on the gates of Europe. They defeated forces sent against them as they moved into what are now eastern parts of Poland and Hungary, setting off what can only be described as a full-fledged panic throughout the continent. The panic was caused in large measure by sheer ignorance. Thanks to the general European disregard for intelligence, there was no forewarning that the mightiest military force the world had ever seen was about to sweep across Europe. All the Europeans knew was that there were a lot of Mongols somewhere out there who apparently were invincible.

However, just as it appeared that Europe was in danger of destruction, what many thought was a miracle occurred. Ogodei Khan, the son and successor to his late father, suddenly died. That caused a succession struggle among the senior Mongol commanders, who rushed back with their armies to Mongolia. Church bells rang all over Europe, hailing this dramatic event. Theologians concluded that only divine intervention could explain it.

More thoughtful European minds began to look deeper into the course of events. They soon arrived at an analysis that convinced them Europe could no longer afford to exist in ignorance about the rest of the world. For too long, they concluded, the kingdoms of Europe had reacted to threats from without by walling themselves in, constructing chains of castles meant to make them invulnerable. In effect, that meant Europe simply waited for the next threat to emerge, which, it was assumed, would be halted at the thick walls of those mighty castles. However, what if Europe was assaulted by a threat even greater than the Mongols? What if that threat had new and powerful weapons of which the

Europeans knew nothing? The near-disaster the Mongols represented was instructive. Unless the Europeans began to devote time and effort to finding out what was happening in the rest of the world, the possibility always existed of some unknown threat emerging to destroy an unprepared Europe.

This new way of thinking took firmest root in the Catholic Church, although the reason had more to do with religion than intelligence. The Mongol invasions had made the Vatican aware that there were undoubtedly great civilizations somewhere far to the east, fertile ground for the conversion of new souls. Missionaries began to make their way eastward, intent on bringing whatever peoples lived there into the fold. The first missionaries who finally reached China sent back stunning reports about such marvels as printing, asbestos fireproofing and silk. The reports, accompanied by samples, caused a stir in both the Vatican and among secular authorities. It was quickly realized that the missionaries could carry out a second mission and collect what we now call technical intelligence, the kind of information of immense value to Europe's burgeoning economy. The first target was silk, that wondrous fabric the missionaries had sent back to Europe. Although the silk-making process was a closely-guarded secret in China, missionaries found out that it was produced by silkworms. Chinese authorities foolishly agreed to provide them with a tour of a silk-producing facility, where the visiting missionaries carefully observed how the process worked. They then surreptitiously filched some silkworm eggs and hid them inside their hollowed-out walking sticks. In another operation, a missionary stole the equally-secret Chinese porcelain-making process by pretending to be an ignorant monk who wanted to visit a porcelain factory. There, he asked a lot of naive questions of his hosts, who didn't notice him pocketing a sample of the "China clay" that was the real secret of the porcelain manufacturing process.

ADVANCED TECHNOLOGY

The supreme espionage triumph of the missionaries involved a technology that initially appeared nothing more than a toy. They became fascinated by coloured paper tubes that, when lit, exploded with a loud bang. These tubes, later called 'firecrackers' by Europeans, first appeared in China in 1110. They had been created when Chinese alchemists, ordered to come up with some sort of crowd-pleasing spectacular for the celebration marking the accession to the throne of a new emperor, produced something that delighted the emperor and awed the crowd. Some tubes exploded with a loud bang when a short cotton fuse was lit, while other tubes produced smoke of various colours after they went off. The firecrackers became a staple of all Chinese celebrations, especially the first day of each new year.

The missionaries had no idea what was inside those tubes to make them explode, but they had the sense it was something Europe ought to know about. Samples were shipped westward, including one that wound up in the study of the English friar, Roger Bacon, among whose multiple talents was alchemy. Bacon took the tube apart and extracted a black powder, which he then discovered was a mixture of saltpeter and other chemicals. Bacon, one of early medieval Europe's greatest and most far-seeing minds, realized he was looking at a substance that had a potential far beyond that of a loud toy. He predicted that sometime in the future, the black powder would be transformed into a terrible weapon, one that would dwarf anything the world had ever seen. He turned out to be right. Only a few decades later, Europeans learned how to develop the Chinese formula into something much more powerful – gunpowder. This discovery was to give Europe the single great technological advantage that enabled it to dominate the world.

It was only because the Chinese had an immense respect for 'holy men' of all kinds that they allowed the Western missionaries great latitude. Such freedom for foreigners represented an exception to the tight internal security of a xenophobic empire, a system that was the progenitor of the later security machinery of totalitarian states. It featured what amounted to history's first passport system. Chinese who wanted to move from one province to another were required to have two letters, one signed by a provincial governor authorizing the bearer to travel, the other certifying that the bearer had sufficient funds to live in the province. Roads all over China had government checkpoints, where all travelers had to provide a full explanation of where they were going, along with producing any documents they carried. Agents manning the checkpoints carefully wrote down everything they learned, forming a huge database on

ABOVE: The remarkable Geoffrey Chaucer: soldier, diplomat, scholar, poet, author of *The Canterbury Tales* – and spy.

virtually every man, woman and child in China.

Foreigners, regarded with grave suspicion, were subjected to even stricter controls. All foreigners entering the Chinese empire first had to check in with a government security office. There, an artist drew a portrait of the visitor. If the foreigner later tried to leave the country without registering with the government, copies of the portrait were made and then distributed to government checkpoints on the borders to aid in apprehension. Foreigners could also expect constant surveillance by government spies at every moment they were in the country. At ports, government agents boarded every foreign ship, inspecting and cataloging the cargo and writing down the names of all crewmen. No ship could enter or leave Chinese waters without undergoing this security check. It was a miracle, then, that the early missionaries to China proved so successful in not only obtaining intelligence, but also transferring all kinds of technical data. The data proved of immense value to the European economy. It greatly aided what would become booming porcelain and textile industries that owed their success in large measure to technical espionage.

Like all other Europeans, the English were interested in the treasures the missionaries were sending back home. However, their main intelligence concern centered on a geopolitical fact of life – they were a small power among other bigger and more powerful European kingdoms, all of whom regarded the island kingdom as a rival. That fact, they deduced, put a premium on what we now call political or strategic, intelligence. Defined, it meant information about what was going on inside the crowned heads of other kingdoms, which was where any threat would be formulated. To get that information, what was called 'King's Business' came into being. It was a euphemism for a wide-ranging intelligence operation that used highly-educated men as 'special emissaries' of the English king. By the fourteenth century, somewhere around a dozen such emissaries were busy at work in the royal courts of Europe, officially representing their rulers in assorted diplomatic negotiations, unofficially collecting high-level intelligence. The methods ranged from simply overhearing indiscreet conversations at court to bribing royal scribes to provide copies of secret documents.

Among the emissaries was a scholar named Geoffrey Chaucer who, beginning in 1348, conducted a dozen 'King's Business' missions. Precisely what kind of intelligence Chaucer collected on those missions is lost to history, since the records of the time avoided discussing specifics. Whatever the details, Chaucer's services must have been valuable, for he was later awarded a generous pension for life – a rare largesse. The records of that pension say only he was awarded it for 'long and varied service to his liege'.

Other surviving 'King's Business' records mention operations in France during the Hundred Years War, including the role of one of England's first known foreign intelligence assets. His name was Pierre Cauchon and he was to be the central character in an operation that ultimately backfired and turned into an intelligence disaster.

A French bishop, Cauchon thoroughly disliked the French

BELOW: Joan of Arc. English Intelligence conducted a wide-ranging campaign to destroy and discredit her.

king, Charles VII. This moved him to transfer his loyalty to England's rival claimant for the French throne, Henry VI. When the Hundred Years' War broke out, Cauchon moved to the English-controlled territory of France, where the 'King's Business' recruited him as a spy. The idea was to use Cauchon as an agent to help recruit other sources among French Catholics and at the same time tap into his contacts in the church's establishment to gather intelligence.

Cauchon proved to be a valuable spy, but in 1428, an extraordinary event that neither he nor anyone else could have anticipated suddenly breathed new life into the failing French cause. A young peasant girl named Jeanne D'Arc, claiming to have received visions in which the Archangel Michael told her that God had decided she would save France, convinced the French royal court to give her a military command. Outfitted in white enameled armor and carrying a banner of white and blue with two angels and the word 'Jesus' on it, this remarkable young woman soon rallied an army to her cause. To the shock of the English, she led the French to a number of victories, including recapture of the city of Orleans. The alarmed English realized their grip on France was threatened. Jeanne D'Arc had to be put out of action.

The English achieved that objective on 23 May 1430, when she was captured during a failed French assault on the town of Compiegne. Her captors could have imprisoned her or worse, but that would not have ended her dramatic inspiration for French morale and their willingness to continue the war. The English decided she would have to be discredited in the eyes of the French, so an audacious plan was formulated. Jeanne D'Arc would be put on trial as a heretic and a witch.

Cauchon was enlisted to conduct what was a mockery of an ecclesiastical trial that included a parade of false witnesses attesting to her 'sorcery'. Of the 42 lawyers convened as a tribunal in the trial, almost all were in the pay of the English. The verdict was inevitable and she was found guilty of witchcraft. On 30 May 1431, Jeanne D'Arc was burned at the stake. She was 19 years old. A sign prepared by Cauchon and posted at the execution site declared that she was a "liar, pernicious, seducer of the people, diviner, superstitious, blasphemer of God, presumptuous, misbelieving the faith of Jesus Christ, braggart, idolater, dissolute, invoker of devils, apostate, schismatic and heretic".

Nobody in France believed this crude propaganda. Her execution served only to spur the French to greater efforts against the English invaders, who discovered that, in death, Jeanne D'Arc became a sacred symbol to her countrymen. Over the next two decades, they would evict the English from France for ever. It was an ignominious end for England that avenged her death and the deaths of all those French warriors at Agincourt.

MARCO POLO: THE SPY

WHEEZING FROM THE EFFORT, THE ELDERLY DOGES, RULERS OF THE VENETIAN REPUBLIC, CLIMBED TO THE TOP OF THE TOWER. THEY RESTED A FEW MOMENTS TO CATCH THEIR BREATH, THEN LOOKED OUT OVER THE MAGNIFICENT CITY AND BEGAN TO DISCUSS THE UNTHINKABLE.

It was the spring of 1253. From their vantage point, the doges could see across the harbor, jammed with ships of every size and description, trading vessels from dozens of kingdoms and empires. At the city's piers and docks, armies of stevedores were loading and unloading goods like a huge beehive – signifying Venice's status as the greatest trading center in the known world and source of its vast wealth.

The operative word was 'known', for the doges had received very disturbing news, sufficient to compel a meeting in the greatest possible privacy, high in the tower, away from any prying eyes. The unsettling news had come from the Vatican's missionaries who had traveled east and were now reporting an astonishing series of wonders. The doges had only moderate interest in most of those wonders. Their attention was concentrated on what the missionaries had to say about China as a mercantile empire, especially a huge fleet of ocean-going merchant ships known as 'junks', capable of sailing all the world's seas because of such miraculous technology as the compass. The doges were first and foremost men of business; all of them were fabulously wealthy traders. The reports raised a frightening possibility: a competing Chinese trading empire that one

day would expand westward and perhaps supplant the mighty trading empire of Venice.

The doges concluded that they needed detailed intelligence on this possible threat to their very existence. It so happened that they ran the largest and most efficient intelligence service in Europe. It was a service that took advantage of Venice's position as the world's most important trading center, into which an ocean of intelligence flowed. The service enrolled a lengthy roster of assets among the thousands of merchants and traders who did business with Venice. Among the more valuable were two of the city's most successful traders, the brothers Nicolo and Maffeo Polo. They had contacts with the first Chinese traders just then beginning to establish economic links with Europe to ship goods along the fabled Silk Road caravan trading route. The Polo brothers were enlisted to travel to China in what was officially a journey to discuss expanded trade. The real mission was to collect intelligence on the extent of the Chinese mercantile structure, how it functioned, whether there were any plans to establish a significant trading presence in Europe and anything else of interest they might find.

The Polos decided to bring with them their bright, 15-year-old nephew Marco, chiefly for his precocious talents as a linguist. As things turned out, Marco would immortalize their journey years later in an account that omitted a significant fact – it was among the most successful missions in the history of espionage.

It took over three years for the Polos to finally reach Beijing, where Kublai Khan, successor to his grandfather as supreme ruler of the Mongol empire, had established his capital after his conquest of China. The energetic Marco had mastered four languages on the way – Chinese, Mongolian, Persian and Uighur – while demonstrating an astonishing ability to soak up information like a blotter. Among the more important tidbits he picked up had to do with the personality of Kublai Khan himself. Marco learned that 'the Great Khan' had an insatiable appetite for intelligence. Generals, merchants, traders and scholars all knew that

RIGHT: Marco Polo, famed explorer and star spy for the city of Venice's intelligence service.

LEFT: An oceangoing
Chinese junk, whose
mercantile potential
so concerned the
doges of Venice.

economic intelligence to the doges. It included one they must have found especially pleasing: the xenophobic Chinese merchants had no intention of establishing footholds in Europe. For good measure, the doges also received some valuable items of technical intelligence, including textile looms, astrolabes, compasses and paper.

When the ever-resourceful Marco returned to Europe, he accepted the lavish thanks and a reward of the finest villa in Venice from the grateful doges. He then decided he was sitting on the thirteenth century equivalent of a gold mine – all those remarkable adventures he had experienced. The result was a book, Europe's first popular best-seller. Entitled *Book of Diverse Marvels of the World*, it would later become an enduring classic under the title of *The Travels of Marco Polo*. The travelogue carefully avoided any mention of Marco's intelligence role in the land he called 'Cathay'. He intended the book as a money-making proposition, but was irritated when many of its readers concluded he was simply telling tall tales. Marco found himself openly mocked for claiming, among other fantastic things, that the Orientals used "stones as fuel for fire" (coal) and hunted "lions with stripes" (tigers).

However, the doges believed and that is what counted. Marco himself kept the secret of his career as a spy until 1323, when on his deathbed he confessed to his two sisters that his great adventure was an intelligence mission conceived by the doges. He asked them to reveal the secret publicly at some point in the future, when it no longer mattered. As for his disbelieving readers, he noted, with an enigmatic smile, "I didn't tell in that book half the things I saw."

an audience with him meant an hours-long grilling on an exhausting range of topics, ranging from the religious beliefs of foreigners to the precise number of spears a soldier of a particular army was issued with. Merchants became aware that the Khan's approval for their valuable trade operations in his domains depended in large measure on how well they could satisfy his appetite for intelligence.

Marco was to find knowledge of the Khan's appetite of great value when the Polos reached Beijing. Granted an audience with Kublai Khan as distinguished traders from Europe – a subject of consuming interest to the Mongolian ruler – the Polos let Marco do much of the talking. It was a shrewd choice, for Marco had prepared well. He dazzled the Great Khan with a virtual encyclopedia of everything he had seen and heard during the long journey. Indeed, the Khan was so impressed, he asked Marco to serve as his personal envoy on various diplomatic missions around the Mongol empire. A more perfect situation for a spy cannot be imagined.

LONG-TERM PLACEMENT

Marco was to stay in the Mongol empire another 17 years, finally leaving when Kublai Khan died. During that time, he sent back to Venice a rich harvest of intelligence, including one piece of news that represented his supreme espionage triumph: he learned, straight from the horse's mouth, that the Khan had decided the Mongols would never invade Western Europe. The reason: Mongol intelligence had concluded that Europe was, as they put it, mostly "rocks and trees", useless for the great Mongol herds of horses that were the backbone of the Khan's mobile army. All those horses needed vast plains of grass. Marco also sent westward a treasure chest of

ABOVE: A 1375 depiction of Marco Polo leading a trade caravan headed for Europe along the Silk Road.

LOUIS XV: THE KING WHO KNEW EVERYTHING

AS KING LOUIS XV SWEPT GRANDLY INTO THE BALLROOM AT THE HEAD OF A LARGE ENTOURAGE OF FAITHFUL COURTIERS (INCLUDING TWO OF THE ROYAL MISTRESSES), THE GUESTS AT THE MASKED BALL BROKE OUT IN WILD APPLAUSE.

As they all knew, Louis was a dedicated party animal who never missed a glittering social occasion. His presence meant the evening was certain to be a lot of fun. In that summer of 1754, France's aristocrats were concerned above all with having fun, mainly in an apparently limitless number of such diversions as lavish masquerade balls.

However much the aristocrats regarded their king as a lightweight social butterfly, in fact there was another Louis XV at the ball that night, a man very few of his subjects knew about – a shrewd intriguer who was also Europe's greatest spymaster. They did not know that behind a facade of joyous partying, his real purpose in attending all those social occasions was recruiting spies. Before this particular night was over, he would find a gem, a larger-than-life character who still ranks as the most extraordinary spy in the history of espionage.

Louis' attention was drawn to one of the more striking figures at the ball, a stunningly beautiful young woman dressed in a silken gown. Summoned to meet the king, the young woman with blonde curls and ivory complexion bowed low, immediately revealing something that Louis

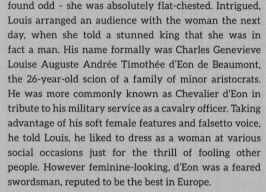

RIGHT: French King Louis XV, whose carefully crafted playboy image served as cover for his management of Europe's biggest espionage organization.

found odd – she was absolutely flat-chested. Intrigued, Louis arranged an audience with the woman the next day, when she told a stunned king that she was in fact a man. His name formally was Charles Genevieve Louise Auguste Andrée Timothée d'Eon de Beaumont, the 26-year-old scion of a family of minor aristocrats. He was more commonly known as Chevalier d'Eon in tribute to his military service as a cavalry officer. Taking advantage of his soft female features and falsetto voice, he told Louis, he liked to dress as a woman at various social occasions just for the thrill of fooling other people. However feminine-looking, d'Eon was a feared swordsman, reputed to be the best in Europe.

Louis instantly decided d'Eon was a perfect recruit for what he called 'The King's Secret', an intelligence agency he had personally created some years before. It was France's deepest secret; an organization of hand-picked agents who were posted in all the continent's important capitals and commercial centers, assigned the task of gathering intelligence about the plans, intentions and diplomatic maneuvers of the major European powers. Operating under deep cover, usually as prominent merchants, the spies of The King's Secret ultimately made Louis the best-informed ruler on the continent.

His newest recruit was assigned to the Russian court of Empress Elizabeth. He was to find out, and balk if possible, any plan for Russia to form an alliance with England, France's traditional enemy. In the spring of 1755, the dashing Chevalier d'Eon, posing as an idle French aristocrat seeking business opportunities in Russia, appeared at Elizabeth's court, where he immediately caught the eye of the empress. He carefully cultivated a friendship and when she admitted she did not like to read, offered her the services of his sister, Genevieve, who would read to her and serve in whatever other capacity the empress might want.

The strikingly beautiful Genevieve, dressed in flowing ivory satin, quickly became a close confidante of the empress, who began to confide Russia's highest secrets and sought her counsel. Genevieve subtly maneuvered

BELOW: The great French victory at Fleurus in 1690, a triumph made possible by France's spies.

where he would be given a comfortable pension on the condition that the Chevalier must always wear women's clothes (Louis oddly believed that d'Eon dressed as a woman was less of a threat than d'Eon dressed as a man). d'Eon again refused. Louis finally gave up, allowing him to settle in England on a £1,000-a-month pension, with the proviso that he kept his mouth shut.

By that point, d'Eon had become a notorious public figure, fueled by whispers about his time in Russia and rumored propensity for dressing as a woman depending on his mood. There were bets laid on whether he was in fact a woman posing as a man or vice versa (confusingly, d'Eon publicly insisted at this point he was a woman) and he fought a number of duels with several men who called him a transvestite. Tongues were further set wagging when d'Eon agreed to a duel with England's best swordsman. An audience that included the Prince of Wales saw d'Eon arrive as a woman wearing a black satin dress. That inspired titters, which turned to shocked gasps as d'Eon easily bested his opponent, finally dispatching him with a thrust between the eyes.

D'Eon died in 1810, at which point authorities conducted an autopsy that finally settled all the speculation: Europe's most fabled spy was indisputably a man.

the empress, something of a bubblehead, into believing that her kingdom's future lay in a close alliance with France. To that end, the empress ripped up a proposed treaty between Russia and England.

THE CHEVALIER UNCOVERED

It was only a matter of time before Elizabeth's ministers, aware that Russia's secrets were somehow finding their way to Paris, focused suspicion on the young Frenchwoman who had become the empress' closest confidante. However, before they could do anything about it, Genevieve d'Eon suddenly and mysteriously disappeared. Her brother expressed regrets that she had unexpectedly been summoned home to France and then disappeared just as mysteriously as his sister. The empress did not learn until many years later that Chevalier d'Eon and his beautiful sister Genevieve were in fact one and the same person.

D'Eon would go on to serve Louis as a spy on other important missions, sometimes as a man, more often as a woman. One of the more important as a man came in 1762, when he was posted to England under diplomatic cover with orders to gather intelligence on English roads and other facilities in preparation for a planned French invasion. D'Eon ultimately concluded that such an invasion would fail, a key piece of intelligence that saved his monarch a lot of grief.

However, the two men would come to a parting of the ways. For some unknown reason, d'Eon was obsessed with becoming French ambassador to England. When Louis said no, d'Eon threatened to go public with revelations about the king's wide-ranging espionage operations. Louis then ordered him to return to France,

ABOVE: The legendary French spy, Chevalier d'Eon, shown in a contemporary illustration as a half-man, half-woman.

THE EMPEROR AND THE LION

The dozen distinguished men of the Society for the Encouragement of French Industry, seated at the large table in a Paris government office, regarded the thin, diminutive man standing before them with something approaching open skepticism.

ABOVE: Napoleon, riding at the head of his staff, surveys his troops after the battle of Austerlitz, the astonishing victory that stamped him an authentic military genius.

LEFT: Napoleon Bonaparte's coat of arms, used on the front cover of the Code Napoleon, his most lasting contribution to European history.

This Parisian champagne-bottler was claiming that he had come up with an invention that would make France the mightiest military power in all history. Thus, he told them, he deserved the prize of 12,000 francs (some £200,000 in today's money) promised by Napoleon Bonaparte to anyone who came up with a scientific or industrial process that would help La Grande Armée achieve military dominance.

Napoleon had personally ordered these men, the best scientific and technical minds in France, to track down every possible innovation that might be of help to his military ambitions. To their dismay, the lure of the cash prize had attracted every crackpot in France. For months, they had listened to a steady parade of nut cases, such as the man who claimed to have perfected 'magic dust' to put entire brigades of British troops to sleep. They stared uncomprehendingly as Nicholas Appert reached into a satchel, withdrew two large champagne bottles and placed them on the table. "This, gentlemen," he announced, "will make the army of France the greatest army in the world."

The men at the table were silent for a moment, then one of them asked, with heavy sarcasm, "Do we presume correctly, Citizen Appert, that you propose to defeat the enemies of France by throwing champagne bottles at them?" "Not at all," an unfazed Appert replied. "It is not the bottle; it is what is inside the bottle." He pointed to several green vegetables floating in some kind of liquid inside the bottle. "These vegetables were sealed inside the bottle approximately three weeks ago, and as you can perceive, gentlemen, they are today just as green and fresh as the day I personally put them there."

Appert launched into a detailed explanation of how he had discovered a way to keep food fresh by boiling it and then sealing it inside an airtight bottle, a process that would maintain the freshness of whatever was preserved for a very long period of time. As he finished, one of his listeners, a military engineer, suddenly leapt from his seat, shouted, "Excellent!" and rushed from the room. He headed directly for Napoleon's office, where he briefed the general on what he had just heard. Napoleon instantly understood and a surprised Appert found himself ushered into the great man's presence. Napoleon pronounced him a genius, told him he

had won the prize of 12,000 francs and then commissioned him to build a factory to turn out many thousands of what Appert called "food in a bottle".

Appert went to work that spring of 1800 turning out a device that Napoleon was convinced would give his army a priceless advantage. Appert's invention would allow French troops to carry their own food, freeing them from foraging or waiting for slow, horse-drawn supply wagons. Troops carrying rations would have unprecedented mobility, able to move rapidly at distances inconceivable in nineteenth-century military strategy. It was, Napoleon decided, France's ultimate weapon.

However, there was no hope that would happen, because only a few weeks later, as the first of Monsieur Appert's wondrous bottles were distributed to French troops, a British spy got his hands on one. He quickly sent it off to London, setting off a chain of events that would result in a grave espionage defeat for Napoleon – just one of many he would suffer at the hands of his most implacable enemy.

When the Appert bottle arrived in London, it was immediately taken to the British army's Ordnance Department, the chief center for evaluating technical intelligence. Quartermasters there instantly realized the significance of the champagne bottle. They issued a plea to the British scientific and technical establishment: find out how the French process works and come up with a version that could be used by the British Army.

The man who successfully answered that call was not a scientist or engineer, but an ordinary London mechanic named Peter Durand. Intrigued by the problem and hopeful of making a tidy profit if he could devise a solution and commercialize it, Durand went to work. He carried out a number of experiments which convinced him that whoever had come up with the idea of food preservation was apparently an expert in bottling champagne, a process that involved keeping the bubbles intact in the liquid until the bottle was opened. That had been achieved by an airtight cork seal kept in place by a tight wire basket. Durand further deduced that the French inventor had made the logical leap: if bubbles could be preserved, why not food?

That process, Durand concluded, involved immersing fresh food in water, boiling it at high temperature to prevent putrefaction, then sealing it inside a bottle by means of an airtight cork. Durand went on to discover this was achieved in the Appert bottle by a mixture of various substances, including an especially pungent French cheese. An ingenious system, Durand concluded, but its weakness was obvious – glass. Even the thickest bottles were subject to breakage, not the ideal material for a combat environment. Although Durand didn't realize it at the time, what he did next would prove to be a revolutionary step in the world's food supply.

Durand had been experimenting with the use of tin, a cheap and widely available metal, for various industrial purposes. The problem with tin was that it was thin and not very strong, making it unsuitable for any use requiring strength. However, in a sudden inspiration, Durand realized the metal would be perfect for preserving food. Instead of a bottle, the food would be preserved, then sealed inside some sort of tin container by means of soldering. He formed a canister of tin, then worked out a system for preserving fresh produce and fruit in it. Thus he created the miracle of canned food and began the revolution in food processing. He called his invention the "tin canister," later shortened to 'can' – the common expression used to this day. His canister was put into large-scale production and less than a year after Appert's invention first entered service in the French army, the British army had an improved version.

The entire episode was a significant milestone in the history of modern espionage. It represented one of the first and most prominent examples of what is known in contemporary intelligence parlance as technical intelligence. What happened in 1800 illustrated the process perfectly. First you learn of the existence of a significant technological development by an enemy, then you obtain a copy of it, subject the sample to expert analysis and finally develop a countermeasure or trump the enemy's technology with an improved version. This process assumed greater importance as the pace of scientific and technical change began to speed up at the beginning of the nineteenth century. Nations learned, occasionally to their cost, that a scientific or technological breakthrough – smokeless powder, breech-loading artillery, rapid-firing 'repeater' rifles, high explosives – could determine victory or defeat in the space of an afternoon. The lesson was clear: intelligence operations to keep tabs on scientific and technological developments were absolutely vital.

There was no greater student – and victim – of this truth than Napoleon Bonaparte. A Corsican artillery officer born of humble circumstances, Napoleon liked to call science "the first god of war". He had no formal scientific training, but from the moment he began his meteoric rise in the French army, he understood that science and technology were undergoing profound

BELOW: French revolutionary Maximilien Robespierre is executed by guillotine during the terror following the French Revolution, ironically a terror he instigated.

ABOVE: Joseph Fouché, Napoleon's ruthless secret police chief, who created the template for the oppression carried out by modern totalitarian regimes.

Napoleon discovered that the great superiority of British guns was primarily the work of Robins, who devised ground-breaking equations that for the first time spelled out the precise forces that propelled projectiles out of guns. It was mathematics that led to dramatic improvements in artillery technology and made British guns the best in the world. Napoleon also learned that the high technical quality of British guns was due largely to the work of another Ordnance Department recruit, James Watt. His steam engines made possible the manufacture of standardized quality military technology on a mass basis, the crux of the Industrial Revolution.

There was something else Napoleon learned about British technological superiority, a facet never discussed publicly – espionage. The Ordnance Department relied on British intelligence to keep it abreast of any foreign scientific and military developments, especially actual samples of new technology. For quite some time, this very efficient system monitored military, industrial and technological developments throughout Europe. However, beginning at the moment when mobs in Paris besieged the Bastille, the attention of British intelligence began to focus most of its attention on France, now a nation controlled by radicals who had made no secret of their intense dislike for their nation's traditional enemy.

changes. He knew this would have important implications for the conduct of war, a subject in which Napoleon had few equals.

Beginning in 1794, he began a serious study of the elements that made Britain the world's greatest military power. The key to that dominance, Napoleon concluded, was the British army's Ordnance Department, which ran a flourishing research and development program to improve British military technology. Operating on the principle that the small nation of Britain had no hope of keeping its empire and surviving among a pack of hungry wolves without maintaining an edge in military technology, it actively recruited among the nation's best scientists for talent to keep that lead.

They included the mathematician Benjamin Robins, who focused his talents on ballistics. This was a subject of consuming concern to Napoleon as an artillery expert.

To keep watch on the new revolutionary government and any new technology it might devise, London's eyes and ears included a number of well-placed assets throughout Europe. These were mostly businessmen, along with diplomats, who were expected to file constant reports with the Foreign Office's very active intelligence section. The most important intelligence operation was centered in Switzerland. It was run by William Wickham, ostensibly the British chargé d'affaires in Bern, but in fact a full-time spymaster. He recruited large numbers of French royalist exiles who had key contacts inside France. Wickham also tapped into the extensive French royalist underground in Europe, which included ex-French military officers who were in touch with fellow former officers now in Napoleon's service.

Meanwhile, the British had not neglected counter-

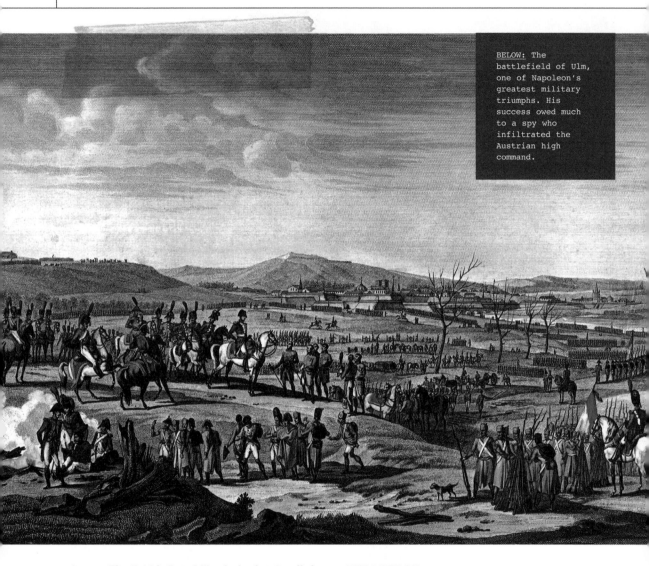

espionage. The British Post Office had what it called a 'Private Office', a secret section that covertly examined letters. It worked in conjunction with the two hundred-year-old Decyphering Branch that cracked enciphered foreign diplomatic communications.

France, Napoleon realized, had nothing approaching the size and efficiency of the British intelligence establishment. However, he was determined to create the French equivalent. It had to be a distinct improvement over the rickety intelligence structure he inherited from the revolutionary regime. In 1793, the Convention had created the 'Central Espionage Bureau' and funded it with 1,300,000 livres. It operated under the revolutionary government's Ministry of Foreign Affairs and was responsible for collecting intelligence about the assorted threats from European powers bent on destroying the revolutionary regime.

EXPANSION

The Bureau enlisted scores of willing spies, but their recruitment depended in large measure on the extent of their revolutionary ardor, not their talent for intelligence collection. Their record was very spotty, as was the regime's chief attempt at counterespionage, the infamous Committee of Public Safety. The theory behind the Committee was that thousands of dedicated French revolutionaries living throughout France would serve as the 'eyes and ears' of the revolution. They would carefully watch for any sign of foreign spies, who then would be reported to the Committee for a drumhead trial and execution on the guillotine.

In practice, however, the system quickly degenerated into denunciation and counter-denunciation by citizens eager to settle old personal scores. Very few spies were caught. The record of another counterespionage force the regime created was not any better. It was called the 'Corps de Garde', a national police force assigned the task of tracking down royalists or royalist sympathizers. However, its members were largely untrained amateurs who too often used their power to shake down alleged royalist sympathizers for profit.

All of this would have to be replaced, Napoleon decided. France must create a new and professional intelligence capability. It needed a foreign intelligence organization to keep watch on the threats that surrounded revolutionary France and a domestic counterintelligence structure that would make France airtight against all hostile intelligence penetrations. Above all, he concluded, France must be able to checkmate the intelligence depredations of its most dangerous enemy – Britain. There was no doubt in Napoleon's mind that a great struggle was in the offing, one that would decide the future of the world. It would pit industrial, autocratic Britain against revolutionary, democratic France. It would be a conflict of opposing ideologies and differing social-economic systems, a titanic battle for dominance of Europe, markets, trade, colonies and commercial supremacy.

In the end, Napoleon would lose that struggle, in large measure because he never succeeded in his goal of achieving a superior French intelligence capability. That failure had a great deal to do with Bonaparte's own personality. Convinced that British spies were lurking everywhere in France (he wasn't far from the truth), Napoleon's first priority was counterintelligence. Almost immediately, he found the perfect man for the job, a strange, sinister and amoral character who would come to be the very personification of a secret police chief. His name was Joseph Fouché. He began life modestly enough as the son of a working class family, before becoming a teacher at Catholic refectories. A mild anti-monarchist, his life was transformed by the French Revolution, which turned him into a radical. His fanaticism was rewarded by the new revolutionary government with appointment as proconsul in one of the departments of France. There, the 32-year-old Fouché quickly demonstrated a talent for domestic terror. He abolished clerical celibacy, ordered all priests to marry or adopt a child within a month, banned Christian funeral services, purged the landed nobility, confiscated the wealth of the privileged, sent hundreds of accused royalists to the guillotine and recruited battalions of informers to spy on their neighbors.

Such zealousness in the revolutionary cause earned him a promotion into the revolution's inner circle, which was undergoing a personnel problem. The problem involved the important post of Minister of General Police of the Directory, the revolutionary government's internal security high command. Nine ministers had come and gone, each of whom proved incapable of managing such an important task. Given

his record to that point, Fouché was the ideal candidate for the job. Armed with unbridled power to impose the will of the revolutionary government throughout France by any means he thought necessary, Fouché soon proved his ruthless talents for such work. When the people of Lyons revolted against the harsh policies of the government, Fouché had 1,906 of them arrested, then executed by guillotine. When that did not appear to end the revolt, he sent in troops who slaughtered protestors with cannon fire. "Terror, salutary terror," Fouché proudly reported to Paris, "is now the order of the day."

Such unbridled terror made Fouché infamous among the revolutionaries and very nearly got him killed. Robespierre, envious of the minister's popularity among the revolutionary government's most radical faction, began to maneuver against him – the clear prelude to Fouché's inevitable arrest and execution. Well-informed of the approaching danger, thanks to informers around Robespierre he had recruited, Fouché made his move. He threw in his lot with Napoleon Bonaparte, who was conspiring to seize power from the Councils of the Legislature. When the Corsican succeeded, he rewarded Fouché with a new post, Minister of Police.

In that post, Napoleon decreed, Fouché was to blanket France with a network of police, spies and informers. They were to know everything going on inside the country, down to street-level gossip. Fouché would operate with no legal restraints whatsoever; he could arrest and execute anyone he wanted at any time for any reason. He was given a force of 30,000 police to carry out this mission, which was to concentrate on counterintelligence. No foreign agent and no foreign intelligence asset could exist a moment in France without the Minister of Police's army of police and informers becoming aware. Fouché made it clear he was willing to kill anyone he considered disloyal or a threat to the regime. As he chillingly phrased it, "The blood of criminals fertilizes the soil of liberty and establishes power on sure foundations."

Executions were just one aspect of a huge secret police apparatus that Fouché put into place, a mechanism for repression that would later serve as a template for the repressive machinery of Nazi Germany and the Soviet Union. France was overlaid with a network that reached into every nook and cranny. No one felt safe saying anything even remotely political for fear of receiving a visit from Fouché's police in the middle of the night and dragged off to interrogation and prison. Those adjudged guilty of treason (usually defined as disloyalty) or serving the cause of foreign intelligence could expect a trip to the guillotine.

THE POWER TO CONTROL

The press was strictly censored and Fouché's headquarters maintained a huge data bank of files on thousands of French citizens who had come to the attention of the police for one reason or another – including a file on Napoleon himself containing salacious gossip gathered from his mistresses. All French workers had to carry a livret, officially a work permit, but in fact a national identity card intended as a means of population control. The man who presided over all this totalitarian machinery prepared lengthy intelligence reports each day (except Sunday) for Napoleon. These covered a wide range of intelligence, from palace gossip to what arrests and interrogations of foreign agents had revealed. Often, he would include human-interest tidbits to titillate his boss, such as the report concerning a captured female British spy who wrote the information she had collected on her petticoat in invisible ink.

Napoleon devoured those reports avidly. He often sent Fouché notes asking for elaboration about one piece of intelligence or another or suggesting areas where his police minister's agents may have missed something. One note to Fouché, for example, read: "They tell me that very seditious talk goes on at a wine shop on Rue St. Honore. Pay a little attention to these small taverns." Napoleon was most interested in any reports dealing with two subjects about which he seemed obsessed – assassination plots against him and the activities of British spies. He was particularly interested in anything suggesting a convergence of the two. As he was aware, even in the police state that France had become, there were still a good number of people who wanted to murder the man who had become dictator of France, notably royalists determined to restore the monarchy.

Aware of Napoleon's special concern, Fouché concentrated a lot of resources on tracking down and ensnaring royalists. This effort included an extensive mail-monitoring operation that sought to spot any correspondence between royalists operating in France and royalist leaders living in foreign exile. All that work paid off when Fouché's agents were able to forestall a number of assassination plots against Napoleon. During his reign, there was only one actual assassination attempt, a bomb that exploded harmlessly near his carriage as he rode through Paris. Napoleon shrugged off that attempt, but became infuriated when Fouché told him of several plots that involved British intelligence. One that dramatically raised the Bonaparte blood pressure was a plot that reached very close to him – the recruitment by the British of a French officer whose wife happened to be one of Napoleon's mistresses. Perhaps for reasons having to do with resentment over his wife's extramarital relationship, the officer agreed to work for British Intelligence and convince his spouse to kill Napoleon during a very intimate occasion. At the last moment, however, the officer changed his mind and told Fouché of the plot. Napoleon magnanimously forgave the contrite officer, but never again shared an intimate moment with the man's wife.

In terms of the threat from British intelligence, a more important effect of Fouché's internal security apparatus was its severe dampening of British operations in France. Most of those operations depended on royalist assets and as more and more of them were hunted down and arrested, British intelligence suffered accordingly. Fouché also managed to shut down a number of important British operations that did not involve the use of royalists. One involved the recruitment of the inhabitants of Jersey, an island just off the French coast, to collect intelligence on French naval facilities. A Jersey resident involved in smuggling had many contacts in France, so he was recruited to make runs into that country to gather intelligence on what he could see of French military preparations along the coast, as an amphibious invasion of Britain by Napoleon was always a possibility. He managed to make 184 round trips before Fouché's agents finally caught up to him, leading to the rolling-up of the entire Jersey network.

Fouché also demonstrated some skill at the double agent game. One of his more brilliant operations targeted a British diplomat, Francis Drake. Officially ambassador to the German state of Bavaria, his real job was running British intelligence operations directed against France from southern Europe. Drake was one of the most talented agent handlers in British intelligence and Fouché was determined to get rid of him. To accomplish that, he set in motion one of his best agents, Mehde de la Touche, who arrived in London one day with an urgent plea. He described himself as a dedicated (but secret) royalist who was the head of an underground network waiting for the opportunity to overthrow Napoleon. He was seeking covert British help for that task, mostly money. Initially, the British were skeptical. However, Touche, who claimed to have many assets in areas of France near the German border, finally persuaded them of his genuineness. They sent him off to Munich to meet with Drake. As he had in London, a persuasive Touche was able to overcome some early skepticism and finally convince Drake to provide lavish funds for his underground network. The game went on for months, until the British began to get suspicious that all was not well with the Touche network. At that point, Fouché pulled the plug, splashing an account of the episode in French newspapers. Other papers in Europe picked up the story and Drake's diplomatic position was soon made untenable. He returned to London, never again to serve on the continent.

Overall, Fouché could claim remarkable success in bringing all of France under Napoleon's heel while at the same time virtually crippling British intelligence operations. That success was largely attributable to his talents as a secret policeman and counterespionage spymaster, as well as the fact that Napoleon left him alone to perform his duties as he saw fit. However, in the field of France's foreign intelligence, Napoleon insisted on being his own spymaster. That eventually proved to be a formula for disaster.

KEY PERSONNEL

Napoleon's early triumphs owed much to intelligence. His brilliant 1796 campaign in Italy, an achievement that made him world-famous, was highlighted by a decisive defeat of part of a much larger Austrian force that had been delayed arriving on the battlefield because of 'poor transmission of orders'. Or so the Austrian commander claimed. In fact, Napoleon's staff officer for intelligence, Adjutant General Jean Landrieux, had discovered that the Austrian was deeply in debt and had no way of getting out from under it given Austria's notoriously penurious payments to its

generals. Landrieux lavished more than 100,000 gold francs on the Austrian commander (nearly £3 million in today's currency) for his convenient delay.

Some time later, Napoleon personally recruited a man who would prove to be an even more valuable asset, a prominent Alsatian businessman named Charles Schulmeister. Introduced to Napoleon during a state dinner, Schulmeister convinced the general that he could obtain top-level intelligence to aid the projected French assault into southern Germany. It is a tribute to Schulmeister's salesmanship that he was not only able to convince Napoleon of his claim to be a master spy (although he had no espionage experience), but was also able to extract lavish payments for his services. He turned out to be well worth the nearly £2 million Napoleon paid him. Schulmeister showed up in Vienna posing as a

ABOVE: The Duke of Wellington encourages his troops during the Battle of Busaco in 1810, one of a series of victories that destroyed Napoleon's armies in Spain.

disaffected Hungarian nobleman who had spent some time in Napoleon's headquarters, later leaving after becoming disillusioned with the French leader's dictatorial ways. Schulmeister tapped into a deep well of French espionage funds to maintain an expensive life style, as befitted a rich Hungarian aristocrat.

Gradually, Schulmeister drew close to his primary target, Austrian Field Marshal Karl von Mack. Capitalizing on some distant royal family connections to make the final link, Schulmeister befriended Mack. He then hooked him by giving him some intelligence on Napoleon's plans – all of it chicken feed provided by the French. It was enough to convince Mack that his Hungarian friend could be an Austrian spy. Now a double agent, Schulmeister happily agreed to the recruitment. He headed off toward the French lines to collect intelligence while Mack gathered his army at Ulm. Schulmeister returned with a vital piece of intelligence: Napoleon did not plan to capture Ulm and was in fact retreating away from the city. Mack swallowed the bait and moved in pursuit of the retreating French, at which point Napoleon sprang the trap. In one of military history's most decisive battles, he surrounded and then shattered the Austrian army, which lost over 50,000 men. "All praise to Charles," Napoleon said to his staff as he watched thousands of Austrian prisoners being marched out of Ulm. "He was worth 40,000 men to me."

No doubt, but such triumphs as Ulm began to convince Napoleon that in addition to his military genius, he was also a spymaster of genius. He came to believe that his own innate talents, which made him so brilliant a tactician on the battlefield, would serve him just as well in the espionage game. He insisted on being the sole evaluator of intelligence. No officer on his staff could change his mind once he decided what a given piece of intelligence meant. Those decisions tended to be made strictly on the basis of what German military tacticians liked to call 'finger feel', an instinctive sense of what was going on in a battlefield – when to attack, when to maneuver and the precise point of an enemy's weakness. However, intelligence does not work that way, as a series of costly espionage blunders by Napoleon were to prove.

The first defeats came where Napoleon was weakest, on the sea. Aware of that, the British began to organize an efficient naval intelligence system, an effort largely the work of a bright young Royal Navy officer named John H. Bancroft. After carefully analyzing how Napoleon kept in touch with his naval fleets operating in foreign ports, Bancroft learned that his orders were dispatched via a number of fast, small boats. Most of these were piloted by local sailors who worked for French pay, but had no particular loyalty to their paymasters. That meant they were vulnerable to bribery. Bancroft convinced the Admiralty to provide him with sufficient gold to convince the captains of the dispatch boats to delay their arrivals because of 'contrary winds' or some other convenient excuse – sufficient for a team of Bancroft's agents to copy the dispatches and then send them on.

Bancroft also recruited a large network of dockworkers, ordinary waterfront laborers and others in a position to know about the dispositions, condition and movements of the French fleets. They were to play no small role in Admiral Horatio Nelson's uncanny ability to divine French intentions for his great victories that destroyed Napoleon's sea power. One other Bancroft innovation also proved valuable. He noticed that the French newspapers, although under rigid censorship, nevertheless contained plenty of valuable intelligence clues, provided that people with the right kind of knowledge could spot them. Bancroft recruited a number of naval officers with varying areas of expertise to carefully comb the French newspapers for any important clues that had slipped by the censors. The censors for the most part were untrained functionaries instructed to excise only the most obvious information of intelligence value – General Murat's cavalry has departed Toulon, etc. However, they overlooked such valuable items as the announcement that Napoleon was recruiting scientists for "an important scientific expedition". One of Bancroft's readers, who happened to be an Egyptologist, noticed that several of the men listed were prominent Egyptologists. This bit of intelligence told Bancroft that Napoleon was about to invade Egypt.

Napoleon's next intelligence failure occurred in Spain. In 1808, he ignored the advice of his intelligence officers and put his brother Joseph on the throne of Spain, igniting a revolt by Spaniards and Portuguese. They sought help from Britain, setting off a six-year-long struggle, just as French intelligence officers warned would happen. As they tried to point out to no avail, Napoleon would need to send in at least 100,000 troops to keep Joseph propped up on the throne against fierce opposition by the Spaniards and Portuguese, backed by the British army. The French army, they noted, would have to function in a sea of hostile people who were potentially a huge army of spies. It was a disaster waiting to happen, requiring only a talented enemy on the other side who knew what to do with all those potential intelligence assets. Unfortunately for Napoleon, just such a man arrived in Spain to head the British forces – Arthur Wellesley, the Duke of Wellington.

Among other talents, Wellesley was a passionate collector of information, who believed no military commander should commit troops to battle without knowledge in depth about the enemy. Long before he went to Spain, Wellesley had devoted much time to a detailed study of Napoleonic tactics. He immersed himself in the minutiae of how Napoleon maneuvered his troops for battle, how the French logistics system worked, what the French marshals were inclined to do in any given tactical situation and how Napoleon's intelligence system functioned.

Wellesley was well prepared militarily to take on the French in Spain, but he realized that he wasn't nearly as well prepared in the intelligence war. Although the British army had been taught the necessity of good intelligence as a result of its sobering experiences during the American Revolution, the effort was too fragmented. Intelligence tasks were usually split among individual units, with each of them collecting their own intelligence without co-ordinating the results with other units. It was an error compounded by each of the units carrying out their own intelligence evaluation, too often on the basis of inadequate intelligence.

Worse, there was no integration of operational intelligence with strategic intelligence.

Wellesley went to work, completely overhauling the British intelligence system in Spain. His first step was to integrate his army's operational intelligence with whatever was collected by non-military British intelligence. The best such intelligence was being obtained by a talented diplomat-spy, Charles Stuart, the British minister in Portugal. Wellesley learned that among other accomplishments, Stuart had organized a ring of spies in the French port of Bayonne. It was the port through which most of the reinforcements for La Grande Armée in the peninsula passed and was a perfect observation post to determine the French order of battle. For some time, such important

BELOW: Goya's depiction of French soldiers executing captured Spanish guerrillas, a draconian action that failed to end the Spanish insurgency.

strategic intelligence had been sent directly to London, with very little of it winding up in the hands of British forces on the peninsula. From now on, General Wellesley decreed, that intelligence would come into his hands first, to be integrated with his own operational intelligence.

His next step was to set up a centralized system for that operational intelligence. Henceforth, all intelligence would be sent to trained intelligence officers on Wellesley's newly-created staff, there to be evaluated. Convinced that his army's operational intelligence collection needed improvement, Wellesley created an elite reconnaissance force called the 'Corps of Guides'. Composed of hand-picked British cavalry units and recruited Spanish insurgents with intimate knowledge of the countryside, they were led by Wellesley's best cavalry officer, Lieutenant Colonel Coloquhon Grant, a dashing and fearless cavalryman whose men made forays deep behind French lines to keep watch on French dispositions and movements. Those operations were run nearly around the clock to keep intelligence as up-to-date as possible.

DEAD NOT ALIVE

The Spanish insurgents turned out to be Wellesley's best assets. Calling themselves guerrillas (a word that has since passed into the language), they carried out a no-quarters war against the hated occupiers with hit-and-run raids against military installations and French troops. Their greatest value, however, turned out to be the turmoil they caused in French communications. One day, a Spanish guerrilla showed up at Wellesley's headquarters with the severed head of a French dispatch rider he had killed. He asked if the British wanted the heads of other dispatch riders he and his fellow guerrillas might encounter. No, thank you, Wellesley replied, but he was interested in any papers the riders would be carrying. Guerrillas who brought him French dispatches would be generously rewarded.

Soon, there was a steady flow of French dispatches into his headquarters, but Wellesley found them of limited use, since they were enciphered. He then fortuitously remembered that one of the junior officers on his staff, an engineer lieutenant named George Scovell, was a brilliant linguist – a talent Wellesley assumed might lead to an insight into those hidden communications. Given the captured French dispatches, Scovell – who had taught himself cryptography as an intellectual exercise for his restive mind – solved them in seven days. Armed with those decrypts, Wellesley scored a number of tactical victories.

The capstone came on 12 July 1812, when guerrillas turned over a lengthy dispatch they had captured. Given its length, Scovell deduced that it was probably an important message, a deduction further proven when he noted that it was enciphered in a new, more elaborate system. Called by the French 'the Great Paris Cipher', it used 1,400 numbers as code words, further hidden by a super-encipherment system to defeat cryptanalysis. Working virtually around the clock, Scovell finally broke the code and discovered he had decrypted a blockbuster.

The message was from King Joseph himself to the commander of French forces on the peninsula, laying out plans and dispositions for a major French offensive against Salamanca, in northern Spain. Wellington struck first, inflicting over 12,000 casualties, a major French defeat that marked the beginning of the end for Napoleon's adventure in Spain. Within a year, the British and their Spanish and Portuguese allies had driven the French from the peninsula. "I knew everything," Wellesley later said of his intelligence advantage during the peninsular campaign, with only slight exaggeration.

Napoleon would have given his right arm for even a fraction of the intelligence riches that Wellesley enjoyed, but his own intelligence service could not provide it. Even when they did provide him with good intelligence, there was no guarantee that Napoleon would accept it. Witness events in Spain, where Napoleon ignored the advice of his own intelligence apparatus that placing his brother on the Spanish throne and imposing his rule by the presence of La Grande Armée was a recipe for certain disaster.

Napoleon ignored his intelligence apparatus' sound advice about another theater of war, Russia. That mistake would prove even more disastrous. Having learned nothing from events in Spain, in the summer of 1812 Napoleon gathered an army of 450,000 men to crush Russian Czar Alexander – his remaining major rival on the continent. His plan was to mass that army in Poland, then strike into Russia, destroy the Russian army in a series of pitched battles and force Alexander to sue for peace. Napoleon brushed aside the uneasiness of his staff about the huge scope of this plan, noting that seven years before he had destroyed a Russian army at the battle of Austerlitz, regarded as his greatest tactical masterpiece. Napoleon insisted he would crush the Russian army of 1812 just as completely; La Grande Armée would slice through Russia like a knife through butter.

To no avail, the staff officers responsible for intelligence pointed out that Austerlitz had been fought on Austrian territory. Now, the Russians would be defending their homeland, a far different matter. There were even more serious problems, not least among them the fact that the French really had no firm grasp on conditions inside Russia. What would Alexander's reaction be to a French invasion? How did the Russian army intend to fight and just how many resources could the Russians muster? In truth, the French would be marching into Russia blind. Napoleon had suddenly decided on an invasion and his timetable allowed no time for any kind of detailed collection of intelligence.

However, Napoleon had no concern about the unknown; he remained convinced that his own tactical genius could overcome any unanticipated event.

Events soon proved that no amount of tactical genius could overcome lack of information. In June 1812, Napoleon led his huge army into Alexander's kingdom. As he expected, there were a number of set-piece battles, but the first in a series of unanticipated events began to unhinge Napoleon's master plan. To his surprise the Russians simply retreated eastward before they could be completely defeated. On the way, they conducted a scorched-earth policy, destroying everything that could be of use to the French forces. Napoleon was befuddled by the Russian strategy of trading space for time, which prevented him from using his greatest weapon – the Napoleonic battle of annihilation that could utterly defeat an enemy in a matter of hours. Moreover, the scorched-earth tactics of the Russians made his supply problems a great deal worse.

By September, Napoleon had entered Moscow, but it was an empty victory. Retreating Russians had evacuated its citizens and burned the city to the ground (Moscow was largely composed of wooden houses). Napoleon had won a handful of ashes and there were even greater troubles behind him. His long supply line was being harassed by an aroused Russian population that fought as guerrillas. As his logistical system collapsed, Napoleon finally decided to retreat from Russia. By that time, the great Russian winter had struck. His exhausted and starving troops, constantly under attack from all sides as they trudged through the snows, became a disorganized mob. Fewer than 10,000 men managed to make it back to their original starting point, a military disaster of the first magnitude. Combined with the defeat on the Iberian Peninsula, it meant Napoleon would never achieve his objective of becoming the master of Europe.

History has judged the invasion of Russia and the British triumph on the peninsula as the two events that wrecked the Napoleonic grand design. However, there was another, less well-known intelligence error Napoleon committed that would have even more significant long-term historical impact.

The error began in Santo Domingo (present-day Haiti and the Dominican Republic), a Caribbean island few in Europe had ever heard of except as a source for sugar, the substance to which Europeans had become addicted. Its acquisition by France early in the seventeenth century was part of a larger plan to establish a powerful outpost of the French empire in North America, centered on the vast lands known as Louisiana. A 1791 revolt by slaves on the island, led by the charismatic leader Toussaint L'Ouverture, threw out the French. In 1802, Napoleon decided to take it back, part of a larger effort to checkmate British influence in the New World. In Napoleon's conception, France would retake the lands ceded to Spain as a result of the Seven Years War. It would then establish a powerful presence based on control of New Orleans, the trading center that controlled the entire Mississippi basin. Control of that trade would provide France with a money machine to underwrite other imperial adventures.

In 1800, Napoleon induced weak Spain to cede Louisiana back to France. In Napoleon's master plan, the next step was to retake Santo Domingo, another potential money machine. Convinced of the genius of his own plan, he hadn't bothered to collect any intelligence in that area of the world. The lack of intelligence would prove very costly. For one thing, Napoleon didn't know that the new nation of the United States, busily expanding, was already settling areas along the Mississippi and casting covetous glances at New Orleans, which controlled trade along the mighty waterway. The Americans were very uneasy about the return of Louisiana to a man notorious for the kind of imperial ambitions that tended to make all his neighbors nervous. They became even more nervous when, in 1802, Napoleon sent 30,000 troops into Santo Domingo to retake the island, restore slavery and restart sugar production.

Almost at once, everything went wrong. Since Napoleon hadn't bothered to collect any intelligence about Santo Domingo, he failed to realize that the island was infected with yellow fever. It felled thousands of his troops, Europeans who had no resistance against the disease. He also failed to realize that the forces of L'Ouverture had no intention of fighting the mighty army of France on French terms. Instead, they burned everything of potential value to the French invaders, then retreated inland to fight a vicious guerrilla war in which they had all the advantages. The French army slowly bled to death. By 1803, it was clear that France had no hope of winning in Santo Domingo. When French commanders asked Napoleon for another 35,000 troops, he turned down the request and tried to figure a way out.

Now another intelligence failing by Napoleon came into play. He badly underestimated the Americans, whom he tended to regard as a bunch of ignorant savages, especially their president, Thomas Jefferson. However Jefferson, who had once served as the American minister in France, had set up an extensive intelligence network of diplomats and merchants. They kept him well-informed of the troubles Napoleon was undergoing – not the least of them financial as the Santo Domingo fiasco drained the French treasury. At precisely the right psychological moment, Jefferson played his trump card: he instructed Robert R. Livingston, the American minister in Paris, to drop broad hints to Napoleon that the United States might be interested in a rapprochement with the British which could include some sort of 'arrangement' about the lands in the southernmost U.S.

As Jefferson intended, the hint raised a specter that Napoleon dreaded: an alliance between the British and the Americans. Since Napoleon had no intelligence that could tell him whether this hint had any basis in reality (it didn't), he could only assume it was probably true. Jefferson's ploy worked. Hard up for cash and now eager to shed himself of the American albatross, Napoleon offered to sell Louisiana to the United States. It was the greatest land deal in history: 828,000 square miles of some of the most resources-rich territory in the world, sold for about eleven cents an acre. In a stroke, the deal set the United States on a course that eventually would make it a mighty world power.

By 1815, it was all over for Napoleon. Decisively defeated at Waterloo and about to be sent into permanent exile, he confronted one last intelligence failure. It concerned his loyal secret police chief, Fouché. Napoleon discovered that his total trust in Fouché had been misplaced. Fouché had been secretly negotiating with the Allies for quite some time, mainly about his own future in a France without Napoleon. Summoned to an audience with his master, Fouché had no sooner walked into the room when Napoleon shouted at him, "I ought to have you shot!"

"I cannot agree with you, sire," Fouché calmly replied, without even a blink of fear. His calmness had everything to do with his intimate knowledge of how Napoleon's mind worked. As he was aware, Napoleon admired courage, above all. He knew that standing unflinchingly before a man whose very name once inspired fear in all of Europe was a guarantee he would live.

He turned out to be right. Napoleon stared at him for a moment, then kissed him on both cheeks. "Go," he said, with a wave of his hand. The two men never saw each other again.

After Waterloo, Napoleon was surprised to learn that he would not be executed by the triumphant Allies. He was further surprised to learn that Allied leaders had been talked out of a plan to put him on trial and execute him by his most implacable enemy, the Duke of Wellington. Executing Napoleon, Wellington argued, would be the height of hypocrisy; all the rulers of Europe were guilty at some point or another of plotting aggressive war. Napoleon Bonaparte just happened to be better at it than anyone else.

Some years after Napoleon's departure to exile, Wellington learned that, in 1804, the French emperor had hired an assassin to kill him. Wellington shrugged off the news, noting that British intelligence had covertly supported a French royalist plot of assassinate Napoleon at about the same time. Wellington's sanguine mood may have stemmed from his postwar existence as his nation's greatest war hero, heaped with honors and wealth. Part of that wealth was an immense amount of war booty he had taken from Napoleon – including two of the French emperor's most beautiful mistresses.

ABOVE: Toussaint L'Overture, the Haitian revolutionary who bled Napoleon's army white — and set the stage for the Louisiana Purchase.

CHAMBRES NOIR: SECRET WRITING

CRYPTOGRAPHY, THE SCIENCE OF SECRET WRITING, WAS BORN AT THE SAME TIME AS ESPIONAGE. THEY SHARE A COMMON GENESIS.

The moment human beings realized that their survival depended in large part on knowing what other human beings were doing, they also realized their most secret communications had to be kept from prying eyes. Cryptography, the method used to achieve that, involves two forms of secret writing – codes and ciphers. Although the two terms are commonly used interchangeably, they are in fact somewhat different.

A cipher transforms plain text into numbers by a specific 'key' that scrambles the plain text letters into a series of numbers unscrambled by a recipient who knows the key. To demonstrate how that works, here's a simple cipher system that uses the numbers one through seven as the key. The cipher would be written this way:

	1	2	3	4	5	6	7
1	A	B	C	D	E	F	G
2	H	I	J	K	L	M	N
3	O	P	Q	R	S	T	U
4	V	W	X	Y	Z		

To encipher the message 'Come at once', begin with the left column, then match the letter with the vertical column. Thus, the enciphered message would read:

13 31 26 15 11 36 31 27 13 15

Commonly, the encipherment is written in five-figure groups, so the message as transmitted would read:

13312 61511 36312 71315

Using the same one-to-seven key, the recipient would make the same grid shown above and decrypt the message.

A code is a system that substitutes plain text with numbers from a codebook, which is a list of words with their numerical code equivalents. The code words are four-digit numbers – 2301 for 'machine gun', 2689 for 'mortar' and so on. A message prepared with the use of a codebook is readable only to a recipient with the same codebook. Those books can range from just a few pages to a thick volume. A naval codebook, for example, would have to include a large number of code words to cover the many words used in naval terminology.

SETTING AND SOLVING

Ever since the first known codes and ciphers were developed in the ancient Middle East, cryptanalysis – the science of solving them – has run on a parallel track. Indeed, the entire history of secret writing can be summarized as a race between offense and defense, with neither side ever able to gain a permanent advantage. The race really began in 1412, when Arab mathematicians arrived at a crucial insight: all languages have specific patterns of letter frequency. Known as frequency analysis, this determines that English, for example, most frequently uses the letter 'E'. That means at least 13 per cent of all the letters in any given message written in English will be 'E'.

The Arab insight provided cryptanalysts with a powerful weapon, one familiar to the solvers of newspaper cryptograms. Looking at a cipher message known to be written in English, they will apply frequency analysis to determine which number occurs with most frequency. If for instance it is 26, they can infer that may mean 'E'. If the inference proves correct, they will have a crucial foothold into gradually solving the message as frequency analysis determines letter after letter. To foil frequency analysis, cryptographers have developed a number of refinements. These include 'additives' (adding one- or two-digit numbers that are

RIGHT: An FBI cryptanalyst works to crack a German message during World War II, using methods made obsolete by the advent of code machines.

One-time pads make the cryptanalyst's job nearly impossible, since every message is truly random. However, the system is time-consuming, a real drawback if a long message has to be transmitted or when speed is of the essence. For that reason, modern cryptography has come to rely on code machines that automatically encipher messages at the sender's end and transmit the messages to twin machines at the receiver end, which also decrypt the messages automatically.

Such machines can transmit reams of messages very quickly. Theoretically, code machines are unbreakable, since they can instantly generate huge numbers of random numbers. However, they have proven vulnerable to attack by computers.

With the advent of the microchip, computers have come to dominate cryptography. So-called super computers designed for cryptographic work can run through millions of possible number combinations in the proverbial blink of an eye to unlock cipher keys and deduce codebook additives. In 1979, the Cray-1 supercomputer specifically developed for the U.S.A.'s National Security Agency, had an average speed of 80 MFLOPS (80 million floating point operations), meaning it could perform that many mathematical computations each second. In 2006, its successor, known as CHAMP, had a computing speed 350,000 times faster.

Modern cryptography is largely a race between these mind-boggling machines, one breed generating codes and ciphers running into the trillions of numbers at a keystroke, another breed uncovering them with equal speed. No one can predict whether cryptographers or cryptanalysts will ultimately come out on top. All that can be said with certainty is that the struggle will go on, probably forever.

changed frequently), 'transposition' (rearrangement of the letters), 'substitution' (jumbling the letters in the plain text by a prearranged system) and constantly changing the key for cipher messages.

The ultimate counter to frequency analysis came in the 1930s, when Soviet intelligence perfected the so-called 'one-time pad'. The pad is actually a refinement to an existing codebook; each sheet of the pad contains a different series of random numbers. Those numbers, called 'additives', are added to the coded message, then the sheet is thrown away, never to be used again. Both recipient and sender have copies of the same pad and use the same sheet of numbers in tandem. The technique, known as 'super-encipherment' causes real difficulties for cryptanalysts, since the additives make the coded message random.

To see how a one-time pad works, assume that a sender wants to dispatch the following message: FIRST DIVISION MOVES EAST TONIGHT. He consults his codebook, which uses the following four-number groups to represent those words: 2222 2413 2624 2517 2941. He writes those numbers on one line. Then he consults a sheet of random numbers in his one-time pad, writing them underneath the coded message. The result will look like this:

Coded message: 2222 2413 2624 2517 2941
One-time pad addition: 4012 1985 6321 3246 1397

The two lines are added together, producing the actual message that will be dispatched:

6234 4398 8945 5763 4338

The recipient consults his own one-time pad and 'strips' the message by subtracting the additives. He then consults his codebook to decode the message.

HIS TRUTH IS MARCHING ON

A heavy spring rain began falling on Washington, D.C., just after dark on the night of 21 April 1861.

It drove the federal sentries to seek shelter – perfect cover, U.S. Army Major Thomas Jordan realized, for his mission. He hurried to a large home not far from the White House. There its owner, a vivacious 44-year-old widow named Rose O'Neal Greenhow, ushered him inside.

Only nine days before, the Civil War had begun with the Secessionist assault on Fort Sumter. What followed was the first of the modern wars, a bloody struggle that in four years advanced the art of war faster than the previous five centuries. It was a war that introduced semi-automatic weapons, aerial reconnaissance, the forerunner of the machine gun, long-range artillery and the ironclad warship with moveable turret that revolutionized naval warfare.

A CIVIL AFFAIR

Yet ironically, although intelligence played an important role in the conduct of the war, espionage was largely an amateur affair using methods familiar since the time of the Bible. There was not a single espionage innovation during the conflict, a somewhat surprising development, considering the extent and success of American espionage during the Revolution. However, in the 86 years since then, the United States – safe behind two oceans that isolated them from the wars in Europe – virtually neglected military preparedness and anything having to do with espionage.

When the Civil War broke out, neither the Union nor the Confederacy had an intelligence agency of any sort and no cryptographic organization. The military did not even have any trained scouts. Both sides realized they would need intelligence, but without any professionals available, there was only one recourse – amateurs, meaning anyone willing to volunteer to be a spy. The results were mixed, as demonstrated by what happened that rainy night in Washington.

As Major Jordan hurried toward the Greenhow house, he was wearing the blue uniform of the Army of the United States. However, he would not be wearing that uniform for much longer; a Virginian, he had decided to resign his

commission and join the Confederate cause. Before leaving Washington, Jordan was determined to create an espionage network that would provide intelligence on the Union forces gathering strength in the capitol, a direct threat to Richmond, the Confederate seat of government, only 60 miles away.

Jordan had no experience in intelligence, but he was aware that Greenhow was a known Confederate sympathizer. She had wept in the Senate Gallery four months before when U.S. Senator Jefferson Davis of Mississippi made his farewell speech, in which he resigned his seat and announced his intention to head the Secessionist movement. More importantly, she was the center of Washington's social life, dining and partying with the city's elite and friends with a wide variety of politicians and military officers. No one could have been in a more perfect position to collect important intelligence. He asked her to become his spy.

Greenhow unhesitatingly agreed and at that moment began a career in espionage that would make her a Civil War legend. It was a career all the more remarkable because she never made any effort to conceal her pro-Confederate sympathies. It was also a tribute to what apparently was her magical power over friends and lovers. Even after her pro-Secessionist sympathies had become notorious, the most rabidly pro-Union officials continued to show up at her home for her glittering dinners, parties and, in some cases, something more. In that last category was Senator Henry Wilson of Massachusetts, chairman of the Committee on Military Affairs (and a future Vice President under Ulysses S. Grant), and Colonel Erasmus D. Keyes, military secretary to General Winfield Scott, commander of all Union forces.

How much useful information she was able to extract from such bedmates as Wilson and Keyes remains unknown. However, it is known that on 21 July 1861, the Confederates inflicted a stinging defeat on union forces at Bull Run Creek on the road to Manassas, Virginia, turning back the first offensive of the war by Union forces. As General P.G.T. Beauregard, the victorious Confederate commander later revealed, much of the Confederate success was due to intelligence provided by Greenhow, particularly the precise strength and order of battle of Union forces advancing toward Manassas. The defeat shocked Washington. What had been thought would be a quick war to brush aside the much smaller and weaker Confederate military would now be a much greater struggle. This would not be a short war.

There was another conclusion the Union high command reached. There was no doubt that the Confederates had been informed, with great precision, about the plans and dispositions of Union forces. That kind of intelligence could only have come from a Confederate spy in Washington with access to high-level sources. That spy must be found.

At this point, Greenhow's fate intersected with that of another interesting character. His name was Allan Pinkerton, a 42-year-old Scotsman who had emigrated to the United States 19 years before. He had worked as a police detective in Chicago before leaving the force in 1850 to found his own private detective agency, the Pinkerton National Detective Agency, which specialized in tracking and capturing

train robbers. Its Chicago headquarters featured a sign with a huge eye and the company slogan 'We Never Sleep'. The slogan reflected the vaulting ambition and inflated opinion of himself that were Pinkerton's chief characteristics.

When the Civil War broke out, Pinkerton wrote a letter to President Abraham Lincoln, boldly proposing to head up an intelligence service for the Union, despite the fact that he had no experience whatsoever in intelligence. Lincoln did not reply, so Pinkerton pulled strings. George B. McClellan, a railroad executive who had used Pinkerton's service, was now a major general commanding the Division of the Ohio. Pinkerton wrote to him, reminding the general of their previous business. McClellan, aware that he needed some sort of intelligence operation, but without the vaguest idea of how to create one, quickly agreed to Pinkerton's proposal. McClellan now had a chief of intelligence. Oddly, he insisted that Pinkerton remain a civilian and that he operate under a military cover name 'Major E.J. Allen'.

In the wake of the defeat at Bull Run and a shake-up in the Union high command, McClellan was named to command the Army of the Potomac. He brought the detective along as his intelligence sachem. At that point, Pinkerton began to call himself "Chief of the United States Secret Service", although he was no such thing. He actually worked only for McClellan, not the entire Union Army and, in terms of intelligence he was not the only spy chief around.

Lieutenant General Winfield Scott, commander-in-chief of the entire Union Army, had his own intelligence chief, an ex-policeman named Lafayette C. Baker. Other Union generals had their individual chief spies, usually officers entrusted with scouting operations. Abraham Lincoln himself had his own personal spy – William A. Lloyd, a publisher of railroad and steamer guides in the South. Early in the war, Lloyd asked Lincoln for help in continuing his business. Lincoln agreed, but suggested that his travels in the South had more than commercial value. He recruited Lloyd as a spy, with a salary of $200 a month (about $4,000 in today's currency).

For the next four years, until the end of the war, Lloyd sent a letter each week to the family of one his employees who lived in Maryland. The family then dutifully delivered the letter, unopened, to the White House. Each letter contained Lloyd's observations about what he

ABOVE: Confederate spy Rose O'Neil Greenhow, with her daughter, at the Old Capitol Prison in Washington, D.C., after her arrest by Pinkerton's agents.

ABOVE: General George McClellan, cheered by his troops, a sentiment not shared by President Lincoln, who accused him of "a case of the slows".

had seen in travels around the rail network in the South, with emphasis on troop concentrations and fortifications under construction. Lincoln, who kept his relationship with Lloyd strictly private, found his intelligence a useful check on what his generals were telling him.

FAMOUS NAME

Pinkerton was in what can only be described as an intelligence free-for-all, with no centrally directed intelligence effort. However, he was determined to become the Union's intelligence czar. For that reason, he avidly leaped at his first major assignment from McClellan after reaching Washington – find the Confederate spy who had caused the disaster at Bull Run. Pinkerton was convinced that if he could succeed, the achievement would make him the Union's most celebrated intelligence agent, a sure road to intelligence supremacy.

His hunt for the Confederate spy got off to a good start when he learned that Union troops advancing on Manassas during the Bull Run battle had overrun a Confederate outpost, in which they found papers and maps. Addressed to Confederate General Beauregard, the papers appeared to be material from a spy, since they outlined which Union units were assigned to the assault on Manassas and their strengths. These reports were routinely filed away and nobody had made an effort to find out who had written them. Pinkerton took a close look at the papers, noticing that they were written in a feminine hand. Instantly, he decided the author almost certainly was Rose O'Neal Greenhow, whose open Confederate sympathies had aroused the suspicions of some Union officers.

In an effort to prove it, Pinkerton assigned six of his detectives to conduct an around-the-clock watch on Greenhow's home. They reported a steady procession of politicians and senior military officers into the house, which convinced Pinkerton that he was on the right track. Final proof came a few nights later, when Pinkerton personally joined two detectives surveilling the house. Informed that a man in uniform had gone into the house a short time before, Pinkerton climbed onto the shoulders of one of the detectives and peeked through the parlour window. He saw the man in uniform hand over a map, then adjourn to another room with Greenhow. They emerged an hour later arm in arm and, with a kiss from Greenhow, he left. Pinkerton was shocked, for he recognized the man as an officer assigned to the provost marshal's office in Washington.

It was enough. A week later, Pinkerton burst into Greenhow's house with three detectives and arrested her on charges of "being a spy in the interest of the rebels and furnishing the insurgent generals with important information relative to the movements of the Union forces". Pinkerton searched her house and found a trove of highly incriminating material, including a simple word code Greenhow used to convey her intelligence. Armed with the code, Pinkerton had no trouble understanding what this message really meant: 'Tell Aunt Sally that I have some old shoes for the children and I wish her to send one down town

LEFT: Lafayette C. Baker, the Union Army's chief intelligence agent and a bitter rival of Pinkerton, whom he despised.

to take them, and to let me know whether she has found any charitable person to help her take care of them.' (I have some important information to send across the river and wish a messenger immediately. Have you any means of getting reliable information?)

She was put under house arrest. Pinkerton visited her each day, trying to get her to tell him the names of her couriers, who her control was and the system used to move her intelligence from Washington to Richmond. She refused to discuss any of those subjects and Pinkerton finally gave up. Greenhow was to spend ten months in the house, until it was discovered she was trying to smuggle out messages, at which point she was put into the Old Capitol Prison (now the U.S. Supreme Court building). Under the prevailing customs of the time, women spies were not executed and in fact were usually exchanged during routine prisoner-of-war exchanges. That happened to Greenhow in 1862; she went to Richmond, from where the Confederates sent her to England to work as propaganda agent for the cause. She returned to America in 1864 aboard a Confederate blockade-runner, but was drowned when the ship ran aground.

Pinkerton attempted to trump his capture of Greenhow by penetrating the Confederacy. He used her word code to dispatch messages via volunteer couriers sympathetic to the Confederate cause (actually some Pinkerton detectives). The idea was lame-brained; since the Confederates were aware that Greenhow had been captured, they were instantly aware that any messages from her were obviously phoney. The failure did nothing to advance Pinkerton's drive to become the supreme head of all Union intelligence. To make matters worse for that ambition, his chief rival, Lafayette C. Baker, had developed a strong dislike of the insufferable Pinkerton, whom he was determined to destroy.

Baker himself was not scoring any points in the espionage game, a subject he knew nothing about – as he demonstrated in his first foray into espionage, during the Bull Run campaign. Baker got the idea of infiltrating Confederate lines by posing as a Tennessee photographer named Samuel Munson. However, his habit of photographing only Confederate troop concentrations and earthworks quickly convinced the Confederates he was a spy. They arrested him for espionage, but finding no incriminating papers of any kind on him, they simply exposed all his photographic plates to sunlight and sent him back to Union lines. Baker returned to Washington in some disgrace. It was a career downturn further worsened when his patron, General Scott, was assigned the blame for the Bull Run disaster and forced to retire.

However, Baker was nothing if not resilient. He tapped into some powerful political contacts and got himself appointed as 'special provost marshal for the War Department'. The vague title actually meant that Baker was now in charge of all counterespionage operations for the Union, a definition that included not only catching Confederate spies, but tracking down deserters and 'subversives' – a catch-all term that included anyone suspected of harbouring sympathies for the Confederacy. By vigorously rounding up perceived enemies of the Union, Baker hoped to earn the gratitude of the Lincoln administration, which would reward him with appointment as intelligence supremo of the Union cause.

Meanwhile, Pinkerton decided he would achieve his own goal of intelligence dominance by establishing a strong Union espionage presence in the Confederacy. His idea was to send agents into Richmond, establish a base and then recruit sources inside the Confederate government and military high command. A lofty goal, but Pinkerton did not have a stable of trained espionage agents for such a task. The best he could do was Timothy Webster, a former New York City Police detective noted for his ability to recruit underworld sources. Believing Webster could accomplish the same thing in Richmond, this time among secret Union sympathizers, Pinkerton sent him into the city under cover of a secessionist acting as a courier for messages from Confederate sympathizers in Baltimore.

Webster's first move was to ingratiate himself with Brigadier General John Henry Winder, who was Richmond's provost marshal and whose duties included counterintelligence. Webster was aware that Winder's life was dominated by a sad circumstance. Like many families in the Civil War, the Winders had divided loyalties. While Winder was a dedicated senior officer of the Confederate Army, his son William was a Union Army officer based in Washington. Webster put Winder deeply in his debt by volunteering to carry letters between Winder and his son. A grateful Winder then rewarded the Union spy with something almost beyond price – a special military pass that authorized him to travel wherever he wanted in the Confederacy.

INFORMATION FEED
A spy's dream, Webster was soon sending Pinkerton detailed reports on a wide range of topics, ranging from the state of fortifications around the city to the effect of food prices on Southern morale. Additionally, he had become friends with Confederate Secretary of War Judah P. Benjamin, who entrusted him as a courier delivering documents to covert Secessionists in Baltimore – all of which were given to Pinkerton for copying before being sent on. However, just as Webster's operation began to reach full flower, in February 1862, his reports suddenly stopped.

Pinkerton sent two of his men to the city to find out what had happened. They reported that Webster had fallen ill with inflammatory rheumatism and would be out of commission for an indefinite period. They had just sent off that dispatch when disaster struck. Several Richmond residents recognized the two agents as former residents of the city. Since they were now working under different identities, it was clear they were spies. Thrown into prison, they were threatened with hanging if they didn't reveal why they were so interested in the medical condition of the sick Secessionist named Webster. To save their lives, they betrayed Webster, who was hanged as a spy on 29 April 1862, despite a personal plea from Lincoln to Jefferson Davis to spare his life.

The operation involving Webster was to serve as the intelligence prelude to what McClellan decided would be the decisive military action to end the Civil War – an all-out assault on Richmond. To carry it off successfully, McClellan would need detailed intelligence on the Confederate forces guarding the capitol. Moreover, he was a notoriously cautious general who tended not to move unless he was absolutely certain of what he was facing on the battlefield.

BELOW: A milestone in the history of espionage. Thaddeus Lowe's spy balloon is launched on 1 June 1862, near Confederate lines in Fair Oaks, Virginia.

He pressed Pinkerton for solid information on Confederate forces, but that was something his intelligence chief couldn't provide. After Webster's death, he had one remaining operative working inside Richmond, an asset named Elizabeth van Lew. Born of a wealthy Richmond family, van Lew was educated in Philadelphia, returning as an ardent abolitionist. When the Civil War broke out, she ignored the contempt of her social peers by caring for hospitalized Union prisoners. She began helping some of them escape, occasionally hiding them in the attic of her family's mansion. It was but a short step from there to espionage. She began sending intelligence reports about various tidbits she picked up in conversations with other residents of Richmond and what she could see of Confederate military dispositions.

She had talked her mother into releasing the family's slaves and they were now enlisted to carry her intelligence messages to Washington. It was a shrewd choice of couriers, since Southerners believed that blacks were too mentally deficient to perform such duties as espionage couriers. The ex-slaves, bowing and scraping in the exaggerated gestures of respect that further convinced Southerners of their inferiority, devised several ingenious methods to transmit van Lew's messages. One involved using scraped-out eggs hidden among real eggs; another hid messages among a stack of paper patterns carried by a seamstress.

However ingenious their transmission, the intelligence provided by van Lew was limited. It was restricted to what she personally observed and overheard. She had no overall picture of Confederate strength or intentions and, since she was not a military expert, she could not evaluate what she saw of Confederate military technology. The solution would have been the patient development of intelligence networks inside Richmond, but McClellan was in a hurry. He was under constant pressure from Lincoln to use his numerically superior army to destroy General Robert E. Lee's Army of Northern Virginia. At the same time, he was eager to achieve a magnificent victory that would enhance his political prospects (the politically ambitious general was already looking ahead to his candidacy in the 1864 presidential election). Pinkerton found himself under increasing pressure from McClellan for precise intelligence.

In response, Pinkerton committed a monumental blunder. He decided to become his own intelligence agency. He set about collecting information on the Confederates that he personally evaluated and submitted in the form of reports to McClellan. However, because Pinkerton had no training as an intelligence agent, he made several serious mistakes in the process of insisting on his own unique system of intelligence collection. One involved his idea of determining Confederate battlefield strength by counting the number of regimental flags in evidence, then multiplying by 2,500 – the standard strength of a Confederate regiment. Pinkerton did not realize that very few Confederate regiments were up to their authorized strength; many were at half-strength because of heavy casualties.

Another blunder involved the idea of determining enemy strength by counting the number of their campfires at night; assuming that about six men would be gathered around a typical fire during a night bivouac, simply multiplying the number of observed campfires by six would give an accurate picture of how many troops were at a given site. As any soldier could have told him, Pinkerton's method was highly misleading. Depending on the weather and availability of wood, the number of soldiers gathered around a campfire varied wildly.

What made Pinkerton's intelligence even more suspect was the fact that the Confederates quickly deduced that he was basing his estimates of Confederate strength on some very shaky quantitative methods. They soon began an extensive deception campaign designed to mislead him. They fashioned logs into 'cannon', ignited hundreds of campfires without any soldiers around them, built elaborate unmanned fortifications and equipped platoons with large, bright regimental flags for units that didn't exist.

The result was wildly inflated estimates of Confederate strength, which McClellan used as justification for not moving aggressively against Lee's army. "A case of the slows," Lincoln complained, but McClellan insisted he was vastly outnumbered. He claimed precipitate offensive action against the presumed mighty Confederate host would result in grave defeats and, possibly, the end of the Union cause. It remains a matter of historical debate whether McClellan was simply using Pinkerton's estimates – which he knew were exaggerated – as justification for his super-cautious approach or he actually believed them.

HARNESS TECHNOLOGY

One clue that he believed what he wanted to believe came from an interesting character named Thaddeus Lowe, a 29-year-old balloonist, who had talked the Union Army into converting his novel contraption, once displayed at county

BELOW: Confederate dead at Antietam, the price of the worst intelligence failure in the history of the Confederacy, when Union forces found a copy of General Robert E. Lee's operational orders carelessly lost by a courier.

LEFT: Major General Ulysses S. Grant, who learned a hard lesson from his intelligence lapses at Shiloh.

The whole matter of Pinkerton's intelligence estimates came to a head on 13 September 1862, in an extraordinary incident when the greatest intelligence disaster in the history of the Confederacy took place. In a cornfield near Antietam Creek in Maryland, two union soldiers on patrol found an envelope lying in the grass. When they opened it, they discovered three cigars wrapped in the paper. The paper turned out to be Lee's Special Orders 191, his plan for an ambitious four-pronged offensive, three of which were aimed at Harpers Ferry, the fourth at Hagerstown, Maryland. The document, probably dropped accidentally by a Confederate courier, made its way up the chain of command to Pinkerton and McClellan, who realized they had just been handed a golden opportunity.

"I have all the plans of the rebels," McClellan wrote Lincoln. The President wondered why, if the commander of the Army of the Potomac had such priceless intelligence, he wasn't moving immediately to crush the enemy once and for all. The answer was that McClellan was being McClellan; seduced by the continued warnings from Pinkerton about a huge Confederate army of nearly 100,000 men (in fact, Lee only had 35,000 men to McClellan's 95,000). He dithered for four days and

fairs, into the world's first aerial reconnaissance vehicle. He built several tethered balloons that floated up to 1,000 feet over Union lines, from which Lowe, using a spyglass, could see 25 miles in all directions. What made his system truly revolutionary was his next innovation: attaching a telegraph cable to the balloon.

With a Morse code operator aboard, Lowe dictated what he was seeing aloft, which was then instantly transmitted to the ground. Assigned to McClellan's Army of the Potomac, Lowe made a number of valuable contributions to Union tactical victories by his ability to spot Confederate troop movements. However, he encountered a cool reception in McClellan's headquarters whenever he got into the business of estimative intelligence. The general did not want to hear anything from Lowe about overall Confederate strength, especially when the balloonist tried to tell him that Pinkerton's estimates were wildly off the mark.

when he finally moved he blundered into a meeting with the Confederates at Antietam Creek, setting off a terrible battle that resulted in nearly 26,000 casualties. A badly bloodied Lee finally retreated. Characteristically, McClellan, convinced of Pinkerton's alarmist estimates of a huge Confederate force, did not pursue.

Lincoln was infuriated at McClellan for his failure to pursue a beaten Lee and destroy his army. However, the Union's narrow tactical victory was sufficient for the President to issue the Emancipation Proclamation, the document that made a Union strategic victory certain. By transforming the war into a crusade to destroy slavery, Lincoln's perfectly-timed move meant no foreign nation would enter the war on the side of the Confederacy in what would have amounted to an alliance to preserve slavery.

Nevertheless, Lincoln decided that McClellan would have to go – along with his intelligence chief, the man responsible for all those inflated estimates of Confederate strength, estimates that in Lincoln's view had prolonged the war. On 7 November 1862, Lincoln relieved McClellan of his command. Pinkerton immediately resigned, petulantly taking with him all the intelligence he had accumulated since the beginning of the war.

If Pinkerton thought that his act would blind the Union cause, he was immediately proven wrong. McClellan's successor, General Joseph Hooker, was not only a fervent believer in intelligence, he wanted only rock-solid accurate information. To get it, he ordered creation of the Bureau of Military Information, the first military intelligence agency in U.S. history. Hooker commissioned his deputy provost marshal, Colonel George H. Sharpe, to organize the Bureau, staff it with whomever he thought of value and get to work.

Sharpe, a brilliant New York lawyer, didn't know anything about espionage, but he was an organizational genius who quickly put together a first-class intelligence agency. He recruited throughout the entire Army of the Potomac for the best and brightest officers, finally enlisting 70 men with college degrees and varying special knowledge. In turn, they formed several separate sub-bureaux each assigned a specific task. One collected tactical intelligence, another concentrated on debriefing prisoners of war – integrating whatever tidbits they revealed into cross-checked reports. Another unit carefully combed through Southern newspapers, searching for revealing items that had slipped past censors, while still another performed the Bureau's most odious intelligence collection task, searching through the bodies of dead Confederate soldiers for letters and other documents that might contain useful intelligence.

Under Sharpe's direction, the Bureau became a first-class intelligence organization. Its supreme triumph came in the spring of 1863, when Sharpe prepared a nine-page report on Lee's army that predicted a Confederate thrust into Pennsylvania. It contained a detailed order of battle that outlined Lee's forces precisely, along with the critical intelligence that Lee had informed his officers the army would undergo "long marches and hard fighting, in a part of the country where they would have no railroad transportation". This was a good description of the country around the town of Gettysburg, where, on 1–3 July 1863, an alerted Union army defeated the Confederates in the Civil War's most decisive battle.

A GREAT GENERAL

Hooker's replacement as commander of the Army of the Potomac was General Ulysses S. Grant, who had made his military reputation with a series of spectacular victories in the western theatre of the war. Initially, Grant had no interest in intelligence, a fault that very nearly cost him his entire command. On the morning of 6 April 1862, Grant's army was camped near a log meeting-house called Shiloh Church in rural Tennessee. They were just beginning to wake up and make breakfast when Confederate troops suddenly attacked their outer lines, then rampaged through the camps, snatching up uneaten breakfasts as Union troops hurriedly retreated. Facing imminent disaster, Grant rallied his troops and, with help from his gunboats on the Tennessee River, poured artillery fire into the Confederate ranks, finally defeating them during a two-day battle. However, the price was high – Grant's army suffered 10,000 casualties.

Grant, a man who learned from his mistakes, freely admitted that the near-disaster at Shiloh was due solely to his neglect of intelligence. Relying almost exclusively on the mostly unreliable reports of Confederate deserters for his intelligence, Grant was misled into believing the enemy was more than 20 miles away. Grant did not bother verifying those reports or send out any scouts. After the battle, Grant summoned one of his best officers, Brigadier General Grenville M. Dodge. He ordered him to create an intelligence apparatus to insure that nothing like Shiloh would ever happen again. Dodge, in civilian life a railroad-builder, had no intelligence experience, but had a natural talent for espionage. He created a special information-gathering unit that used a wide variety of sources, including runaway slaves, Unionist sympathizers in Confederate territory and his particular favourite – women spies. Many Southerners believed that women lacked the 'gumption' for espionage work, which meant women often could move more freely between the lines than men.

This organization worked with another Dodge creation, the Corps of Scouts, a unit of the best cavalrymen he could find. He personally conducted a rigid training program, instructing them in such tricks of the trade as estimating the strength of an enemy unit by measuring the length of road occupied by a column of soldiers. He preferred to use Southern Unionists for his Corps of Scouts, correctly reasoning that their intimate knowledge of the local terrain was a big advantage.

Dodge was among the first intelligence officers to understand that the Union's best intelligence assets were slaves. They hated their Southern masters, had intimate knowledge of Confederate fortifications because they did the actual construction work and, since they served in a variety of support tasks for the Confederate army, had firsthand knowledge of the locations and conditions of rebel troops. Lincoln's Emancipation Proclamation gave Dodge a powerful recruiting weapon, since it guaranteed freedom to all slaves within Union military jurisdiction.

The practical effect was a flood of runaway slaves to Union lines, each of them with at least a few tidbits to pass on to Dodge's agents. Indeed, the slaves provided so much information it was collected separately in a category called

'Black Dispatches'. Even more valuable were slaves who agreed to remain in bondage as agents in place to provide the Union with intelligence. The star spy among them was, at first glance, the most unlikely. However, the small, gentle slave named Harriet Ross Tubman was not a woman to be underestimated.

Tubman's life in the covert world began in 1855, when she fled a Maryland plantation on which she had been born 35 years before. She was driven to flee after being whipped and struck in the head with a scale weight, an injury that caused her terrible pains and seizures for the rest of her life. She made her way north along the Underground Railroad, at which point she could have settled in the North to live the rest of her days as a free black. However, Tubman was determined to help her fellow slaves still suffering in Maryland, so she returned there for the dangerous task of conducting runaway slaves along the Underground Railroad. By 1861, she had led 300 slaves to freedom (including her own elderly parents), all the while dodging patrols of slavecatchers with tracking dogs determined to catch the 'little nigger woman' who was removing so many of their valuable human assets.

Experience in the world of the Underground Railroad prepared Tubman for her next role – Union spy. In 1861, she volunteered to work as a spy in her native Maryland, where she provided intelligence on the networks of Southern sympathizers that Confederate intelligence was attempting to recruit. A year later, she was asked to work in a Union foothold on the south-eastern coast of South Carolina, where there was a desperate need for intelligence on the sea of Confederates that surrounded it. Tubman went to work, turning the Union enclave into a magnet for slaves fleeing to freedom, all of whom she debriefed for anything they might know of intelligence interest. She also set up networks of slave spies throughout South Carolina, an effort that produced huge amounts of valuable intelligence.

Union officers were bemused by the sight of this woman, barely five feet tall, who seemed to have inexhaustible energy despite the constant pain she suffered, but no one doubted her abilities. Her most spectacular achievement was a brilliantly-planned Union night raid up the Combahee River to destroy a major Confederate supply depot and free some 750 slaves from a nearby rice plantation. The Union colonel who led the raid appointed Tubman as his second in command, the only known instance of a slave serving as an officer actually giving orders to troops. The feat led to her nickname of respect among Union officers – 'the general' – and at her death in 1913, she was buried with full military honours. It was largely the effectiveness of Tubman's slave-spy network that led Robert E. Lee to lament in a report to Jefferson Davis, "The chief source of information to the enemy is through our negroes."

Lee's rueful complaint was not the only Confederate admission that the South was overmatched in the espionage war with the Union. After Grant took over command of the Army of the Potomac, he brought Colonel Sharpe, his brilliant intelligence chief, with him. As he had in Tennessee, Sharpe organized a vast, sprawling intelligence web (including hundreds of runaway slaves enlisted as spies) that produced much valuable intelligence. By 1864, so much intelligence was flowing into Grant's headquarters at City Point, Virginia, a clerk in the Confederate War Department in Richmond noted in his diary, "The enemy are kept fully informed of everything transpiring here." That was no exaggeration. Among Sharpe's assets in the rebel capitol was Samuel Ruth, superintendent of the Richmond, Fredericksburg and Potomac Railroad. Although considered among his fellow southerners as an ardent Secessionist, Ruth was in fact a secret Unionist who made contact with Sharpe's Bureau through Elizabeth van Lew.

Ruth not only provided intelligence on Confederate Army movements over his railroad, he also arranged to retard certain critical shipments of war supplies and deliberately slowed the repair of vital railroad bridges. Continuing problems on the railroad caused Confederate officials to wonder whether all of them could be attributed to the natural course of events. Finally, it was decided that Ruth was working for the Union and he was arrested. He coolly denied being a Union spy, aware that he had no incriminating documents lying around. A few days later, as Richmond newspapers complained about the "hysterical" arrest of one of the city's most prominent citizens, Ruth was released for lack of evidence. He went right back to sending intelligence to Sharpe until the end of the war.

PROPAGANDA AND INFLUENCE

The Confederate espionage defeat extended overseas, where the government of Davis sent agents to achieve three goals: convince both France and Great Britain to join the war on the Southern side; procure arms and secretly build warships in European yards to break the Union naval blockade. The Confederates were aware that public opinion in Britain and France was strongly opposed to slavery, so their first objective was to change that opinion. The Confederate Secret Service, its main intelligence organization, earmarked nearly $200,000 for a 'propaganda fund' that paid out bribes to British and French journalists to write pro-Confederate newspaper articles. Those taking the bribes got a bonus – Havana cigars and American whiskey. The fund also paid for the publishing of 125,000 copies of a pro-slavery tract ostensibly produced by 'the Clergy of the Confederate States of America', a fictional organization.

The Confederates never succeeded in overcoming the British and French revulsion over slavery and they experienced a similar lack of success in their other two goals. The problem was that they were up against a very ruthless and talented Union spymaster named Henry Shelton Sanford. Officially the U.S. minister to Belgium, he was in fact the head of Union intelligence in Europe. President Lincoln, aware of the importance of Europe in the covert war, gave Sanford lavish secret funds to spend as he saw fit. Like just about everybody else involved in espionage war between North and South, Sanford had no background in intelligence, but he did have a good instinct for intelligence operations. He demonstrated this by balking the full range of Confederate secret operations in Europe.

First, he hired a battalion of British police detectives, luring them to moonlight for him with generous salaries. Then he recruited a whole series of local sources, including mistresses of Confederate agents and their landlords. With this dual set of assets, Sanford was able to develop a detailed picture of just which Confederate agents were operating in Britain and France and what they were doing. He also bribed factory agents to tell him what the Confederate agents were paying for supplies (whereupon he had Union purchasing agents outbid them) and shipyard officials to provide all the details on covert Confederate shipbuilding.

The chief target of Sanford's operation was James D. Bulloch, a former U.S. Navy officer who had joined the Confederacy. In 1861, Bulloch was assigned to Europe to head the covert Confederate shipbuilding program. He had managed to get one ship built and sent to America before Sanford decided the shipbuilding program must come to an end. Bulloch's second ship, which he code-named in messages back to Richmond as '290', was finished and ready to sail when the U.S. Department of State, using intelligence from Sanford, went to court with a legal claim against the shipyard for violating British neutrality laws.

RIGHT: The Union's most remarkable spy, the ex-slave Harriet Tubman, heroine of the Underground Railroad.

Concerned the ship would be seized by British authorities, Bulloch decided he would have to spirit it out of its berth in a Liverpool shipyard. To accomplish that task he devised a clever deception operation. A 'pleasure cruise' of the ship was announced and he recruited nearly a hundred men and women to pose as passengers. As Sanford's spies observed these people – dressed in their Sunday best and happily promenading on the deck while the ship slowly sailed down

the River Mersey – they concluded that the vessel was in fact embarked on a pleasure cruise. However, once the ship was out of the sight of Sanford's agents, it suddenly stopped. A tugboat pulled alongside and took off the 'passengers'. Ship 290 – now christened the Alabama – then fired its boilers for maximum speed and raced for the open ocean.

Bulloch congratulated himself on a great covert triumph, but he soon learned it was about to turn to ashes. The first blow came when he found out that one member of the Alabama crew was a spy for Sanford – the ship's paymaster, Clarence Yonge. After the Alabama crossed the Atlantic following its escape from Liverpool, the ship stopped in Jamaica for reprovisioning. Yonge left the ship there, claiming pressing personal business. He then actually boarded a Union ship and headed back to England, where he met with the U.S. ambassador, Thomas Haines Dudley. Yonge imparted some critically important intelligence. The Alabama had been built with sockets in her decks and other fixtures for guns, along with powder tins – hardly the standard equipment for a supposedly commercial vessel.

Dudley put that information into an affidavit for a court suit demanding that the British government observe the neutrality laws by ending the construction of what were clearly Confederate warships in British shipyards.

There was more. Sanford's agents discovered two additional Confederate ships under construction in British shipyards, both of which had underwater metal rams. This was standard equipment for warships of the time, used to rip holes in wooden hulls. As the American ambassador noted acidly in a snotty note to the Foreign Office, Great Britain had an odd definition of what constituted a "commercial ship". The British began to waver and they became further unsettled when Dudley passed on a message from President Lincoln: if the British permitted completion of those two ships and the Confederates took possession of them, the United States would regard such an act as a British declaration of war against the United States. Finally, the British gave in. The ships were seized as violations of British neutrality and later sold to the Royal Navy.

Bulloch now realized there was only dwindling hope for

his operation to succeed. It was dealt a final blow in June 1864, when Sanford's spies learned that the Alabama – which had racked up a spectacular record as a commerce raider of Union shipping – had put into the French port of Cherbourg for emergency repairs. Thanks to the telegraph, Sanford was able to forward this vital intelligence to the captain of the *U.S.S. Kearsage*, a Union warship then in a Dutch port. The *Kearsage* immediately sailed for Cherbourg, took up a position just outside the three-mile territorial limit and waited for the Alabama. Finally the Confederate ship left the port and took on the Union ship in a two-hour battle watched by 15,000 spectators ashore, a battle that ended with the sinking of the Alabama.

A dejected Bulloch wrote a detailed report to the Confederate Secretary of the Navy that concluded there was no longer any hope the Confederacy could covertly build warships in Britain, change British and French public opinion or convince either nation to become an active ally. The reason for that total defeat, Bulloch wrote, could be ascribed mostly to Union intelligence. "The spies of the United States are numerous, active and unscrupulous. They invade the privacy of families, tamper with the confidential clerks of merchants and have succeeded in converting a portion of the police of this Kingdom into secret agents of the United States..."

Bulloch's report was written in 1864 and reflected the general tenor of Confederate morale at that point. In a word, morale was bad. Clearly the war was being lost and nothing the Confederacy could do would change that. The North was too powerful, too numerous and too determined to be defeated. What made it all worse was the growing realization at the highest levels of the Confederate command structure that whatever they might decide to do would be an open book to an increasingly pervasive Union intelligence. Official Confederate government and military reports written at the time are replete with pessimistic references to the impossibility of keeping anything secret from Union spies. The pessimism was justified, for in fact by 1864 the Union had achieved total victory in the intelligence war, most importantly in the field of communications intelligence.

Both sides in the Civil War had access to one of the century's momentous inventions – the telegraph – and were aware that it promised a revolution in military communications. Even far-flung commands could now be coordinated and orders could be dispatched with a speed thought unthinkable decades before. Both sides were also aware that this modern miracle always had an important implication: what could be sent could be intercepted. At the outbreak of war, both the Union and the Confederacy began a major effort to read the telegraphic communications of the other side.

The Union began with an advantage because of superior organization. All its telegraphic communications were centered in an agency of the best telegraphers in the country – the U.S. Military Telegraph (USMT). Drawing its operators mainly from Western Union, USMT connected all Union military commands with each other and the War Department in Washington. The agency also included a number of civilian cryptographers with experience in encrypting sensitive business communications. Their expertise was now put to work encrypting Union military communications, devising a relatively simple, but difficult to crack, codebook that telegraph operators found easy to use. The system used what the cryptographers called a 'routing code', meaning the scrambling of words in a prearranged pattern before actually enciphering them. The Union communications system was a model of efficiency, handling more than 4,500 telegrams a day.

Meanwhile, a secret unit of the army's Signal Corps targeted Confederate telegraphic communications. The Union codebreaking task was made that much easier by some fundamental errors committed by the Confederate communications system. Like the North, the Confederates created a separate organization – in the South's case the Signal Service – to handle telegraph messages between military commands and Richmond. It differed from the Union counterpart in two important respects. One, it was a military unit, staffed only by military personnel who had only rudimentary training in telegraphy. Second, it did not enlist civilian cryptographers. Instead, the Confederates used barely-trained soldiers whose grasp of the field was something less than total. As a result, Confederate secret communications were cryptographically weak.

INSIDE KNOWLEDGE

Union codebreakers were delighted to discover that the Confederates used only three keywords during the entire war, making decryption that much easier. Moreover, they used a cipher system known as the Vigenere substitution cipher, a sixteenth century cipher that had previously been broken many times. Worst of all, the Confederate telegraphers, overwhelmed by heavy traffic and lack of skill in encipherment, often enciphered only the important parts of a message. For example, in early 1863, Union agents intercepted a message sent by Confederate President Jefferson Davis to one of his generals that began:

> BY THIS YOU MAY EFFECT O___TPGGEXVK
> ABOVE THAT PART ____HJOPGKWMCT____
> PATROLLED...

It did not take long for a cryptanalyst, using simple guesses, to deduce that the first word jumble was 'crossing' and the second was 'river'. Aware that the Confederates used the Vigenere cipher, the cryptanalyst would then use the early decryptions to build a grid, with which he would deduce the keyword: CompleteVictory. From there, the rest of the message was easily deciphered. The Confederates never grasped the elementary fact that enciphering only part of a message allowed cryptanalysts too many 'cribs' in solving a message.

A Confederate cryptographic innovation late in the war, a crude cipher cylinder, proved of little help. The cylinder consisted of two concentric disks marked off in a series of numbers. To encipher a message, an operator would receive a keyword (say, 476) and align that with the inner disk equivalent, which would be a different number, the actual number used in message. However, the disk was hopelessly flawed so long as the Confederates insisted on enciphering only part of their messages. By 1863, Union tapping of Confederate telegraph lines and decrypting the messages had become so pervasive, General Lee ordered his officers to "send no dispatches by telegraph relative to... movements, or they will become known."

The Confederates also came up short in another phase of the communications war, tapping telegraph lines. The problem was that while there were a number of daring Confederate cavalry operations that managed to tap Union telegraph lines, these only gave them enciphered communications that were useless unless they could be deciphered. However, the Confederates lacked sufficient numbers of cryptographers with the requisite skills to accomplish the task. Therefore, intercepted Union messages – some of which may have afforded Confederate generals a tremendous advantage – simply lay around, unread. The Confederates became so desperate, they placed advertisements in Southern newspapers that contained the texts of captured Union messages, begging any reader with knowledge of how to solve them to contact the War Department immediately.

The Confederate cavalry that performed such tasks as tapping Union telegraph lines represented the cutting edge of the South's intelligence. From the day the war began, the Confederacy tended to regard espionage as largely a military function, with an emphasis on collecting tactical intelligence – the location and strength of advancing enemy forces, location of their supply depots, etc. Confederate military commanders tended to be strict traditionalists in such matters of intelligence. In their perception, spies were largely lowlifes out of uniform who deserved to be hung when caught. Scouts, on the other hand, were honourable military professionals in uniform who collected intelligence.

True, that line could become blurred, exemplified by the man who was the South's greatest spy, Benjamin Franklin Stringfellow. He began his espionage career as a scout assigned to Robert E. Lee's 'eyes and ears', the cavalry unit of the Army of Northern Virginia headed by Major General James (Jeb) Stuart. Grandson of a Revolutionary War hero, Stuart disliked the term 'espionage' to describe the scouting missions he conducted behind Union lines. He typified the Southern mystique that surrounded its most glamorous military unit, dressing like a seventeenth century cavalier, complete with a large black plume and golden star. Many of his men demonstrated similar sartorial flamboyance.

It was not the kind of outfit considered useful for intelligence operations, but since Stuart didn't regard himself as a spy to any degree, he saw no reason for a disguise. Stringfellow, his best and most daring scout, disagreed. Galloping around the countryside in uniform was all well and good, he argued, but had its limitations. A Confederate in uniform was an enemy soldier while in Union territory and thus had no hope of obtaining intelligence from Union sympathizers. He further noted that Stuart's forays included attacks on Union supply trains, which meant he was combining intelligence with direct military action. It was a combination that didn't mix well. The moment Stuart's cavalrymen fired a shot, they had advertised their presence, hardly the right atmosphere for intelligence collection, which mandated as much invisibility as possible. Stuart listened patiently, but was unpersuaded as Stringfellow argued that a Confederate scout in civilian clothes, operating under cover, would be able to collect a lot more intelligence from people unaware they were dealing with the enemy.

Stringfellow decided to demonstrate how his theory could work by talking Stuart into letting him operate in Union-occupied Alexandria, Virginia, in civilian clothes. He had a rudimentary knowledge of dentistry, which he used to pose as a dentist's assistant. He entered Alexandria – a key supply and troop rotation base for the Union – and talked himself into a job with the town's leading dentist. It was not an accidental choice; careful reconnaissance had revealed to Stringfellow that the dentist performed dental work on a number of Union officers who often could be careless when discussing the war with him. He listened carefully and, by putting various clues together, was able to send Stuart accurate reports on Union troop movements.

Stringfellow followed that accomplishment with an even better one, infiltrating Washington in the guise of a dentist – a profession for which he had diligently studied, sufficient for him to earn a dental license. He went out of his way to offer his services to Union forces stationed in the city, often travelling to various encampments to handle dental emergencies. Soldiers grateful for the services of a dentist willing to travel to their camps and pull an infected tooth did not notice that the friendly dentist always seemed to take a route that allowed him to see as many units as possible. Nor did they wonder why this chatty dentist seemed so interested in local military chatter – which units were being withdrawn from the front for rest and refitting, which units were getting ready for offensive action, how many reinforcements were arriving from other theaters.

"Your information," Stuart told him, "may be worth all the Yankee trains that I attack." However, he remained unconvinced that he should convert his other scouts into that dirty word, spy. He held that view right to the end, on 11 May 1864, when he was killed outside Richmond in a Union ambush by a unit specifically tasked with hunting down Stuart and his cavalry. The man in the black plume had no spy to tell him of this unit and its deadly mission. His death, the last great intelligence failure of the Confederacy, symbolized its overall espionage defeat. His superior, General Robert E. Lee, a father figure to the dashing cavalry commander, wept when he heard the news of Stuart's death.

Less than a year later, he surrendered what remained of his shattered forces to General Ulysses S. Grant, whose intelligence organization had relentlessly tracked the Army of Northern Virginia, always aware of their location and strength. As he left the surrender ceremony at Appomatox, Lee gazed at the great numbers of Union soldiers gathered in the area. "I had no idea there were so many," Lee said – the ultimate epitaph for Confederate intelligence.

Not too long after Lee's surrender, an arrest in Canada illuminated the darker side of confederate intelligence. It involved an attempt to win the war by mass murder and its unlikely progenitor was a distinguished, soft-spoken Kentucky physician named Dr. Luke Blackburn.

Known for his expertise in treating yellow fever, Blackburn appeared in Bermuda in late 1864, volunteering his services to the local government to combat a major yellow fever epidemic. Blackburn was also a fervent Confederate supporter, a fact that brought him to the attention of the U.S. Consul in Bermuda. He wondered about the official cover story explaining Blackburn's supposedly selfless offer volunteering his services – that he intended only to help victims and simultaneously conduct research on the disease for which he was regarded as the country's leading expert. But the consul's suspicions were aroused when he learned that Blackburn was covertly collecting the clothes of yellow fever victims who had died. A strange action – and the consul decided to probe further.

Finally, one of Blackburn's assistant, afflicted by a guilty conscience, revealed that Blackburn had ordered him to transport a trunk of victims' sweat-stained clothing and blankets to Canada, from where it would be distributed to points in the northeastern United States and given to "charity cases". The idea, he said, was to infect thousands of people in the north who wore the clothes, setting off a pandemic as they came into contact with other people. And there was more. One special valise contained expensive dress shirts that had been rubbed against the clothing of yellow fever victims. It was to be presented to President Lincoln as a gift from "grateful supporters".

Fortunately, thanks to a serious scientific error, there were no mass deaths. Like all other medical authorities of the time, Blackburn believed that yellow fever could be transmitted by contact between the infected and non-infected, including contact with a victim's clothing. Not until nearly four decades later was it discovered that yellow fever is, in fact, spread by the bites of the aedes aegypti mosquito. Nevertheless, the intent of Blackburn's operation was clear and it was an operation that was sponsored by the Confederate intelligence service, to which Blackburn had proposed the idea of winning the war by a weapon of mass destruction.

In May 1865, after the collapse of the Confederacy, Blackburn fled to Canada, but Union agents tracked him down and put him on trial on charges of conspiracy to commit mass murder. Despite the testimony of his accomplice turned prosecution witness, Blackburn was acquitted. Legally a free man, he returned to Kentucky, where in 1879 he was elected governor. After his death, a small monument was erected on his grave that described him as a "good Samaritan".

THE PURLOINED LETTER: MEXICO AND THE FRENCH

IN THE AUTUMN OF 1865, MEXICANS LIVING ALONG THE RIO GRANDE BORDER WITH TEXAS SAW SOMETHING THEY HAD NOT SEEN IN SEVERAL YEARS – BLUE-COATED AMERICAN TROOPS IN FORCE.

These were not just any troops; they were among the most elite units in the entire Union Army, cavalrymen of General Philip Sheridan, one of the famous heroes of the recently-concluded American Civil War.

No sight could have cheered the people of northern Mexico more. Three years earlier, the reformist government of Benito Juarez had been driven out of Mexico City by French troops. Juarez had fled to a small enclave in northern Mexico, where he desperately tried to organize resistance to the French occupation, hoping all the while for help from the United States. However, the Americans, locked in a terrible civil war, were in no position to help. Now with that war over, the Americans had turned their attention to the French military occupation of Mexico. They were determined to end this European threat to their southern border.

Juarez discovered that the Americans had no intention of eliminating that threat by invading Mexico outright and attacking the French. Such an act would lead to war and war was something the reunited American union, weary of bloody struggle, did not want. Instead, the French would be driven out by America's first covert war, one which would demonstrate that the Americans had come a long way in the dark arts of espionage. In the plain-spoken general known popularly as Phil Sheridan, they had a very talented spymaster.

Sheridan was among the reformers in the Union Army who had overhauled its creaky intelligence system. During his greatest military triumph, the 1864 campaign in the Shenandoah Valley, Sheridan had established a group of trained intelligence operatives under military control. These replaced the haphazard system of scouts collecting information from local civilians and deserters – notoriously unreliable sources. Known as 'Sheridan's Scouts', the intelligence unit collected every possible scrap of information, ranging from the strategic to the tactical. This was then evaluated by experts on his staff. The unit included teams of expert cryptographers who deciphered coded dispatches stolen by yet another intelligence unit that specialized in waylaying enemy couriers.

RIGHT: Emperor Napoleon III of France, whose attempt to check the growing power of the United States led to a disastrous gambit in Mexico.

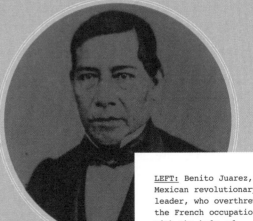

LEFT: Benito Juarez, Mexican revolutionary leader, who overthrew the French occupation with the help of a covert operation by American intelligence.

LEFT: A contemporary
version of the
execution in 1867 of
Emperor Maximilian, the
puppet ruler imposed on
Mexico by France, and
two of his generals.

Sheridan now deployed his spies in Mexico, where they soon wove an extensive intelligence web that provided a very complete intelligence picture. What the spies learned was disturbing. The French had invaded Mexico in 1862 under pretext of collecting debts owed by Mexico, but the real reason was Napoleon III's ambition to create a Mexican outpost of the French empire to check the rising power of the United States.

To that end, Napoleon had convinced Maximilian, the younger brother of the Austrian Emperor Franz Joseph, to become the emperor of Mexico – at the point of 30,000 French bayonets. In 1864, Maximilian arrived in Mexico City to take the throne, convinced by Mexican monarchists and Napoleon that he would be welcomed by the Mexican people as their enlightened despot. However, the Mexican people made it clear that they had total contempt for Maximilian, who seemed incapable of grasping the simple truth that they wanted no part of a German-speaking foreigner selected by the hated French occupiers to rule them.

Sheridan, aware that the unpopularity of a European monarch foisted on them had created the perfect conditions among the Mexicans for an insurgency, began covertly arming Juarez's guerrilla bands. The classic insurgency formula came into play. Increasing attacks by Juarez's guerrillas led to increasing repression by the French and Maximilian. That in turn led to more recruits for Juarez's army, which carried out more attacks, which led to even greater repression and so on. Juarez's increasingly effective attacks relied on intelligence collected by teams of Sheridan's spies and Mexicans they trained in military reconnaissance operations.

COVERT OPERATION

Sheridan's covert operation was supported by another American intelligence operation, this one run by Secretary of State William H. Seward. Known primarily in American history for what was derisively called at the time 'Seward's Folly' – the purchase of Alaska from Russia – Seward was in fact a highly intelligent, very shrewd diplomat well-versed in the espionage arts.

During the Civil War, aware of the French threat to the south, Seward adroitly carried out a diplomatic tap dance. He suggested to Napoleon that he accepted the fiction of French involvement in Mexico merely to collect foreign debts. At the same time he subtly conveyed President Abraham Lincoln's uneasiness over what might be interpreted as plans for a permanent French occupation of Mexico as exemplified by the figure of Emperor Maximilian – Napoleon's puppet. Meanwhile, he set up an intelligence network of American consuls and diplomats that kept tabs on just what Napoleon was planning. Seward also used America's first non-military communications intelligence operation, a group of telegraph clerks and cryptographers he recruited, who kept watch on Napoleon's communications with Mexico.

It was the communications intelligence network that in late 1866 came up with a priceless piece of intelligence – an enciphered letter they intercepted. It had been sent by Napoleon to his commanding general in Mexico City announcing his conclusion that the Mexican adventure was costing too much in terms of blood and treasure and must come to an end. He ordered the general to formulate a secret three-stage withdrawal plan that would remove the French military presence over a two-year period. The withdrawal, Napoleon revealed, was part of a larger plan – get the United States of America to agree to a joint occupation of Mexico with France and create an interim government which would exclude the hated Juarez, whose men had killed a lot of French soldiers.

Armed with that intelligence, Seward suddenly stepped up pressure on Napoleon. The United States, he curtly informed the French ambassador, was a supporter of Juarez, so any plan to exclude him was a non-starter. There would be no joint occupation, interim or otherwise; France must withdraw immediately from Mexico. The Americans began pouring in more arms and supplies to Juarez while Sheridan led showy military maneuvers along the border to convince Napoleon that an American military assault might be imminent. He finally gave in, abruptly ordering his troops to withdraw, much to the dismay of Maximilian, who stubbornly decided to stay in Mexico and fight on.

Hopelessly misinformed to the end, Maximilian believed that he and a small band of supporters somehow could rally Mexicans to their cause. However, that support never came and he was captured. On the morning of 19 June 1867, the only emperor in the history of Mexico and two of his surviving generals were shot by a firing squad.

THE SECRETS OF RUE PEPINIERE

Among the Belgians who lived near anywhere the large mansion at 10 Rue Pepiniere in German-occupied Antwerp during the fall of 1914, the very address was something mentioned only in whispers.

LEFT: Elsbeth Schragmueller, the legendary 'Fräulein Doktor' of German intelligence who devised the modern system for training intelligence agents.

They had learned to avoid walking anywhere near the building. The German military patrols that guarded it routinely picked up pedestrians on Rue Pepiniere and subjected them to hostile interrogation, accusing them of being spies for even daring to look at the place. Those who made the mistake of openly speculating about what was transpiring there could expect to be rounded up and thrown into prison.

Something evil must be going on inside that mansion, the Belgians decided. How else to explain all those guards, the rolls of barbed wire to keep out intruders and the cars with black curtains in the windows that sped in and out of the place at all hours of the day and night?

WORLD EVENTS

Not evil, exactly. The Belgians could not have known that inside the ornate grey building a revolution in espionage was taking place, one that reverberates to this day. Nor could they have known that this revolution had been brought to life by the most unlikely character in the history of espionage, a reclusive female academic who never worked a day in her life as a spy. It was the central oddity in the very odd career of the espionage legend known as Fräulein Doktor.

When war broke out in August 1914, Elsbeth Schragmueller was a brilliant 26-year-old economist who had just earned her doctorate at the University of Freiburg (her dissertation was on medieval stonecutter guilds). A fervid German patriot, she volunteered her services as an infantry soldier. That was out of the question, but bemused German officers realized that her obvious intellectual capability – including fluency in English, French and Italian – could be put to use somewhere in the war effort. The best they could come up with, to Schragmueller's frustration, was the army's Postal Censorship Bureau in Brussels, where hundreds of censors pored through every piece of mail, searching for clues to intelligence spies were transmitting in the guise of ordinary correspondence.

Almost at once, Schragmueller realized the operation was a failure. As she informed her shocked superiors, almost all the people assigned to censorship duty were untrained drones of narrow vision who looked only for the obvious, such as 'Aunt Millie tells me she saw 10 geese in Namur yesterday' (my source reports 1,000 Germans bivouacked at Namur) or soldiers' letters that included too much specific military information. Look what they missed, she told her superiors: the bill of sale sent to a bank detailing the sale of the family farm carefully listing the number of chickens, pigs, cows, horses and farm implements that had been sold (various types of German units observed, along with their strengths); and this letter from a woman recounting the results of a sailing regatta to her sailor boyfriend, telling in detail which sailboats in each class had won individual races (the number and types of German warships in the harbour).

In a presentation that dazzled her listeners, she demonstrated a system of textual analysis she had developed, which would reveal which sentences in a given letter were probably conveying intelligence. This system of textual analysis, she argued, should be made part of a rigorous course of instruction for people assigned to censorship duty. Those people should be talented college graduates from a wide variety of professions with the kind of backgrounds that would help them to spot even the subtlest attempt to slip espionage through the mails.

The Bureau followed her suggestions, which dramatically increased its effectiveness. Word of this remarkable woman and her abilities reached the senior officers at the upper level of German military intelligence, who had an even bigger challenge in mind – reforming Germany's espionage education system. As Schragmueller discovered, Germany had seriously neglected its intelligence capabilities in the decades prior to World War I and was now paying the penalty. The Germans needed a lot of spies for myriad intelligence tasks in three theaters of war. It was a need they were trying to fill quickly by churning out spies from three spy schools set up in occupied Belgium. It was very much of a hurry-up operation; hundreds of recruits were being rushed through a quick one-week course. Little wonder, Schragmueller noted, why the first graduates sent off to the Western Front were arrested almost as soon as they crossed enemy lines.

Given a free hand to solve the problem however she saw fit, Schragmueller concluded there was no way German intelligence could be improved so long as the current training regimen remained in place. Sending graduates out into the cold equipped with only a rudimentary knowledge of codes, invisible writing and use of cover was tantamount to murder. Schragmueller drastically revised the curriculum and just about everything else at the schools, creating the first real systemic method for training spies, adopted years later as a template for all modern intelligence training courses.

The three German spy schools were consolidated into one large school on the Rue Pepiniere in Antwerp. Under Schragmueller's radical new system, no one would be recruited for training at that school without careful vetting to determine if they were prepared to make the effort required to become trained spies. She did not want the dregs of society, the usual recruiting base for intelligence agencies. What she wanted were intelligent people who were strongly motivated to help the German cause. Those who passed that first hurdle were taken to the school in cars with black curtains blocking the windows. When they arrived, they confronted a tall blonde woman in civilian clothes who announced she was their 'director' and went on to inform them how they would spend the next 15 weeks of their lives.

Students would occupy 12 hours each day with intense instruction in the espionage arts (use of cover, invisible inks, sketching military installations, codes). They would live in private living quarters at the school, forbidden contact with other students. They would be known only by a number and they would wear masks at all times (so they could not give away the identities of fellow students if later captured). At the conclusion

BELOW: One of the more successful products of British Intelligence's WW I propaganda operation, a poster that popularized the image of Germans as barbaric 'huns'.

of the course, they would be given a 'final examination' consisting of an assigned espionage mission somewhere in friendly territory. If they succeeded in the mission, they would then be assigned a real mission behind enemy lines. Those who failed would be washed out, informed they would never work for German intelligence and sent home with the warning that if they ever told anyone what they had experienced at the school, they would be executed.

By the spring of 1915, the French and British counterintelligence services became aware that a sudden vigour and professionalism had infused German intelligence. A new wave of German spies demonstrated considerably better skills than the first generation of Germany's agents, who had been rounded up in wholesale lots. It took a while to determine the reason for this new professionalism, but finally a number of Schragmueller-trained assets who had been arrested, confronting the choice between immediate execution and revealing what they knew, confessed their recruitment for German intelligence. The story was always the same. A trip by car with black-curtained windows to a big mansion in Antwerp, the blonde woman who directed their training, an intensive course of instruction and their 'final examination', usually an assignment to contact a 'traitor' with information to impart. The student was to adopt a cover and evade the efforts of German agents to arrest him, using countersurveillance techniques he had been taught.

POWERFUL FIGURE

The common thread that ran through all the confessions was the striking character of the Germans' new espionage trainer. No one knew her name (since she pointedly never told them), but one of her graduates, arrested in northern France, noted a slip-up in the school's tight security. One day, he overheard one of the German officers there address the 'director' as Fräulein Doktor. That offered a clue: in German culture, which reveres higher education, male holders of a doctorate are respectfully addressed as Herr Doktor and an unmarried female doctorate holder is addressed as Fräulein Doktor.

With that scrap of information, the British sought to find out just who Fräulein Doktor was, infiltrate her spy school and put her out of commission. They failed in all three goals. They never did discover that the director was Elsbeth Schragmueller (her real identity was not revealed until after the war), nor were they ever able to get anywhere near her. As they discovered, trying to track Fräulein Doktor was like trying to find a ghost. Schragmueller lived at various addresses under multiple identities (including an old washerwoman), seldom spending more than a few nights at a particular address.

In the end, however, it did not matter; the British decided that if they couldn't catch the real Fräulein Doktor, nonetheless a mythical one could prove useful as a propaganda symbol. In short order, the popular press was filled with stories about the amazing German superspy named Fräulein Doktor, the buxom blonde Teutonic goddess whose ruthlessness included shooting especially doltish students dead with a pistol. These lurid stories served their purpose. The stalemate on the Western Front, in which thousands of British soldiers were sent to their deaths by incompetent generals, could now be explained away, at least in part, by the efforts of a German superspy who cunningly obtained British offensive plans.

The truth, of course, was much more prosaic. After the war, Schramueller, who never married, returned to civilian life, working quietly as a lecturer in economics at the University of Munich. She was appalled by the exaggerated accounts of her role inspired by British propaganda, which flowed into postwar accounts as fact. She always refused to discuss her wartime role in German espionage – except in 1932, when a woman being treated in a Swiss sanatorium for addiction to opium claimed to be the legendary Fräulein Doktor. Schragmueller emerged from obscurity to vigorously deny it, then turned away all requests for interviews and rejected lavish offers for her memoirs. She died in 1939.

In reality, German intelligence had nowhere near that kind of capability portrayed in British propaganda. Neither did the other participants at that early stage in the war. In fact, there was a heritage of near-total intelligence blindness at the beginning of the war. Indeed, it can be argued that this blindness was largely responsible for the cataclysm in the first place.

Beginning in 1885, the powers of Europe arrived simultaneously at the conclusion that war was inevitable. They believed it was the only way to resolve the irreconcilable differences among rival powers over colonial empires, perceptions of encroaching danger, revenge for past geopolitical injustices and competing economic interests. To prepare for what they all believed would be a short, decisive war in the Napoleonic mould, the nations formulated elaborate war plans that included detailed mobilization schedules. At the first indication that the outbreak of war was imminent, a nation's standing army would move to its pre-ordained battle stations, to be followed by the mobilized reserves.

In espionage terms, that mandated what was called at the time 'sure knowledge', a very precise intelligence estimate of the military capabilities of the other side. Such knowledge would allow an attacked nation time to go on the defensive while a decisive counterattack plan could be formulated, based on the intelligence about the opponent. As a result, intelligence became the province of the military, narrowly focused on collecting detailed technical and tactical details.

ABOVE: Colonel Alfred Redl of the Austro-Hungarian General Staff, blackmailed into treason by the Okhrana, czarist Russia's intelligence agency.

were quite convinced that they knew everything worth knowing. They could point to walls of filing cabinets filled with reports on every possible item of intelligence interest. They knew how the new French 75-millimeter artillery's recoil mechanism worked, how the turrets on German battle cruisers traversed, how the British cavalry deployed on the battlefield, the precise thickness of Serbian frontier fortifications, the exact number of Russian troops that would be mobilized in the first 24 hours of war.

True, they knew everything – except what they needed to know. German intelligence knew how fast a British infantry soldier could reload his rifle, but did not have the first clue how Great Britain would react when Germany carried out an important step in its war plan – the invasion of neutral Belgium. They did not know for the simple reason the Germans had not bothered finding out. Austro-Hungarian intelligence had detailed information on the precise numbers of Serbian artillery pieces that would be deployed in the event of war, but had not made any effort to find out the implications of Russia's vow to enter the war on Serbia's side in the event of an attack by Austria-Hungary. Every intelligence agency confidently predicted a short war won by grand offensive sweeps, having failed to study the lessons of the Russo-Japanese War of 1905, which showed that the machine gun and rapid-firing artillery had shifted the advantage decisively to the defence.

COMPROMISING SITUATION

Even the most notable pre-war intelligence success had only limited usefulness. That success involved the recruitment by Russian intelligence in 1913 of Colonel Alfred Redl of the Austro-Hungarian army's general staff The Russians discovered that Redl was a paedophile, information they used to set him up with a young boy and photograph the results. Threatened with exposure, Redl turned over everything he could get his hands on, most importantly Plan 3, the Austro-Hungarian mobilization and deployment plan in the event of war with Russia. However, Redl was subsequently arrested. At that point the Russians could only assume that the Austrians would learn of his betrayal of the plan, which, obviously, they would change.

The narrow focus on tactical intelligence was a recipe for disaster as events in 1914 proved. Seven European nations literally stumbled into war that summer, each one of them convinced their victorious armies would be home 'before the leaves fall'. The Belgians sat contentedly in their 'impregnable' fortresses that blocked any German advance, but their intelligence never bothered to find out what the Germans planned to do about those fortifications in event of war. Thus, they were unaware that the Germans had developed special siege artillery that would reduce the forts to rubble.

An example of this was a voluminous French intelligence report of 1913 on the German army that even included such mind-numbing details as the precise dimensions and operating philosophy of cook wagons used to prepare food for troops in the field.

Gathering such intelligence, a humdrum task that didn't require much in the way of sophisticated training, was largely handled by military attaches assigned to embassies. It was supplemented by material from low-level spies, most of them paid assets recruited among foreigners. Their work was directed by resentful officers on general staffs who had little or no training in intelligence and considered their work a dead-end job. Most had been assigned to intelligence work largely because they were deemed to lack the right stuff for combat command. As every officer understood, combat command was the only route to higher promotion and honours.

By 1914, the intelligence agencies of the European powers

RIGHT: Some of the 100,000 Russian prisoners captured at the battle of Tannenberg, a military disaster caused by lapses in Russian radio security.

French Intelligence, obsessed with Alsace-Lorraine, the former French province lost to Germany during the Franco-Prussian War 44 years before, assumed without any evidence that the main German effort would occur in that area. With no insight into German military thinking or planning, the French failed to spot, almost until it was too late, a million German troops pouring into northern France.

German intelligence knew a lot about British battlefield weapons and tactics, but had no idea of what Great Britain planned to do with its army. As a result, it missed the movement of the British Expeditionary Force (BEF) to the continent, a crucial intelligence lapse that moved an infuriated Kaiser Wilhelm to ask his chagrined ministers, "Am I surrounded by dolts?" British intelligence knew a great deal about the German navy – except its operational plans when war broke out. Consequently, the British failed to realize that the Germans would not, as assumed, use their U-boats as scouts for the main fleet. Instead, they would use them as warships. In the early days of the war, two Royal Navy cruisers, sailing without any antisubmarine protection, were sunk in 14 minutes by a single German submarine.

This drum roll of intelligence disasters was the product of Europe's espionage organizations, which were largely dysfunctional. The central problem was that they were seriously behind the times. Despite the clear warnings, beginning during the American Civil War, that warfare was changing dramatically, intelligence organizations failed to keep up with the rapid pace of change. While warfare was being revolutionized by such technological developments as the telegraph – which now permitted the rapid movements of mass armies – intelligence was stuck somewhere around the age of Napoleon. No country developed a centralized intelligence system to collect and evaluate intelligence. Cryptography was haphazard at best and putting virtually all intelligence in the hands of the military meant that intelligence was largely a matter of bean-counting, a hopelessly narrow obsession with the compilation of data on the numbers of troops and weapons of the other side.

The most dysfunctional intelligence organization was that of France. Following the disaster of the Franco-Prussian War, the French realized that a large part of the reason for their defeat was a lack of intelligence on the Prussian enemy. To rectify it, a new section, called the Deuxième Bureau, was created within the French General Staff. It had responsibility for everything related to intelligence. This was an organizational mistake, for like armies everywhere, the route to promotion and success was in the combat arms, which attracted the best officers. Intelligence, regarded as a career-killer, was staffed with mediocre officers who spent most of their time manoeuvring to get transferred. In any event, most of them knew next to nothing about intelligence, and had no intention of learning anything about the subject.

To make matters worse, the Bureau was riven by rivalries and dissension. This climaxed in 1894 in the case of Colonel Alfred Dreyfus, a General Staff officer charged with betraying military secrets to Germany. Anti-Semitic fellow officers attempting to cover up the real traitor, another General Staff officer, who had framed Dreyfus, a Jew. Revelation of the cover-up several years later undercut public support for the General Staff. When a left-wing government took power in 1908, it severely pared the staff's budget (including the Deuxième Bureau) and intelligence languished.

There was no Dreyfus case in Germany, but its intelligence void was equally large – as Colonel Walter Nicholai was to discover. A junior officer on the German General Staff, Nicholai, who knew nothing about intelligence, found himself summoned one day just after the outbreak of war and ordered to take command of Germany's intelligence. The organization, Nicholai was stunned to discover, consisted of the grand total of 13 men – one senior General Staff officer supervising 12 junior officers. There was worse news to come. Nicholai was told that his official title as 'chief co-ordinator' included, besides directing intelligence, supervision of all German propaganda operations and censorship. He was then informed that he was to accomplish all this with a budget of only 470,000 marks. When Nicholai asked why Germany was spending so little on intelligence, he was told that since the war would last only a few months, there was no necessity to spend a lot of money. He was further unsettled when he was buttonholed by General Erich Falkenhayn, Chief of the General Staff, who told him, "Do tell me how things are with the enemy. I hear nothing about that."

While Nicholai was trying to figure out how he was supposed to run an intelligence organization with little money and few men (desperate, he enlisted 50 policemen as his first intelligence recruits), his counterparts in Russian intelligence, the Okhrana, could count on nearly 8,000 agents and a vast sub-network of informers and assets. It also had its own cryptographic section and communications network. A formidable intelligence organization on paper, it was badly focused. Obsessed by internal security threats from an increasingly restive Russian population, czars had used the Okhrana as a tool of internal repression. By 1914, the organization had only one foreign station, in Paris. However, even that station's efforts were diverted from foreign intelligence to spying on Russian exiles.

The inevitable result was that when war broke out in 1914, the Okhrana had no idea what Russia was facing. The Russian strategy for war was simple. The bulk of the 'Russian steamroller', its vast reserves of manpower, would simply march west and crush the Germans on the way to Berlin. But crush what? The Okhrana had no intelligence whatsoever on German forces in East Prussia, the German province on the other side of the Russian border, nor did it have any information on how the Germans would react to a Russian invasion. Two large Russian armies crossed the border totally blind, with no idea where the German army was, how many Germans there were and what those forces intended to do. It is hard to imagine a more disastrous set of circumstances under which an army marched into war.

THE COST OF WAR

However, the First and Second Russian armies that blundered into East Prussia on 26 August 1914 suffered from a handicap – communications. The Okhrana had zealously guarded its monopoly over cryptography, which meant the Russian army was the poor stepchild, woefully short of equipment and trained personnel. It was so short, in fact, that the armies in East Prussia were reduced to broadcasting operations orders in the clear. The astonished Germans who heard those transmissions manoeuvred the Russians into a huge trap near the town of Tannenberg, inflicting 122,000 casualties in the first of a series of military disasters that would destroy Imperial Russia.

The Okhrana was not about to bear any blame for one of history's worst intelligence disasters. Assigned by the government to conduct an investigation into what happened at Tannenberg, the Okhrana concluded that the defeat could be attributed solely to treason by the Minister of War. The evidence? He had a Jewish wife who spent a lot of money on clothes and a week before the battle he had written a letter to a friend in Austria. In the letter he mentioned that because of bad weather 'long walks are out of the question'. This was a coded message, the Okhrana insisted, revealing Russian operational plans for the invasion of East Prussia. He was sentenced to life in prison.

No such lunacy afflicted British intelligence, but like the other intelligence services of Europe, it had very little insight into what was happening on the continent. The British depended to a great extent on volunteer amateur spies, beginning a tradition that would become a hallmark of British intelligence for many years. The roster of volunteer spies included the famed explorer Richard F. Burton, who provided intelligence on what he had seen during his

embarked on a massive build-up of the Kriegsmarine. They openly predicted an eventual war with Great Britain, a war they claimed would be won by Germany's 'mailed fist' – its High Seas Fleet. Not since the days of Napoleon had the British felt so threatened. The popular press began to be filled with scare stories about the growing German military threat, along with a sub-text about a great German espionage menace seen as the essential prelude to what many people believed was an invasion that might take place any day.

It all came to a head in 1903 with the publication of a novel by the Anglo-Irish writer Erskine Childers, who also happened to be an amateur spy working for the Foreign Office. Titled *Riddle of the Sands*, the novel features a yachtsman named Carruthers (interestingly a real amateur spy for the Foreign Office), who discovers a secret German invasion plan while sailing off the Frisian Coast. Carruthers and a companion also uncover a vast German espionage network on England's eastern coast, directed by the ruthlessly cunning "Herr Dollman" – a perfect caricature of an evil German spymaster, complete with "Hunnish features" (whatever that meant).

The book was a sensation, becoming one of the great best-sellers of the age. Childers' avowed purpose was to rouse public opinion to demand action by what he considered lassitude by the government and the Royal Navy in reacting to the 'German menace'. He succeeded in that goal. There was a public outcry, a reaction that had a great deal to do with a common perception that the novel was actually barely-disguised fact. Many believed that there really was a massive German invasion in the offing, assisted by a German espionage effort that had penetrated every area of British life.

In espionage terms, the important effect of the book was its impact on the British government. The Committee of Imperial Defence concluded that there was no factual basis for Childers' alarming scenario, but at the same time realized it really had no idea of the dimension of the German threat. It commissioned several studies of the

travels in Arab lands, and Robert Baden-Powell, founder of the Boy Scouts, who worked as a spy for the British army. Baden-Powell's forte was steganography, the art of concealing intelligence information in ordinary-looking artwork. In the years before World War I, Baden-Powell took advantage of his extensive world travels to reconnoiter military fortifications. Known as an inveterate sketch artist of birds and insects, especially butterflies, Baden-Powell, a national hero and expert on static defences worked even the tiniest detail of fortifications he surveyed into his drawings, a technique he performed so subtly it was impossible to spot without knowing his system.

Intelligence did not become a serious proposition in Great Britain until the early part of the twentieth century, when the worst spy scare of modern history convulsed the country. The scare was touched off by the spectre of an increasingly bellicose Germany, whose naval leaders problem, which concluded no one really knew, but it was reasonable to deduce that (a) there were probably a lot of German spies already at work in Britain; and (b) there was a growing German threat that required a major intelligence effort to monitor. The result in 1909 was the creation of the Secret Service Bureau, initially divided into military and naval sections. A year later, these morphed into the Home Department responsible for counterespionage (eventually MI5) and a Foreign Department for espionage (eventually MI6).

The foreign intelligence component of this new structure was not able to create much in the way of networks on the continent by the time World War I broke out, except for assets developed in neutral Holland and Switzerland as active listening posts for spying on Germany. The star asset in Switzerland was the novelist Somerset Maugham. His adventures in espionage were later included in his Ashenden stories about a British agent (a thinly-disguised portrait of himself) in Switzerland during the war. The stories are full of derring-do exploits by a James Bond-type agent, although in reality Maugham's espionage work in Switzerland was much more humdrum. It involved mainly keeping tabs on the movements of German government money through Swiss banks and diplomatic tidbits picked up from junior diplomats he befriended. Maugham roamed the country under cover of 'research' for his novels and what he collected was sent to London concealed among the pages of manuscripts mailed to his British publisher. An especially ingenious method of espionage communication, since Swiss Customs officers were not likely to patiently pore through hundreds of pages of a manuscript to search for pages that didn't belong there.

TOUGH DECISIONS

Communications were always the Achilles heel of all spies working behind enemy lines. Even assuming an agent could obtain good intelligence, there simply was no easy, quick method for getting that information back to headquarters. Most intelligence was perishable. Learning that the Second Infantry Division was being redeployed to another section of the front was of no value unless that intelligence could be rapidly imparted. To solve that problem, the Germans, British and French trained carrier pigeons to carry messages in the form of tiny writing on lightweight rice paper attached to a bird's leg. However, as that practice became widespread, front line troops were ordered to shoot any bird on sight.

The British and French then came up with a technical solution that would solve two problems at once – aerial reconnaissance. The idea first occurred to French intelligence, which one day assigned a Paris studio photographer to ride in the observer seat of a scouting plane.

When the plane overflew German lines, the pilot grasped the belt of the terrified photographer as he leaned out of his seat and aimed his box camera at the ground below. The results were sensational: clear pictures of German trenchworks and fortifications, along with troop concentrations. The British refined this first attempt at overhead espionage by developing new large-aperture cameras that could take pictures of wide swaths of land. The chief virtue of aerial reconnaissance was that it eliminated the need for a spy to infiltrate behind enemy lines to scout those trenchlines while providing a foolproof method of transmitting that information. Unless, of course, the enemy shot down the reconnaissance planes...

That is exactly what happened. As everybody began to understand the tremendous value of those pictures taken from nearly a mile up, planes were armed with machine guns to shoot them down. That made the lives of observers in the planes a dangerous proposition. However, they were a picnic compared to the heart-stopping existence

BELOW: An American observer in an observation balloon above the Western Front. He had to be alert for enemy fighter planes that targeted the spy balloons.

of the observers who worked aboard a subsidiary aerial reconnaissance operation – observation balloons.

In an idea borrowed from Thaddeus Lowe's innovation during the American Civil War, the balloons were tethered up to 2,000 feet above the front lines. Aboard was an observer with a mapboard, field glasses, and a telephone hook-up to the ground. He would observe the enemy positions, which he would send over the telephone link as instantaneous intelligence, then update a tactical map. All the while, he had to be alert for the sound of an approaching airplane engine, since the standard method of eliminating espionage by balloon was to shoot down the balloon. Not an especially difficult task, since even one tracer bullet was enough to convert the gas bag into an inferno. With the approach of an enemy plane, the observer had to leap from the basket under the balloon and parachute to the ground. His life, obviously, depended on good timing.

Judged overall, these overhead reconnaissance operations produced only spotty results. Those results were especially frustrating to Germany, since so many of their other intelligence operations had gone wrong. Among the worst failures was a total intelligence disaster in Great Britain. It was a reality in sharp contrast with the popular perceptions that arose during the great spy scare of a country honeycombed with German spies. The Home Department mounted an extensive effort to find them, but failed to turn up any, for a very good reason – they did not exist.

At about the same time that the Home Department came into being, German intelligence decided that it was time to create espionage networks in Great Britain, part of the preparations for the war certain to come. The problem was that the Germans had no spies to send there and no idea of how to find any. In desperation, they turned to an ex-private detective named Gustav Steinhauer, whose sole claim to any kind of espionage expertise was a brief period working in the United States as an industrial spy. A plodding incompetent, Steinhauer took up residence in London under cover of an émigré German businessman (the thinness of the cover was necessitated by his thick German accent). Steinhauer travelled throughout the country, recruiting assets. By July 1914, shortly before the outbreak of the war, he had managed to enlist a grand total of 26 spies, most of them German émigrés who had been living in Great Britain for years. Unfortunately for German intelligence, they were individually and collectively incompetent, with extremely limited access to any kind of useful information.

For communicating with his superiors in Germany, Steinhauer recruited a German émigré baker named Karl Ernst to serve as a letterbox. Reports from Steinhauer's agents would be collected by their spymaster, then taken to Ernst, who would put them in the form of a letter addressed to German intelligence cover addresses in the Netherlands.

ABOVE: Gustav Steinhauer, the hopelessly inept head of German intelligence operations in Great Britain during World War I.

After the outbreak of war, it did not take long for postal censors to wonder why the owner of a small bakery was writing so many letters to the Netherlands, all of them accounts of family gossip with an odd emphasis on numbers (obviously military information).

Two other Steinhauer assets, Dutch émigrés, demonstrated similar incompetence that attracted the unwanted attention of postal censors. With covert funding from Steinhauer, they opened a cigar store in Portsmouth. The idea was that they would carefully monitor Royal Navy ship movements in and out of the harbour and pass on that information to a cover address in the Netherlands via letters that would conceal the information among ostensible orders for cigars. However, the censors could not fail to notice that this small cigar store had an astonishing amount of commercial correspondence, including orders for 48,000 cigars in ten days.

Steinhauer, bombarded with increasingly urgent requests

from the German navy for intelligence on its British counterpart and impatient with his assets' inability to obtain any useful information, decided to carry out some espionage himself. Posing as a fisherman, he went to the naval base at Scapa Flow and used a knotted line to measure the water depth of the anchorage. This was an interesting tidbit of intelligence, but hardly the kind of information that would provide any useful insight into the plans of the Royal Navy. Meanwhile, as his irked superiors noted, Steinhauer had somehow missed the dispatch of the BEF to France – a massive troop deployment that moved from ports his assets were supposed to be watching.

Frustrated by the Steinhauer ring's failure to obtain any useful intelligence, especially about the Royal Navy, Berlin decided on a radical solution. It was one that would have tragic consequences. At the end of 1914, an American tourist bearing a passport in the name of Charles A. Inglis arrived in Southampton. His real name was Hans Carl Lody, a lieutenant in the German Kriegsmarine who had been assigned the mission because he had once served on the Holland–America Line, where he picked up a fluent command of English. However, that was the sole qualification he had for his mission, which was to gather intelligence on the Royal Navy; he had no intelligence training whatsoever. He was to transmit the information to a cover address in Stockholm in letters to 'relatives'.

The 'tourist' immediately headed for Portsmouth, where he attracted attention by asking a lot of detailed questions about warships in the harbour, the kind of questions no ordinary tourist would ask. Lody further attracted attention to himself by including rabidly anti-German statements in his letters, which he thought would be a good way to convince anyone reading those letters that whoever wrote them could only be what he said he was, a very pro-British American. Of course, it had precisely the opposite effect. The postal censors wondered why an American tourist would hector his Swedish relatives with anti-German diatribes. The rest of the letters contained awkwardly-phrased accounts of his 'visit' to England, which turned out to be a crude letter code reporting information on Royal Navy ships.

Scotland Yard detectives entered the hotel room where he was staying and noticed that his clothes were made by a Hamburg tailor and had the name 'Lody' stitched on an inside pocket, a colossal violation of elementary espionage tradecraft. No doubt: 'Inglis' was a spy. Only a few months after entering Great Britain, with virtually nothing to show for all his trouble, he was arrested, convicted by court martial and on 6 December 1914, was shot by firing squad. Earlier, the Steinhauer ring had been rolled up and with Lody's death, German intelligence in Great Britain collapsed, never to revive.

THE AMATEUR ROLE

While German foreign intelligence was suffering disaster after disaster, the new British MI6 was initiating a series of operations whose success would depend on British intelligence's greatest resource – talented amateur spies. Their ranks included a very unlikely spy, a soft-spoken nurse whose fate would have a major effect on the course of the war. The spy's name was Edith Cavell, who was among the first assets recruited in Belgium after the German invasion in 1914. An English nurse who had been working at the Berkendael Institute in Brussels, Cavell stayed on after the German occupation when the institute became a Red Cross hospital that treated French, British and Belgian wounded soldiers.

However, the hospital was also being used to hide troops, most of them British, who had been cut off by the German offensive. A Belgian underground group, working with British intelligence, set up an operation to smuggle the soldiers to safety in neutral Holland. Cavell worked tirelessly with the group, providing false papers for the smuggling of 200 soldiers out of Belgium. Eventually a traitor within the underground group betrayed the operation to the Germans. Cavell was among those arrested. She was charged with 'conducting soldiers to the enemy', a charge she defiantly and proudly admitted to. On 12 October 1915, she was shot by firing squad.

In a time when hundreds of thousands of men were dying in battle, the death of an obscure nurse in Belgium would not have usually been a cause celebre. However, Edith Cavell's death occurred just as the British government decided to create a new entity: the War Propaganda Board.

Propaganda as a sub-species of espionage is as old as the Bible, but the British version introduced a number of innovations to make it a formidable weapon of war. First, it operated in co-ordination with both the military and intelligence, using information from both for maximum effect. Second, it recruited the cream of the literary and academic establishments for first-class propagandists, including John Buchan, the spy novelist (*The Thirty-Nine Steps*) and the Oxford historian Arnold Toynbee. Third and most important, its propaganda carefully distinguished between German militarism and the German people. It argued that the war was not against the German people, but a crusade in the name of civilization to destroy the evil militarists who had dragged Germany into a senseless war.

The first great achievement of Wellington House (as the War Propaganda Board was commonly called after the government building in which it was headquartered) was a campaign that elevated Cavell's death into the war crime of the century. In this version of events, Cavell was a completely innocent angel of mercy, the victim of spike-helmeted brutes in jackboots, prototypical 'Huns' who became the stock villains in British propaganda. Popular artists commissioned to illustrate Cavell's death portrayed a young, beautiful woman (a considerable deviation from the real Cavell, a plain-looking 50-year-old matron) tied to a stake as grinning Huns prepare to shoot her.

This version of her end, which omitted any mention of the work she did for British intelligence, was the cutting edge of a brilliantly successful larger propaganda campaign about the 'rape of Belgium' by the brutal German military. Like other British propaganda campaigns, it was careful never to stray too far from the truth. In the case of Belgium, the fact was that the Germans, harassed by Belgian insurgents, had carried out a number of reprisals against civilians. This was sufficient raw material for the British to magnify that into a portrayal of a land crushed under German jackboots, its cultural treasures destroyed and its people brutalized.

There were ripples everywhere from the British propaganda operation, the most important of which was felt in the United States. There, it began to whittle away at American neutrality, part of a covert action operation that would turn out to be the most successful such operation in the war. It would also prove to the decisive factor in Germany's defeat. The success owed much to yet another unlikely spy, aided by the ineptitude of German intelligence.

In the autumn of 1914, Captain Guy Gaunt of the Royal Navy arrived in Washington, D.C., with the official title of naval attaché at the British embassy. In fact, his real role was to head all British intelligence operations in the United States, including propaganda. Washington was the most important British intelligence target in the world, since the Americans were vital to the British war effort. First, Britain needed the arms U.S. factories were supplying, along with the war loans from American banks. Second, a keystone of British policy was to draw the U.S. into the war on the Allied side. Third, German intelligence operations, which threatened the arms pipeline and were exerting a maximum effort to keep the Americans out of the war, had to be balked.

It was a complex challenge. Within a year, it became clear that Gaunt was not up to it. A swaggering, boastful character in love with the drama of espionage, Gaunt was as subtle as a heart attack. Within a short time, there were few people in the U.S. government who weren't aware that he was head of British intelligence in America, with a mandate to drag the country into a European war. Not the kind of covert subtlety needed for the task at hand, although Gaunt made a number of close friends in the American establishment. These included the young Assistant Secretary of the Navy, Franklin D. Roosevelt, and the Dulles family. Their youngest son, Allen, sat enraptured as Gaunt recounted tales of his adventures in the espionage world. However entertaining, Gaunt's antics began to cause deep unease in London, where the first head of MI6, Mansfield Smith-Cumming, realized he needed another man for the job.

RIGHT: Edith Cavell, the British nurse and spy whose execution by the Germans in 1915 provided the British with a priceless propaganda opportunity.

BELOW: Captain Guy Gaunt, head of British intelligence in the United States early in World War I, whose careless talk and self-promotion led to his recall.

Part of Cumming's calculation that Wiseman was the right man for that important job centered on his international banking experience, which included several years working as a banker in the United States. There, he established close links with the upper level of the American financial establishment, which was pleasantly surprised to encounter, for the first time, a British banker who did not look down his nose at them. Additionally, Cumming was aware that Wiseman had come to like Americans and had a firm grasp on the intricacies and subtleties of American politics and culture – usually subjects of deep mystification to his countrymen.

In October 1915, Wiseman arrived in the United States under a cover Cumming thought would give him greater freedom of action – head of the British Purchasing Commission, ostensibly concerned with arranging U.S. arms sales to Britain. Wiseman went right to work quietly courting influential opinion-makers, politicians, and government officials. He concentrated much of his attention on Colonel Edward M. House, a rich Texan and noted political operator who had played a key role in getting President Woodrow Wilson the Democratic nomination for President and, subsequently, his election in 1912. Thereafter, House became one of Wilson's closest advisers. Wiseman read his quarry well. An insufferable egotist, House fancied himself an expert on international relations and a lot of other subjects as well. He liked to hear himself talk, much of it arrant nonsense, but Wiseman found it all quite "insightful". Wiseman went out of his way to praise House's views on one topic or another. He and House became close friends, a bond that drew Wiseman deep into Wilson's inner circle, where he began to gain Wilson's ear. Wiseman played his hand carefully, avoiding any kind of overt hectoring. Aware of how the mind of Wilson, the former college professor, worked, he waited for the right opportunities to put forth his arguments in the form of academic analysis. Summarily, it amounted to German militarism as a grave threat to the Western world, a threat in which the United States had a large stake. A triumph of the German militarists meant the death of democracy and self-determination Wilson hoped for Europe.

His choice of a replacement was inspired. He picked a full-blooded British aristocrat named William Wiseman. A former Cambridge boxing blue, he had a baronetcy dating back to 1628 and a career in international banking. Wiseman presented the very picture of a man of the British upper class, including an air of quiet superiority. Behind that facade was a deeply committed British patriot and a very shrewd and resourceful covert operator. That talent came naturally; he had never worked in intelligence until Cumming recruited him in 1915. At the outbreak of war, Wiseman had volunteered for army service, but after being gassed in Flanders was invalided out of military service. Eager to serve the war effort, he asked for some sort of important work to do, an eagerness that moved Cumming to enlist him for MI6. Cumming sent him off to Scotland Yard for a brief, one-week course in the rudiments of espionage, then announced his new recruit would be assigned to America, there to take over from Gaunt.

Fortunately for Wiseman, German intelligence demonstrated an astonishing ineptitude in the United States, carrying out a number disastrous operations that served only to prove the darkest assertions of British propaganda. The most serious German misstep was a decision to conduct sabotage operations against the arms pipeline that began on American soil. These operations included bombs placed against cargo ships transporting military supplies to Europe and a number of spectacular explosions. Amongst these was the blowing up of a huge stockpile of ammunition awaiting shipment at a storage site called Black Tom in the East River between New York and New Jersey. The explosion, which could be heard three states away, blew out windows in Manhattan and damaged the Statue of Liberty.

A LACK OF EFFECT

Clearly, German intelligence had not thought through the decision for sabotage. For one thing, it could have no real practical effect. American manufacturers collected the insurance checks, then simply manufactured more guns and artillery shells. No amount of sabotage could disrupt an arms pipeline that was earning the manufacturers immense profits, to say nothing of all the jobs it had created. Americans wanted to remain neutral, but as the old American saying had it, 'Business is business'. For another, sabotage was hardly the way to win the battle for U.S. public opinion. No American could tolerate the idea of foreign spies running around the country, blowing up things.

Those sabotage operations had an unintended and highly damaging consequence for German intelligence. Aware of the American unease over what the Germans were doing, Wiseman established close relations with the two chief components of America's modest intelligence establishment: the U.S. Army's Military Information Division (MID) and the Secret Service (at the time responsible for counterespionage against foreign intelligence operations in the U.S.). Wiseman's offer to provide any intelligence he had on German agents involved in sabotage paid off when he gave the Secret Service the name of a low-ranking German diplomat whom he believed was the contact conveying orders between the German embassy and the saboteurs.

Secret Service agents began an intense surveillance of the New York-based diplomat. One day riding the subway carrying a briefcase, he fell asleep. Suddenly awakening and realizing that the train had reached his stop, he leaped from his seat and quickly left the car – leaving the briefcase behind. Agents immediately seized it. The papers inside were pure dynamite: a detailed outline of plans for German sabotage operations and propaganda. They were returned to furious German diplomats who demanded the recovery of "diplomatic documents", but not before copies were made that Wiseman then leaked to several major newspaper publishers he had befriended.

The newspaper leak, which severely damaged German efforts to keep the U.S. neutral, were part of an extensive British propaganda operation in America. Wiseman retained tight control of that operation, arguing that the United States represented a unique situation, one not easily understood by propagandists in London. In effect, Wiseman was his own propagandist, carefully shaping what London produced into material that would work effectively in the United States. He was aided in great measure by still more German blunders, especially its decision to instigate unrestricted submarine warfare that threatened the lives of American seamen. The sinking of the Lusitania in 1915, in which 1,498 passengers and crew perished, including several hundred Americans (among them Alfred Vanderbilt), provided Wiseman with a golden opportunity. He took full advantage of it, with a full-blown propaganda campaign that portrayed the sinking not as the mistake of a U-boat captain (which in fact it was), but an act of deliberate barbarism by German militarists willing to slaughter the innocents. Support for Germany in American public opinion began to crumble.

The final blow came by means of another, final, German blunder. That blunder was born on the grey morning of 4 August 1914 – the very day that Great Britain declared war on Germany – when the cable-laying ship Telconia slipped out of its port and sailed to a point off the coast of Germany. The ship lowered grapples and, over the next hour, pulled up and cut the telegraph cables connecting Germany with the United States. As the British intended, that meant German communications with America would now have to be sent via a powerful radio station just outside Berlin. The British began to intercept those signals and were rewarded with a flood of messages, but all of them were encoded. The next step, obviously, was decoding all that traffic, but that presented a problem.

The problem was that Britain's cryptographic capability, once the best in the world, had been allowed to deteriorate. Since the most important military communications before World War I involved naval messages (the British were the first to equip warships with radio communications), responsibility for codes and ciphers had been assigned to the Naval Intelligence Division (NID) of the Royal Navy. The task was handled by a secret unit known only as 'Room 40', after the number of the office they occupied in the Admiralty building. Its chief, Captain (later Admiral) William Hall had very few cryptanalysts to handle the large numbers of intercepted German messages piling up in his office, so he decided his first priority was to find more cryptanalysts and fast. But where?

Hall knew a lot about naval communications, but very little about cryptanalysis – so little, he believed people who liked to solve crossword puzzles would make great

CLASS OF SERVICE DESIRED
Fast Day Message
Day Letter
Night Message
Night Letter
Patrons should mark an X opposite the class of service desired; OTHERWISE THE TELEGRAM WILL BE TRANSMITTED AS A FAST DAY MESSAGE.

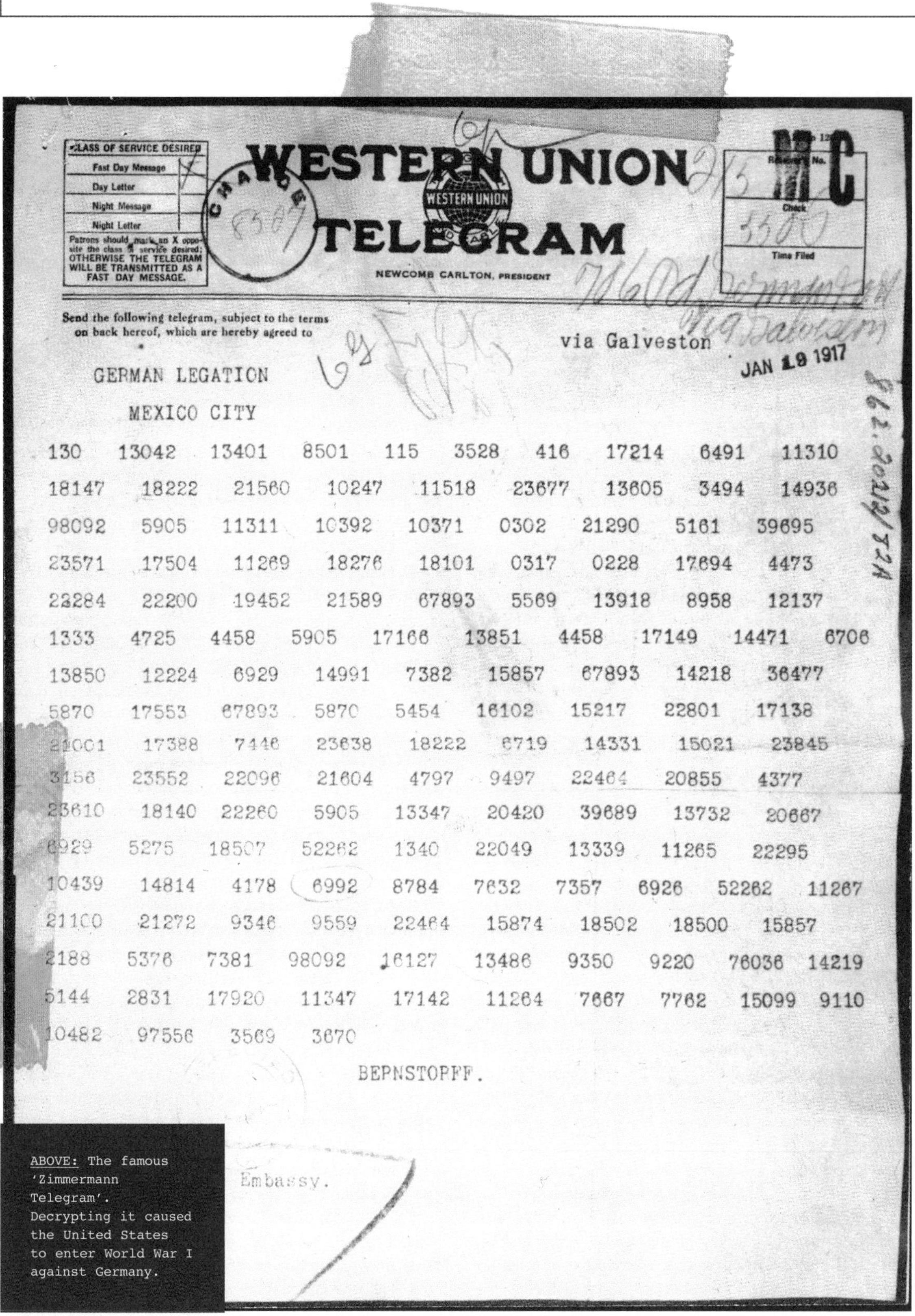

WESTERN UNION TELEGRAM

NEWCOMB CARLTON, PRESIDENT

Receiver's No.
Check
Time Filed

Send the following telegram, subject to the terms on back hereof, which are hereby agreed to

via Galveston

JAN 19 1917

GERMAN LEGATION

MEXICO CITY

130 13042 13401 8501 115 3528 416 17214 6491 11310
18147 18222 21560 10247 11518 23677 13605 3494 14936
98092 5905 11311 10392 10371 0302 21290 5161 39695
23571 17504 11269 18276 18101 0317 0228 17694 4473
22284 22200 19452 21589 67893 5569 13918 8958 12137
1333 4725 4458 5905 17166 13851 4458 17149 14471 6706
13850 12224 6929 14991 7382 15857 67893 14218 36477
5870 17553 67893 5870 5454 16102 15217 22801 17138
21001 17388 7446 23638 18222 6719 14331 15021 23845
3156 23552 22096 21604 4797 9497 22464 20855 4377
23610 18140 22260 5905 13347 20420 39689 13732 20667
6929 5275 18507 52262 1340 22049 13339 11265 22295
10439 14814 4178 6992 8784 7632 7357 6926 52262 11267
21100 21272 9346 9559 22464 15874 18502 18500 15857
2188 5376 7381 98092 16127 13486 9350 9220 76036 14219
5144 2831 17920 11347 17142 11264 7667 7762 15099 9110
10482 97556 3569 3670

BERNSTORFF.

Embassy.

ABOVE: The famous 'Zimmermann Telegram'. Decrypting it caused the United States to enter World War I against Germany.

cryptanalysts. It sounded like a crazy idea, but he turned out to be right. One day, Hall was chatting with a fellow naval officer, Captain Alfred Ewing, Director of Naval Education, who casually mentioned that he was passionately devoted to solving crossword puzzles, the more difficult, the better. Hall immediately talked him into joining Room 40. Ewing in turn recruited fellow crossword puzzle fanatics and, in just a few months, Hall had a first-class group of cryptanalysts, all of whom easily mastered a course in codes and ciphers.

They went on to a number of cryptanalytical triumphs – especially cracking German naval codes used to communicate with its fleet of commerce raiders, leading to their destruction. However, early in 1917, the cryptological equivalent of an atomic bomb landed in their laps. It would lead to fulfilment of Wiseman's greatest goal, getting the United States into the war on the side of Great Britain.

For quite some time, Hall's team had been attacking what they called Code 0075, the highest level and most difficult German code, used primarily to transmit sensitive diplomatic messages. The code used some 10,000 groups of numbers to represent random words and phrases. The Germans considered it very secure, given its complexity, but Room 40 managed to break it. On the morning of 17 January 1917, one of Hall's best cryptanalysts, Nigel de Gray, walked into his office and asked him, "Do you want to bring America into the war?" He then handed Hall a decrypted telegram from German Foreign Minister Arthur Zimmermann to his ambassador in the United States, J.H. von Bernstorff. Hall nearly fell out of his chair as he read the message, which informed von Bernstorff that Germany would begin unrestricted submarine warfare, which would bring Britain to its knees and that war with the United States appeared inevitable. It went on to tell the ambassador that Germany planned to offer an alliance with Mexico. In return for their support of German war aims, they would be awarded American territory lost after the Mexican–American war of 1847.

De Gray urged Hall to release the telegram immediately; there was no doubt that when the Americans learned of it, a declaration of war against Germany was inevitable. "You boys think you do a very difficult job," Hall replied, "but don't forget I have to make use of the intelligence you give me and that's more difficult." He was right. Releasing the telegram was not that simple. First, it would reveal that the British had broken the highest level German code, which would be instantly changed, wiping out a precious British advantage. Second, the Americans had to be convinced that the telegram was not a forgery designed to stampede them into war. Third, the Americans would deduce that if the British were reading so difficult a code, it was reasonable to assume they were reading high-level American communications, too.

DECIPHERS

The problem was finally solved when the British learned that von Bernstorf, as protocol required, sent a copy of the message from Zimmermann to the German ambassador in Mexico. However, he made the grave mistake of sending it in a very low-level code. Working with American agents, the British burglarized the German embassy in Mexico City and stole a copy of the von Bernstorf message. Hall's people quickly decoded it (not much of a feat, since they had the original) and it was that version which the British gave to President Wilson and the Americans.

Wilson was furious, an anger reflected by the public at large when the 'Zimmermann Telegram' was released to the press on 1 March, complete with a fairy tale about how it had been obtained via a theft of the document in Mexico City. Zimmermann made things all the worse for Germany by publicly admitting the authenticity of the message, apparently unable to grasp why the Americans were so angry. Some weeks later, Wiseman listened in satisfaction as Wilson told him that he would ask the Congress for a declaration of war against Germany.

With that, Wiseman could reflect on a covert mission that had succeeded in achieving something once thought unachievable, bringing the United States into the war and the one sure guarantee of an Allied victory, although he was the first to admit, his job had been made all that easier by German errors. Fundamentally, those errors can be laid at the doorstep of German intelligence, which from the first moment failed to provide Imperial Germany with even the most basic insight into the reality of the United States. History exacted a steep price for those errors.

Among the important effects of Wiseman's operation was the strong bond forged between American and British intelligence. It was a relationship that would play a key role in the next great war and beyond. The lasting effects of another major success of British intelligence during the war were much more problematical, largely because the warnings of one of its greatest amateur spies went unheeded.

If ever there was a perfect espionage recruit, it was Gertrude Bell, one of the twentieth century's more remarkable women. Fluent in Arabic, Persian, Hebrew, Turkish and various local dialects, she was the first woman to earn a first in modern history at Oxford. She then won fame as an explorer of the Arab lands, at the time largely a mystery to the world. By 1914, when the Foreign Office intelligence section added her to its roster of amateur spies, Bell had travelled more than 25,000 miles all over the Middle East, in the process spending 700 days riding a camel. There was little Bell did not know about this great blank area on most maps, for she made it a point to spend her time not with the sheiks, but among the common Arab tribesmen, "in the goat tents" as she put it. As a result, she had an unequalled encyclopedic knowledge of the lands and peoples of the Middle East, including its Turkish occupiers. It was the Turkish overlords of the Ottoman Empire who most interested British intelligence: would they join Germany as an ally? If so, what threat did that represent to vital British interests in the Middle East? What would the Arab tribes do in the event of a war between Great Britain and Turkey?

To answer those questions, the Foreign Office rounded up a group of people with Middle East expertise for a new organization called the Arab Bureau. Headquartered in Cairo, it was basically an intelligence organization designed to pool whatever intelligence was collected throughout the Middle East. Bell was its star asset, an indefatigable spy almost constantly on the move as she reached deep into the Arab sources she had recruited over the years for information.

There was not much Bell didn't know about the Turkish military dispositions and plans, along with vital intelligence on just what the Arabs planned to do. Her wide range of sources included a spy ring of Zionist settlers in Palestine – the linchpin of the Turkish military structure in its Middle East empire.

Bell's knowledge was so extensive, she was recruited to moonlight for British military intelligence, whose attention was fixated on the Suez Canal. Loss of that vital waterway was unthinkable, so a high priority was intelligence on any Turkish military threat against it. Bell predicted that the Turks would indeed join the German side in the war and they would attempt at some point to threaten the Suez Canal. However, she added, the Turkish military was spread thin and lacked modern weapons.

Military intelligence found her intelligence so valuable she was given a commission as a major in the British Army, even though she and the generals did not see eye to eye. Their differences centered on the Arabs. Bell argued that the military was missing a golden opportunity in not recruiting the Arabs as fighters. As she pointed out, most of the Arabs despised their Turkish oppressors and would welcome any help in throwing off the yoke. To her annoyance, the military's estimate of the Arabs was coloured by racism. The British military considered them a bunch of dirty savages who were too divided by clan and tribe to be of any use.

Despite that attitude, Bell was undiscouraged. She proposed a daring plan for a covert action operation that would dwarf anything British intelligence had ever attempted. The plan called for enlisting the Arabs in a huge guerrilla warfare campaign. Aided by British arms and support, they would sweep through the deserts, using their superior mobility to cut rail links and isolate the Turks in their garrisons. As the British military began offensive operations in Turkish territory, the Arab guerrillas would operate behind Turkish lines, serving as eyes and ears for

ABOVE: Gertrude Bell, British Intelligence's star agent in the Middle East, who devised the plan to use the Arab Revolt to undermine the Ottoman Empire.

the British while cutting Turkish communications and making life a living hell for isolated Turkish units. The model for her plan was the Spanish guerrilla campaign that played so critical a role in the defeat of the French on the Iberian peninsula during the Napoleonic wars. As she noted, British army commanders initially denigrated any idea to use the oppressed Spaniards, men they considered ignorant peasants incapable of fighting La Grande Armee. Fortunately, for the British, the Duke of Wellington overruled them.

It is a tribute to Bell's tenacity and her vaunting reputation among senior military officers that she wore down the opposition and was finally able to gain approval for her plan. She had just the Arab leader in mind to lead what would become known as the Arab Revolt – Amir Faisal ibn-Hussain, chief of the Hashemites, the largest Arab tribe and one of her most important intelligence assets. The next step was to appoint a British liaison officer who would oversee the British arms supply pipeline to the Arabs and serve as Faisal's military adviser. Bell rummaged among the Arab Bureau personnel, finally emerging with an inspired choice – archaeologist and amateur spy, Major T.E. Lawrence.

Bell could not have predicted the spectacular success of 'Lawrence of Arabia', but she could see beyond the Arab Revolt. What she saw were dark times ahead, not a vision welcomed by British intelligence. In the euphoria of victory, she insisted, Britain was badly misreading postwar reality, treating the conquered Ottoman Empire in the Middle East like a birthday cake to be divided among celebrants. The war had released the powerful force of Arab nationalism and now it could not be forced back into the bottle. Eventually, she predicted, it would sweep across the Middle East. Fuelled by the region's natural resource that was already proving vital for Europe's industry, the resurgent Arabs would one day turn against the powers that had thwarted their right to self-determination. Above all, she warned, Britain's cynical arrangement in Palestine, based on promises to both the Zionists and Arab nationalists the British had no intention of keeping, was a time bomb that one day would detonate, with catastrophic results.

However, British intelligence was no longer listening to its star agent. In a time when the Middle East was being arbitrarily carved up into European geostrategic spheres of influence with no regard for Arab aspirations, what she had to say was not welcomed. Like Lawrence – who also was sickened by what had happened in the postwar Middle East – Bell's tragedy was that she had outlived her usefulness. On 12 July 1926, finally worn down by her struggles with the mindset of British intelligence and discouraged by what was happening in the desert lands she loved, she committed suicide.

The success of the Arab Revolt represented one of the few intelligence successes by any of the warring powers during World War I. Otherwise, the record was pretty barren; on both the strategic and tactical level, espionage agencies consistently missed important intelligence, failed to gain any insight into their enemies and, above all, failed to understand the nature of total war. The extent of that general myopia can be summarized by the Russian Revolution, which every single intelligence agency missed.

When the revolution broke out, the British Foreign Office sent an urgent telegram to the Moscow embassy, demanding to know why the intelligence contingent there had somehow failed to anticipate the event (despite widespread unrest and a tottering regime) and what it all meant. In reply, the embassy sent off a reassuring cable that the revolution was "nothing serious", insisting it was a revolt, not a revolution. German Intelligence also missed it, but quickly sought to pour some kerosene on the fire by arranging for the transport of the most radical Russian political exile, Vladimir Lenin, to Russia. It was a move the Germans would come to regret.

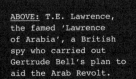

ABOVE: T.E. Lawrence, the famed 'Lawrence of Arabia', a British spy who carried out Gertrude Bell's plan to aid the Arab Revolt.

EYE OF DAWN: MATA HARI

FROM THE MOMENT SHE ENTERED THE COURTROOM CLOSELY ESCORTED BY TWO ARMED SOLDIERS ON THAT UNSEASONABLY WARM AUTUMN DAY IN 1917, ALL EYES WERE FOCUSED ON THE SHORT, PLUMP WOMAN.

She then looked calmly at the array of seven senior French Army officers constituting the court martial that would determine her fate.

"Margareta Zelle," the presiding officer began intoning as he read from the official charge sheet, "you are charged with espionage activities inimical to the security of France." It took him nearly 20 minutes to read all the charges, a breathtaking catalog of espionage extending back to shortly after the outbreak of war and covering a wide range of military and diplomatic secrets. By the time the officer finished reading he had presented a portrait of one of the greatest super spies in history, a woman responsible for a long list of military disasters suffered by France, the brilliant agent who single-handedly almost changed the course of the war. Yet almost none of it was true.

In fact, the only truth in the charges was that Margarete Zelle had been a spy for Germany. She was not a very good spy – useless, actually. She had caused virtually no damage to France. She was not responsible for the failed offensives in which thousands of French soldiers perished or the deadly stalemate on the Western Front in which entire generations of Europeans died.

However, the truth had nothing to do with the case against Margareta Zelle – or Mata Hari to use her better-known stage name. She was charged because it suited the purposes of statecraft to do so and because she was a victim of her own undeserved renown as a super spy. That reputation had been inflated by wildly inaccurate stories in the popular press, accounts which portrayed her as the irresistible femme fatale spy who had used her amazing sexual talents to wheedle France's greatest secrets from generals of the French High Command and senior diplomats.

In this version of events, the French military setbacks – the result of incompetent political and military leadership – could be attributed to Mata Hari, the female super spy. The French public, notoriously susceptible to the plot line of romantic entanglement as the key to most world events, lapped it up and the legend of Mata Hari was born. That legend has portrayed Mata Hari as the greatest, most beautiful and most mysterious spy of all time, but the truth is more prosaic.

ABOVE: Margarete Zelle in costume as the dancer Mata Hari. Despite her reputation as a master spy, Zelle was, in fact, a total failure as a German spy.

THE REAL STORY

Born Margareta Zelle into a middle class Dutch family, she eloped at 18 with a drunken Scottish sea captain who deserted her in 1901. Left with no means of support, Zelle hit upon a brilliant idea. She had once accompanied her ex-husband on a trip to the Dutch East Indies (present-day Indonesia), where she visited temples and watched the graceful female temple dancers. She now reinvented herself as Mata Hari ('eye of dawn' in Javanese), the daughter of Java's greatest temple dancer. She added an extra twist, claiming to have been taught 'secret erotic temple dances' by her mother, which she began to perform at soirees all over Europe. She was a sensation. At a time when public nudity was quite rare, Zelle appeared in a costume of her own design; slowly divesting herself of it she danced, climaxed by a few final movements in the nude.

Zelle now began a second career: well-paid courtesan for senior members of the European establishment. Among them was the chief of police in Berlin, whose duties included counterintelligence. When World War I broke out in 1914, he got the idea of recruiting Zelle as a spy, reasoning that her access to senior French military and political figures would result in a treasure trove of information she could wring from them during pillow talk. However, it didn't work out that way.

Not especially bright, Zelle was underwritten with extensive German intelligence funds to operate in France with a wealthy life style in the circles of the high and mighty. However, she failed to collect much in the way of useful intelligence and the little she did mange to gather became hopelessly confused in her mind. German intelligence persisted, sending her on missions elsewhere in Europe, including Spain, where her control officers included a young German naval lieutenant named Wilhelm Canaris, later head of Nazi Germany's Abwehr intelligence service. All those missions were ignoble failures.

Zelle was not very subtle about her intelligence collection efforts and it was only a matter of time before French counterintelligence deduced she was probably a German spy. They got conclusive proof late in 1916 when their greatest intelligence asset produced the proverbial smoking gun. The asset, oddly enough, was the Eiffel Tower. Originally scheduled to be torn down just before the war, the French made the fortuitous discovery that radio detection gear atop the tower could pick up just about every radio signal for hundreds of miles around – most importantly Germany's. The tower was saved and with the outbreak of war, the French used it to secretly collect German radio traffic. One

ABOVE: Admiral Wilhelm Canaris, chief of the German Abwehr intelligence agency in World War II and one of Mata Hari's control agents during World War I.

of the detected messages, decrypted by French cryptanalysts, discussed the activities of a spy code-named H21. Details made it clear H21 was Mata Hari.

The French decided to turn her into a double agent. She was told her life would be spared if she agreed to spy for France against the Germans. As a test of her genuineness, she was given the names of six French spies operating in Brussels. It was a test she flunked. Within two weeks they were rounded up by German counterintelligence and one of them was executed. There was no doubt: Zelle had betrayed them to the Germans. She was a double agent, but trusted by neither side. By 1917, concluding that she had outlived her usefulness, the Germans sent her on a new espionage mission into France, alerting their foreign networks of her mission via a radio message in a code they knew the French had cracked. The French deduced the Germans were discarding her, but decided that although she was of no further use as a spy, she could provide an even greater service as a scapegoat.

What happened next was a foregone conclusion. "Harlot, yes," she told the court martial in a forlorn effort at a defense, "but traitoress, never!" The court martial found her guilty and ignoring an astonishingly large number of requests for clemency from her former lovers, sentenced Mata Hari to death. Just after dawn on 17 October 1917, she was shot by a firing squad and passed into espionage immortality.

THE RED ORCHESTRA

On the morning of 29 December 1917, the caretaker at the Smolny Institute for the Daughters of Noblemen hastened to answer a loud knock at the buildings front door.

LEFT: The 'sword and shield' insignia of the KGB, which grew to become the world's largest and perhaps most notorious intelligence agency.

As he hurried down the grand staircase leading to the marbled entrance hall, he hoped against hope that the young daughters of the wealthy had returned, somehow ready to resume their studies at the best finishing school in all of Petrograd (formerly Saint Petersburg).

However, he knew in his heart that was not possible. The girls were gone for good, having fled with their rich families two months before as the Bolshevik revolution swept across Russia, crushing the old order in its path. "I'm sorry, gentlemen," he said to the half-dozen men at the door. "The institute is temporarily closed."

"Incorrect" said one of them, a thin man with a wispy beard, as they walked past the caretaker into the building. He withdrew a folded piece of paper from his pocket and showed it to the caretaker. It was apparently some sort of official document of the new revolutionary government announcing that the Smolny Institute henceforth was to be the headquarters of something called the All-Russian Extraordinary Commission Combating Counterrevolution, Speculation, Sabotage and Misconduct in Office.

"I have not heard of this organization," the caretaker said. "You will, I assure you," the man with the wispy beard replied. "Comrade, your work here is finished. The oppressor classes will not be returning. From this moment, only the important work of the revolution will take place in this building. You will vacate it by two o'clock this afternoon."

RED DAWN

With that, Feliks Edmundovich Dzerzhinsky began his mission to save revolutionary Russia. It marked the onset of an extraordinary career that would make him the greatest spymaster in the history of espionage, the man who created and moulded the largest and most accomplished spying organization the world had ever seen. However, it would turn out to be a very troubling legacy.

Vladimir Lenin liked to call Dzerzhinsky 'Iron Feliks', an entirely accurate nickname. Born in 1877 to a wealthy Polish family, Dzerzhinsky turned his back on his family when, as a 20-year-old university student, he joined the Social Revolutionary Party (SRP). As a Marxist political

organization determined to overthrow the existing order, little wonder the party attracted the close attention of the Okhrana, which worked actively to destroy it. The SRP was driven underground, where Dzerzhinsky worked as a courier between party cells and exiles abroad, his first experience in the clandestine world. He was arrested several times by the Okhrana and spent most of his youth in Siberian prisons, forced to work in coal mines. As a result of that experience, he contracted tuberculosis, the disease that would plague him for the rest of his life.

The experience also formed the man Lenin so admired: hard, iron-willed, totally ruthless and utterly dedicated to the cause of revolution. However, there were other qualities that made him a singular figure: acute intelligence, clear-headedness and a distinct talent for espionage. He also had the heart and soul of a secret policeman. It was that aspect of his personality that most drew Lenin to this slight man with the wispy beard who was often wracked with violent coughing that brought up blood. Lenin first met Dzerzhinsky in 1903 during a crucial moment in the Bolshevik movement, the political split with the SRP. Dzerzhinsky threw in his lot with Lenin's Bolsheviks, an act that put him in Lenin's debt.

Lenin, a shrewd judge of men, immediately bonded with the Polish revolutionary who, to a large extent, was a reflection of himself. As they became close friends, Lenin understood his new friend's psyche was dominated by a single obsession: achieve the revolution that would destroy Imperial Russia and, eventually, take over the world. For his part, Dzerzhinsky saw Lenin as the one man capable of achieving that revolution. It was to Lenin that he now dedicated his life and unquestioning loyalty.

"Power was just lying around in the streets, waiting for us to pick it up," Lenin would often say about the Bolshevik revolution in October 1917. However, in truth the coup was a bold gamble, fraught with danger and it was Dzerzhinsky who did the most to make it succeed. Several months before the revolution, Lenin had appointed Dzerzhinsky head of what he called the "security subcommittee" and charged him with the task of ensuring the success of the Bolshevik seizure of power. Dzerzhinsky had only a few dozen men and several old cars to achieve the task, which appeared insurmountable. The small Bolshevik movement's enemies included the forces of Alexander Kerensky's provisional government then in power, the more numerous SRP opponents and various anti-Bolshevik factions – any one of which, or a combination of all three, could snuff out a Bolshevik putsch in an instant.

Dzerzhinsky moved with decisive swiftness. He ordered a roundup of all the Okhrana officers he could find and told them they could either support the Bolsheviks or face imprisonment. With the Okhrana neutralized, Dzerzhinsky's men then seized all of Russia's communications – the post, telegraph, telephone and civilian messenger services. All 'non-Bolsheviks' were banned from using any of these communications, which meant that when Lenin carried out his coup, his enemies, especially the Kerensky government, had no idea of what was happening until it was too late.

It also meant that the communications blackout gave Lenin precious time to consolidate his power before his opponents could mobilize a countercoup.

However, it was one thing to seize power; it was quite another to keep it. Holding on to power presented even more serious obstacles than the actual coup. Russia was still at war with Germany, which was seizing huge chunks of Russian territory while its forces were decimating a demoralized Russian army. There were also large forces of anti-Bolsheviks (known as 'Whites') who vowed to depose Lenin's revolutionary government. This threat was made further dangerous by indications that they might receive support from the British and French, alarmed by Lenin's vow to take Russia out of the war.

Lenin now entrusted Dzerzhinsky with a new task: defeat the enemies of the revolution and consolidate Bolshevik power throughout Russia. In early December 1917, Dzerzhinsky created the organization that became more familiarly known by its Russian acronym – Cheka. It was an impressive-sounding organization, but did not have much in the way of impressive assets. Dzerzhinsky had a grand total of 130 men under his command, most of them ex-Okhrana agents he had dragooned. He did not fully trust these men who were once oppressors, but kept them on anyway since there were not many Communists in Russia with the necessary intelligence and internal security skills the Cheka needed. The only other assets consisted of six old cars and a new headquarters in the former girls' school in Petrograd (now renamed Leningrad).

However, the Cheka had one supreme asset – Feliks Dzerzhinsky. With a furious energy that belied his crippling illness, he filled the Cheka ranks by recruiting thousands of brutal and semi-educated men, mostly the dregs of Russian society. He informed them they would be the 'sword and shield' of the Bolshevik regime. That meant they would fan out all over Russia, rounding up the 'enemies of the revolution', defined by Lenin as anyone who defied his government in any way. These perceived opponents would be either thrown into prison or, more often, executed on the spot. Their families received a short, curt notice that they had been found guilty by the Cheka of unspecified 'counterrevolutionary activities' and liquidated.

"We stand for organized terror," Dzerzhinsky

ABOVE: The novelist W. Somerset Maugham, among the most famous of Great Britain's roster of amateur volunteer spies.

announced, opening a dark chapter in Russian history known as the Red Terror. During the next two years, his organization executed more than 50,000 people and imprisoned 100,000 more while he enlarged the Cheka a hundredfold. It quickly outgrew its headquarters in the girls' school and was moved to much larger quarters in a former insurance company building in Moscow on Lubyanka Street, remodelled to include a prison. The new address soon became the most infamous in Russia as citizens by the thousands disappeared behind its walls. In a small office on the third floor, Dzerzhinsky, constantly wracked by coughs, worked up to 20 hours a day under the glare of a single powerful electric light, poring over records and files. Every so often, he would be brought a stack of death warrants to sign, a task he performed without ever once even bothering to look at the names.

By the early months of 1918, the Cheka had grown to a force of more than 100,000 men (and a few women). It had established tight control of the Bolshevik-held part of the country, aided by thousands of local informants. Dzerzhinsky had created a police state, no mean feat in a country racked by a civil war and foreign military intervention. It was on that latter problem that he next focused his attention.

As Dzerzhinsky understood, the foreign intervention represented the single greatest threat to the Bolshevik regime. Alarmed over the regime's plan to negotiate a peace agreement with Germany that would release nearly a million German troops for the Western Front, Great Britain, France and the United States had sent military forces into Russia. This was done under various pretexts such as to guard Allied military supplies sent to Russia and ensure they did not fall into German hands. However, the military forces were part of an overall covert action plan by the Allies to destabilize, then overthrow, Lenin's regime in favour of the Whites, who would continue the war against Germany. In November 1917, the British sent one of their best amateur spies, W. Somerset Maugham, to Russia. His mission was to aid Alexander Kerensky, head of the provincial government, in a propaganda campaign urging the Russians to fight on. Too late, Kerensky told him; the Russian army didn't want to fight anymore.

At this point, Dzerzhinsky demonstrated yet another of his espionage talents: counterespionage. He recruited the best counterintelligence agents he could find among ex-Okhrana types willing to work for the revolutionaries and organized them into a new section specifically targeted against the emerging Allied intelligence effort inside Russia. He also went looking for a deputy who would head up the counterespionage operation and found him near at hand, one of his leading bloodhounds who had been tracking down 'counterrevolutionaries' in the Moscow area. His name was Jakov Peters, a Latvian revolutionary with an English past and an English wife.

ACT TWO

Peters had fled to London in 1903, after running afoul of the Okhrana for his revolutionary activities, and there he worked as a pants-presser and joined an anarchist group. That group carried out a botched jewel robbery in which four policemen were killed during a shootout. Peters was charged as one of the robbers, but was acquitted in a trial that featured the most famous alibi in British legal history: he claimed to be at home building a mousetrap when the robbery occurred. He went to Russia when the Bolshevik revolution broke out and offered his services to Dzerzhinsky. Although Peters had no intelligence training or experience in counterespionage, he quickly proved his talents as a hunter of spies who had been sent into Moscow by the Whites. It was a record that convinced Dzerzhinsky he would be the ideal choice as his deputy for counterespionage.

Dzerzhinsky and Peters soon formed a general outline of the Allied operation. It was run out of the British and French embassies and overseen by British diplomat Robert Bruce Lockhart. A number of Russians had been enlisted as assets, many of them by a veteran MI6 agent dispatched to Russia for the operation, the Russian-born Sidney Reilly. He was a man who would become a figure of consuming interest to the Cheka.

Dzerzhinsky and his deputy decided the best attack point was via the Russian assets. Peters discovered that two British military attaches working in the Bruce-Lockhart operation were very careless in their recruiting approaches. That set the stage for an approach to them by the commander of the Latvian troops who served as Lenin's inner guard. The commander, a colonel, reported that his troops had become seriously disillusioned and were ready to rebel.

The colonel, who actually was working for Dzerzhinsky, played his part well. The British took the bait and Reilly showed up with 1,200,000 roubles to finance an anti-Bolshevik coup. From there, it was pure end game. The Cheka used the penetration to get inside the Allied operation. Then they struck, rolling it up in a wave of raids and arrests. Several British agents managed to flee the country, among them Reilly, who was sentenced to death in absentia. Dzerzhinsky was determined to get him, a goal he would achieve a few years later with the Cheka's first major foreign espionage operation, a masterpiece of an espionage sting known as the Trust.

The idea behind the Trust operation was ambitious – create a phony anti-Bolshevik underground in Russia. This would be used to achieve the double aim of luring support from White Russian exiles abroad and Western intelligence agencies – and possibly their assets – into the web. The

ABOVE: Sydney Reilly, the legendary British spy who tried to snuff out the Bolshevik revolutionary government.

opening move of the chess game came in 1921, when an ex-Czarist official whom Dzerzhinsky had recruited to the Communist cause travelled to Europe and contacted a number of people he once knew in Russia. He recounted that although he was now an official in the Bolshevik government, he retained secret allegiance to the monarchist cause. He had discovered there were a number of others with similar views and they had organized themselves into an underground movement they called Trest (Trust). They slowly and carefully built the organization into a widespread shadow government, ready to overthrow the Lenin regime. Aware that both the exiles and Western intelligence would be suspicious, Dzerzhinsky played carefully. His agent made no rash promises or demands, simply inviting exile groups to send representatives into Russia to see for themselves.

What happened next amounted to pure espionage theater. Representatives of exile groups were sent to Russia, at each step of the way shepherded by agents of the Trust. It was all very impressive. The Trust agents smuggled them across the border via secret crossing points only they knew. Once inside the country, the representatives were passed along a chain of Trust members who operated like clockwork, complete with complex recognition signals and the highest standards of security. Apparently, hundreds of support agents were working for the Trust. The final touch was a secret meeting with the Trust's senior leadership at a dacha deep in the woods near Moscow, during which grand plans for the return of Russia to the monarchy were outlined. The exiles were pleasantly surprised to see that the Trust had organized an 'underground church' where Eastern Orthodox rites were performed in defiance of the Bolshevik government's ban on religion.

When the exile representatives returned, their reports caused a sensation. There were subsequent visits by other exile representatives and soon all doubt was washed away: the Trust unquestionably was genuine. Any last vestige of distrust was removed when the Trust arranged for the daring 'escape' from prison of the brother of a prominent exile. Since many of the exiles were working as assets for Western intelligence agencies, what they had seen quickly reached the ears of their controllers. The controllers were initially sceptical, a doubt removed when the exiles continued to travel back and forth across the border, experiencing first hand the astounding depth and breadth of the underground movement. The intelligence agencies of a half-dozen countries, including the British, recruited members of the Trust inside Russia. A small river of intelligence began to flow westward, reporting, among other fictions, that Lenin had decided to forego his goal of world revolution and would now concentrate strictly on developing Russia's economy. Trust reports also portrayed a very strong Russian military force (at considerable variance from the truth).

As Dzerzhinsky was the first to understand, this elaborate shell game could be continued only for so long. At some point, a slip-up among the hundreds of agents he had posing as everything from Russian Orthodox Church priests to border guides would give the game away. Before that happened, Dzerzhinsky and Peters wanted to ensnare their two top priority targets. One was Sidney Reilly, the British agent who had just managed to escape the dragnet during the rolling up of the Allied covert action operation in 1918. The other was the most dangerous of the Bolshevik regime's exile foes, Boris Savinkov, who was based in Paris. The Cheka knew that Reilly and Savinkov were close friends, a relationship that suggested Reilly was funnelling MI6 funds to him (actually, he wasn't). Savinkov, an old Socialist Revolutionary, was the leader of a large number of diehard members of that party still in Russia – an incipient internal threat Dzerzhinsky wanted to stamp out. So long as Reilly and Savinkov were operating out of the Cheka's reach, they represented danger.

Savinkov, suspicious that an anti-Bolshevik organization the size of the Trust could survive in a police state, for quite some time resisted the idea of going to Russia, even when exiles came to him with reports of the wonders they had seen with their own eyes. However, Dzerzhinsky had read his quarry well. The egotistical Savinkov soon heard reports that the Trust leadership held him in high esteem and desperately wanted to meet with him. It was too dangerous for them to travel to the West, but if Savinkov would come to Russia...

Savinkov swallowed it – hook, line and sinker. In 1923, he was escorted across the border by two Trust 'guides' who immediately put handcuffs on him and rushed him to the Lubyanka. Savinkov realized he could expect no mercy, but he apparently decided he needed to warn his fellow exiles – and his friend Sidney Reilly – that the Trust was a fraud. As he was being taken to an interrogation room, he saw a means to achieve it. When his guards' attention was diverted for a moment, he hurled himself out a fourth-floor window.

His death was in vain. For reasons that remain unexplained, Reilly ignored the clear warning signal that the Trust was a fraud and decided to go to Russia to see for himself if the underground organization was as effective as so many exiles claimed it was. Whether Reilly went as a mission for MI6 or strictly on his own remains a matter of dispute. In any event, the Trust arranged an elaborate welcome, even providing a stamp for Reilly to use on a letter he posted to his wife after he arrived in Russia, meant as a signal that he was okay and that the Trust was genuine. However, the moment he put that letter in a postal box, the Cheka grabbed him. When it finished emptying Reilly's head of whatever he knew, he was shot.

The Cheka tried to keep the game going by having the

Trust spread the word that border guards had killed both Reilly and Savinkov because they had failed to follow the proper security procedures and did not use Trust guides to cross the border. It might have worked, except that a senior officer with Polish intelligence was suspicious the intelligence he was receiving from the Trust on Russian military strength was cooked. In early 1924 he conducted an in-depth analysis, comparing what the Trust was telling him with incontrovertible facts established by his own agents. The result was sobering. Every single piece of intelligence he had received from the Trust was false. He rang the alarm, warning other intelligence agencies and all contacts with the Trust ceased. However, the damage had been done. For nearly three years, the Trust was the exclusive source for Western intelligence in Russia. The exile movements were penetrated and two of the new Soviet Union's most dangerous enemies had been eliminated. Above all, the regime had been given precious time to consolidate its power, free from any outside interference. Dzerzhinsky died at this moment of his greatest triumph, finally succumbing at the age of 49 to the disease that had wracked his body for so many years. He had lived long enough to see his Cheka evolve from a few men and a few automobiles to a vast organization of several hundred thousand employees, the biggest espionage apparatus the world had ever seen.

BELOW: Moises Uritsky, Dzerzhinsky's chief of foreign intelligence, laid the groundwork for Soviet Intelligence's brilliantly successful foreign spying operations.

TIGHT ORGANIZATION

The Cheka represented something new in espionage, an entity that combined foreign intelligence and counterespionage in the same organization – a powerful instrument in the hands of the state. At the time of Dzerzhinsky's death, the Cheka was blandly renamed Main Political Administration, more commonly known by its Russian acronym OGPU (the first in a series of organizational name changes that would culminate, finally, in the KGB).

Whatever the name, Soviet intelligence operated with the template that Dzerzhinsky had created. It included a pervasive internal security apparatus featuring border security units that controlled all movements in and out of the Soviet Union; an internal passport system for all Russian citizens; networks of informers on every block and factory; strict oversight over all media; intense surveillance of all foreigners and rigid vetting of all senior military and civilian officials. Dzerzhinsky had gradually weeded out the ex-Okhrana types he was forced to work with in the early days of the Cheka. He replaced them with graduates of new espionage training schools he set up, borrowing a system pioneered by Fraulein Doktor.

In terms of foreign intelligence, Dzerzhinsky realized early in the Cheka's evolution that its greatest recruiting pool existed in the training schools of the Comintern, the Soviet-controlled organization of world Communist parties. Communists from all over the world were selected to attend these schools in the Soviet Union. They were taught the basics of underground work – organizing, clandestine communications, false identities, etc. – for Communist party functionaries, especially those who would operate in countries where the party was illegal and operated strictly as an underground organization.

The Cheka trolled among the thousands of Communists who traveled to the Soviet Union for Comintern training, skimming off the cream of them for its own ranks. The recruitment had several advantages. The first was that these Communists, dedicated to the cause, were not only politically reliable, but would work for no salary. The second and even greater advantage was that they represented a cross-section of the world's nationalities and ethnic groups. For example, using an American Communist solved the problem of having to convert a native Russian into an American speaking flawless American idiom and at ease in the uniquely American culture.

Dzerzhinsky's other great contribution to the evolution of Soviet intelligence was his recruitment of Cheka's senior executives, a process he insisted must be based strictly on talent. He did not want bureaucrats; what he wanted were original thinkers. He wanted the kind of men who instinctively knew where their assets should be operating for maximum effect, which were the key targets, the right time to withdraw a key source as counterintelligence closed in and which assets or agents had been turned and were now feeding back disinformation. The recruitment effort was responsible for a number of brilliant Cheka executives. These included such espionage luminaries as Jakov Peters – his brilliant deputy for counterespionage – and Artur Artuzov, the man most responsible for building Soviet intelligence's first great overseas intelligence networks.

To Dzerzhinsky's regret, another of his sterling recruits, a brilliant man whom he thought at one point would ultimately succeed him as head of the Cheka, slipped from his grasp. His name was Peter Kyuzis, a fanatical Latvian Communist revolutionary, who would enter the espionage pantheon under his revolutionary pseudonym of Jan Berzin. Dzerzhinsky recruited Berzin in 1920 and assigned him to the Cheka's Registry Section, which supervised the agency's first foreign intelligence operations.

To Dzerzhinsky's surprise, his 31-year-old new recruit immediately criticized how his boss was organizing foreign intelligence. Too many of the Cheka's recruits among foreign communists were well-known to police and counterintelligence agencies, Berzin complained. He noted that any active Communist, however well-trained for espionage work, would be too notorious to be effective. He also criticized Dzerzhinsky's espionage training schools, arguing that the instruction was too shallow. For example, operations in Western Europe required sophisticated agents who could operate with ease in an upscale cultural or social milieu where most espionage targets were located (such as high-level government officials and senior government executives).

Dzerzhinsky had no problem with in-house criticism (he preferred a collegial atmosphere in the Cheka's upper ranks), but Berzin, a notoriously blunt and undiplomatic man, irritated him. As their estrangement grew, a third actor entered this little drama – Leon Trotsky, head of the Red Army. Trotsky had become concerned over the exponential growth of the Cheka, fearing its use in the hands of his chief political rival, an up and coming senior Bolshevik leader named Josef Stalin.

ABOVE: Josef Stalin (left), a rising power in the Soviet Communist Party, in 1925, with three other key leaders: (from left) Rykov, Kamenev and Zinoviev. Stalin later murdered them, cutting a swath through Soviet intelligence.

Seeking to create an intelligence counterweight, Trotsky formed the Fourth Department of the Red Army, the Soviet Union's first military intelligence agency. To staff it, Trotsky recruited a number of promising military officers and then went searching for any disaffected Cheka executives willing to switch to the Fourth Department (subsequently renamed GRU). Trotsky became aware of Berzin's estrangement from Dzerzhinsky and enlisted the Latvian to run the new GRU. Berzin agreed to the recruitment on the condition that he be given a free hand to run the GRU as he saw fit, a condition to which Trotsky immediately assented, since he knew nothing about intelligence and was perfectly content to let Berzin handle it on his own.

With that kind of unfettered authority, Berzin created an intelligence agency very much in his own image. Among his first acts was to set up a GRU spy training school, with a much more rigorous curriculum than its Cheka counterpart. Berzin supervised every detail of the training, carefully evaluating students for their ability to operate in particular foreign environments. A man who disdained any kind of organizational chart formality, Berzin became close friends with many of the potential agents, who affectionately called him starik, Russian for 'old man', because of his prematurely aged features.

The students graduated from his school only when he thought they were ready, even his star pupils. That kind of attention to detail would produce some of the greatest spies in the history of espionage. They were men and women of wildly disparate backgrounds – among them a Polish leatherworker, a German housewife and a Dutch antiques dealer – who shared only one common trait: there were all fervently devoted Communists. This was the sole precondition, Berzin was convinced, that would help his spies cope with the tension of operating in an environment where the slightest misstep might land them in a torture chamber or in front of a firing squad. As he often said to his students, his standard for good spies began with their commitment to Communism, followed by three essential character traits: "Cool head, warm heart and nerves of steel."

Berzin planned to send his best graduates to work in the two areas he believed vital to the future of the Soviet Union: Europe and the Far East. Looking far ahead, Berzin deduced that a resurgent Germany and a militaristic Japan would be the two greatest threats to his country. It was vital, he believed, for the GRU to set up extensive intelligence networks in those two areas that would serve as early warning radar, revealing any emerging threat to the Soviet Union. In the event of war, these networks would already be in place, obviating the necessity of creating such networks in wartime, always a difficult proposition. The two spy school graduates he selected for those espionage priorities would achieve everything Berzin hoped, a case study in just what well-trained spies of talent can accomplish.

"I am a Communist because I am a Jew," Leiba Domb often said by way of explaining why he had devoted his entire life to an ideology he was convinced would emancipate the oppressed Jews of Eastern Europe. By the time he was 19, in 1925, working in a leather factory in his native Poland, he was already an activist and agitator among workers for the Polish Communist Party. In 1928, after being arrested for 'revolutionary activities', he was ordered to be deported in lieu of jail sentence. He wound up in Palestine, where he was deported again, this time by British authorities, to France.

Already noted in the Communist world as a brilliant organizer, the French Communist Party enlisted Domb to run its Jewish immigrant labour section. Success in that job led to Domb's selection to attend the Comintern's main training school in Moscow, the University for National Minorities. All students selected for such training were the subject of extensive dossiers prepared by the OGPU during a vetting process. Those that indicated a promising espionage recruit were flagged for a recruitment approach. Domb's dossier was among those flagged, but before the OGPU could recruit him, Berzin, who had been tipped off by a friend in the Comintern about this promising Polish Communist, got to him first.

Domb and Berzin hit it off immediately and the GRU chief had what would become one of his greatest recruits. A short, squat man, Domb radiated a powerful personal energy and an aggressiveness that suggested he would put his head through a wall, if necessary, to get what he wanted. He also projected an air of total fearlessness. As Berzin was aware, he was a man who had challenged people and doctrines he thought wrong, an unusual personality in Communism's rigid, doctrinaire world. To a large extent, he reflected Berzin's own personality, one explanation for the close relationship that developed between the two men. Another was Berzin's realization that in Domb he had found a real espionage gem, a man whose years of underground party work had honed a fine-edged talent for espionage. He sent him to France under the new name of Leopold Trepper – a name that became an espionage legend – to work with a small network. This was mainly to give him some actual experience in intelligence operations and prepare him for the much greater role Berzin had in mind for his star pupil: rezident.

NETWORK SOLUTIONS

In Soviet intelligence practice, the rezident (head of a network) played a very important role. He would not only supervise day-to-day operations of the network, but would also select its targets, manage its assets and decide the final form of the intelligence sent to Moscow. In Trepper's case, Berzin planned an even bigger role: organize and supervise

ABOVE: Leopold Trepper, organizer and head of the fabled Red Orchestra, the successful Soviet intelligence network in Europe before World War II.

Brussels to take over the running of a new company called Simexco (a GRU-funded front company), which specialized in the manufacture of raincoats. A subsidiary company, called Simex, another GRU front, was set up in Paris. Gilbert (actually Leopold Trepper) was an indefatigable businessman, traveling all over Europe, drumming up business – or so it appeared. In fact, he was energetically recruiting assets. Within several months, he had built a series of compartmentalized rings with nearly 200 assets. They included a small ring inside Nazi Germany itself, consisting of a dozen secret anti-Nazis who worked in government jobs.

While Trepper was busy putting his network together in Europe, Berzin turned his attention to the Far East, where the Soviet Union was dealing with an intelligence failure of the first order. The failure concerned the so-called 'pact of steel' between Germany, Japan and Italy that raised the spectre of the worst nightmare Moscow could imagine – hostile powers facing the Soviet Union on the east and west. The Soviets had not learned about the alliance until it was publicly announced, a grave intelligence lapse that led to the recall of both the GRU and NKVD (successor to the OGPU) chiefs of station in Tokyo (and execution for their failure).

The problem was that Japan, a tightly-controlled police state, was a particularly difficult intelligence target. At all costs, Berzin decided, the GRU had to develop a reliable network there. Above all, that network would have to provide early warning of any plan by the Japanese to invade the Soviet Union from the east while Germany attacked in the west. Such a task would require a very special agent for such a task and Berzin had just the man in mind – Richard Sorge. He was still another of the students Berzin personally groomed for espionage immortality.

It was said of the German-born Sorge that his deep Communist convictions were in his blood. His grandfather had been private secretary to Karl Marx and among the first books he read as a small boy was Marx's *Das Kapital*. After enlisting in the German army at the outbreak of World War I, he was wounded twice and spent long convalescences devouring books on Communism. By the end of the war, he

a large network that would cover the entire continent of Western Europe. The target was the new Nazi regime in Germany, where, Berzin concluded, Soviet intelligence procedure had to be rethought.

Both the OGPU and the GRU relied on German Communist Party assets, but Berzin correctly predicted that the party would be outlawed and become the target of a merciless effort to destroy it. (Events proved him right). Attempting to rebuild networks in Germany, especially with native Communists well-known to the Gestapo, was doomed to failure. The solution, Berzin decided, was to wrap Nazi Germany in an espionage web based in bordering states, its tentacles reaching into every possible connection Germany had with other countries. The web would also recruit assets inside Germany itself, using strictly non-Communists.

In early May 1939, Berzin set Trepper in motion. A Canadian businessman named Jean Gilbert appeared in

ABOVE: Richard Sorge, the German Communist and GRU spy who penetrated the Japanese government.

William Johnson, a journalist. He quickly justified Berzin's confidence in him, building a number of networks throughout the country. In the process, he provided Moscow with some important intelligence, including early warning of Chiang Kai-shek's rightward drift and the growing power of a Communist guerrilla leader named Mao Tse-tung. He also provided the first warning that Germany was about to abandon its longtime alliance with China and draw closer to Japan – a warning discounted by the GRU and NKVD rezidents in Tokyo.

Assigned the task of establishing a network in Japan, Sorge reinvented himself, this time as a fervent Nazi journalist whose Communist background somehow escaped the notice of German authorities when they approved his appointment as correspondent in Japan for several newspapers. With that cover established, Sorge went to Tokyo to build his network. He began with several Japanese assets he recruited in China, who now helped him recruit several other sources who shared a common goal: defeat the Japanese militarists who were leading the country to disaster. Eventually, Sorge had a network of 20 assets, along with two German-born GRU agents whom he brought with him to run the network's radio communications.

was a fervent Communist and among the charter members of the German Communist Party. He then followed the standard career path of many Soviet intelligence agents: party work, a judgment by his superiors he was marked for greater things, assignment to the Comintern training school in Moscow and, finally, recruitment. In Sorge's case, he was spotted by Berzin, who added him to his special stable of men and women he believed were destined to become topflight agents.

After graduating from Berzin's training program, Sorge performed a number of early espionage assignments with great skill, a record that convinced Berzin he would be the ideal man to build a network in the Far East. In 1935, Sorge was appointed rezident for GRU operations in China, headquartered in Shanghai. He worked under cover as

His preparations included his own immersion in Japanese language and culture, a deep study that included a library of 1,000 books on Japanese history and politics. As material from his assets began flowing in, Sorge's powerful radio came to life, broadcasting large volumes of material westward. Aware that so powerful a radio might attract the attention of Japanese counterintelligence, adept at tracking down clandestine radios, Sorge installed it on a sailboat kept on the move to defeat any attempt to triangulate it.

Sorge's signals were among a flood of espionage traffic that began flowing into the GRU communications center near Moscow. Most of them came from Europe, including some very clear signals from the Swiss Alps. Those signals were being broadcast by a supplementary, smaller operation Berzin established in conjunction with Trepper's. Based in Switzerland, it was run by Alexander Rado, a Hungarian Communist and veteran GRU agent who headed a news service as cover for intelligence collection throughout Europe. Several of Rado's assets were recruited by another of Berzin's star pupils, Ruth Kuczynski (who preferred to use the name 'Werner', one of her many aliases). Werner served her espionage apprenticeship in China for Sorge, who had enthusiastically reported to Berzin that she had demonstrated a striking ability for espionage, a recommendation that convinced Berzin she would be ideal to run the British section of Trepper's network.

Werner's first task was to find a topflight radio operator for Rado's network. She recruited among British veterans, most of them Communists who had fought on the Republican side in the Spanish Civil War. She finally emerged with one of the best radio operators around, Alexander Alan Foote. His enlistment was the final component of the Rado network, which now set up headquarters in a farmhouse atop a 3,600-foot-high hill in the Swiss Alps. A more perfect espionage location could not be imagined. The farmhouse was very isolated, accessible only via a narrow path; a vehicle could approach the place no closer than a half-mile away. The hilltop location, whose height offered a view that extended many miles in all directions, was an ideal radio site. When Foote set up his radio and tapped out 'CZWRX calling Moscow Center', that signal could be heard with near-perfect clarity at GRU communications headquarters, more than a thousand miles away.

Foote's transmissions were soon joined by other transmissions, amongst them those from Trepper's radios, including his main transmitter on the top floor of a house in Brussels. There were further signals in the ether from Europe: the radios of the other Soviet intelligence entity, the NKVD. All that traffic did not go unnoticed by German counterintelligence, which realized that its sheer volume, all in code, meant only one thing: a major network or networks were at work. The Germans, fond of using musical analogies to describe espionage organizations, instantly collectively christened all those radios Rote Kappelle – Red Orchestra. It was the name by which the great Soviet intelligence offensive became known in espionage history.

EAST AND WEST

The NKVD, like the GRU, was very concerned about Germany and Japan, but any similarity between the two agencies ended there. From the moment Leon Trotsky created the Fourth Department, both agencies were strong rivals, a competition that would plague Soviet intelligence for many years. There were recurring battles over which agency 'owned' a particular asset, such as the moment when the NKVD attempted to recruit a young American State Department official named Alger Hiss, only to be told that he was already functioning as a GRU asset. The rivalry between the two agencies sharpened as one of the most odious characters in the history of Soviet intelligence began his rise to power.

Lavrenti Beria, a Georgian Communist revolutionary who had worked with another Georgian revolutionary, Josef Stalin in the underground struggle against the czar, was among the first recruits of Feliks Dzerzhinsky in 1919. He carried out a number of foreign missions with great skill and by 1930 was head of the NKVD's foreign intelligence section. He had also established a close friendship and working partnership with Stalin. As Stalin was consolidating his power, Beria rose with him. In 1938, Stalin made him head of the NKVD. Beria left foreign intelligence to his deputies and spent most of his time doing the dirty work of Stalin's purges.

Among Beria's victims was a man he hated, Jan Berzin, largely because the GRU chief, who was working in Spain as a military adviser to the Republicans, had the temerity to complain about NKVD excesses there. When a summons arrived for him to return to Moscow for 'consultations', Berzin knew what that meant. So did his deputies, who urged him to flee. However, Berzin, a loyal Communist to the end, declined. "They can shoot me here or they can shoot me there" he said and headed off to Moscow, where he was taken to the Lubyanka and shot within an hour of his arrival.

The purges also cut a wide swath through NKVD ranks. Indeed, 1,373 of its agents were arrested on charges of being 'imperialist spies' of one kind or another; 153 of them were executed and the rest were sent to the Gulag. Another 6,000 agents were fired. This madness was set off by Stalin's paranoiac belief that Soviet intelligence agents who had served overseas (or were even friends with those who had) had succumbed to the blandishments of Western intelligence agencies. It decapitated the cream of Soviet intelligence. Among the victims were Ignace Reiss, a master recruiter who headed agent networks in Western Europe. When he refused a summons to return to Moscow, an NKVD execution squad was sent to murder him. Walter Krivitsky, head of a large GRU network in Amsterdam, where he worked under cover as an antiques dealer, also refused a summons home. However, unlike his friend Reiss, he managed to flee to sanctuary in the United States. So did Alexander Orlov, head of NKVD operations in Spain.

Many of Soviet intelligence's greatest agents perished, including two who had carried off a remarkable espionage operation in Great Britain. Both Arnold Deutsch and Theodore Maly were veterans of Dzerzhinsky's first great recruitment drive among foreign Communists for espionage work. Dedicated Communists, Deutsch (an ex-Austrian academic) and Maly (a Hungarian ex-priest) had the polish and sophistication of highly-educated Europeans with deep experience in the ways of the world – precisely the right background for a very sophisticated recruitment operation. No one knows who came up with the idea, which involved penetrating the British government structure not by the conventional method of recruiting officials, but by setting the clocks on what can be considered espionage time bombs.

In the NKVD's analysis, the British establishment had a narrow pipeline: virtually all of its members were graduates of Oxford or Cambridge. Recruitment efforts would concentrate on promising students at those two institutions, with emphasis on the right kind of political sympathies suitable for moulding. The two NKVD recruiters worked with great skill and subtlety. Prospective recruits were told they were being enlisted for the 'struggle against fascism' or vague variations on the same theme. The words 'NKVD', 'Soviet intelligence' or 'espionage' were never mentioned. Once recruited, the assets were informed that their real value would come in the future, when they would be in some sort of government job and in a position to provide important information.

Deutsch and Maly played their roles perfectly. They treated their newly recruited assets collegially, fellow warriors in the war against evil, while dispensing with such standard tradecraft of espionage as passwords and recognition signals. They also deviated from standard espionage practice by recruiting assets whose value, if any, would not be apparent for years to come. However, Deutsch and Maly succeeded brilliantly, far better than anyone could have dreamed. Before both men were purged from NKVD ranks in 1938, their efforts had been crowned with recruitment of the famed 'Ring of Five', young men of Oxford and Cambridge who would go on to become the most destructive moles in the history of espionage – Anthony Blunt, H.A.R. 'Kim' Philby, Guy Burgess, Donald Maclean and John Cairncross.

The purge of the NKVD also destroyed an authentic genius in the art of propaganda, a man who invented an important technique of modern espionage, the front group. His name was Willi Muenzenberg, a rumpled German Communist who was among Dzerzhinsky's early recruits. Muenzenberg was full of ideas on how the Communist cause could be advanced by using the communications revolution – movies, mass-market books, large-circulation newspapers and magazines. The Communist message, Muenzenberg argued, would be carefully concealed in material about 'world peace' and other such vague generalities.

Muenzenberg also proposed turning propaganda into a weapon of espionage, an idea he got from studying the success of the British propaganda operation in World War I. However, Muenzenberg went a step farther, advocating what he called a 'front group'. Basically, it amounted to the creation of a legitimate-appearing political or cultural organization, using locally-recruited assets and secretly funded by Soviet intelligence. It would advance Soviet interests while at the same time undermining the policies of a target country. Impressed, the NKVD provided him with the funds to get it started and full authority to run it as he saw fit.

The operation would become the most successful in history, a success largely attributable to Muenzenberg himself. He was a wild character of boundless energy who built a huge propaganda empire that at one point included two daily newspapers, an illustrated weekly, dozens of magazines and a movie studio. The key to Muenzenberg's success was credibility. He and his stable of expert propagandists artfully mixed fact and fiction to conceal its Communist origin.

His greatest achievement, which still ranks as the supreme propaganda triumph of all time, was *The Brown Book of Hitler Terror*. Ostensibly the result of an investigation into the Reichstag fire in 1933 by 'objective' people enlisted for a front group, the Brown Book concluded that Hitler and the Nazis had set the fire to justify their suppression of civil liberties in Germany. The book was an artful piece of disinformation, enhanced by a special 'investigation commission' that Muenzenberg put together, using naive prominent people (Muenzenberg called them "fellow travelers") to lend the group credibility. The operation was a brilliant success and highly damaging to Nazi Germany, convincing millions of people that the Reichstag fire was a Nazi conspiracy.

Muenzenberg would go on to create dozens of other front groups, all designed to advance the Soviet cause behind such facades as 'world peace' and 'an end to weapons of destruction'. However, at the very height of Muenzenberg's success, Stalin, for reasons known only to himself, decided his master propagandist had to be purged. Muenzenberg not only refused to return to Moscow for his certain execution, he defied Stalin by publishing an open letter accusing him of despotism. Later, he was found hanged from a tree, a death attributed to 'apparent suicide'.

It is a tribute to the deep Communist convictions in the ranks of NKVD agents that the murder or imprisonment of so many of their fellow agents did not rattle their faith. Among many other examples, Ruth Werner demonstrated the kind of thinking common among NKVD agents who believed that what was good for the party transcended all other considerations. She was married to a German Communist and NKVD agent named Hamburger. One day he was dragged away to the Lubyanka, accused of being a "British spy" and executed. When informed of what had happened to her husband, Werner calmly replied that since he was an "enemy of the people", his death was well-deserved. As she must have known, her husband was nothing of the kind. Such unswerving dedication to the cause explains why Soviet intelligence managed to survive and flourish, despite the bloodbath. Another reason was the weakness of its opponents, especially Germany.

LATE STARTER

Nazi Germany's intelligence structure was born on the morning of 14 June 1931, when one of the more fervid functionaries in the newly-created Schutzstaffel (SS), Hitler's Praetorian Guard, travelled to the chicken farm near Munich of its leader, Heinrich Himmler. Reinhard Heydrich had been summoned to determine his fitness to head up a new Nazi intelligence service, to be called Sicherheitsdienst (SD – security service). When he arrived, Himmler told him to sit down and write out an operating plan for the new organization. He gave Heydrich 20 minutes to perform the task.

Heydrich found himself in a quandary. He didn't have even the slightest idea of how an intelligence service was organized and operated, yet didn't want to indicate his ignorance and thus jeopardize his SS career. Fortunately for Heydrich, Himmler did not know anything about intelligence either, so when he presented an outline of how he thought a modern intelligence service ought to be organized – drawn from spy movies he had seen and spy novels he had read – Himmler instantly pronounced it brilliant. On the spot he appointed Heydrich chief of the SD.

Meanwhile in Berlin, a German naval officer named Wilhelm Canaris, who had dabbled in espionage during World War I (see page 129), was summoned to meet with his superiors, who informed him that he was now chief of the Abwehr, Germany's main military intelligence agency. Canaris' grasp of intelligence was not very firm, so he immediately recruited military officers with intelligence experience to run the agency. He recruited men very much like himself, intense German patriots who regarded the growing power of the Nazis with a mixture of loathing and dread. Later, these men, along with Canaris, would do everything they could to destroy the regime they were supposed to be serving as its eyes and ears.

These contradictory threads of German intelligence now came together in a rickety structure that attempted to operate in a climate of mutual suspicion and antipathy. The result was an intelligence mess that had an inevitable result. Before World War II, Germany was unable to develop even a rudimentary picture of its potential enemies. The strange bifurcated German intelligence establishment played a key role, but an even greater factor was the quirky approach to intelligence by their Fuehrer.

Hitler tended to regard himself as his own intelligence agency. As a man who was convinced he knew everything there was to know, he accepted or rejected intelligence on the basis of whether it fit his preconceptions. He also had the bad habit of mixing politics and intelligence, often ordering German intelligence not to conduct any operations in a particular country so as not to jeopardize some sort of accommodation he had in mind, then ordering such operations to begin when that gambit failed for one reason or another. It was no way to run intelligence, as exemplified by German intelligence's problems in Great Britain.

Hitler ran hot and cold on the subject of the British. Sometimes he believed he could reach an accommodation under which the two countries could divide the world between them; other times believed the British were his most dangerous enemies who had to be destroyed. Authority to conduct intelligence operations inside Great Britain was subject to these fluctuations, which was especially upsetting to the German military, which was desperate for intelligence on the state of its British counterpart.

The Luftwaffe, in particular, had an acute need for specific intelligence on a number of mysterious towers that were built during the 1930s along Britain's eastern coast. Anticipating a future war between Germany and Britain,

ABOVE: Laventri Beria, the odious head of the Soviet NKVD, the organization which was the precursor of the KGB.

LEFT: The German
zeppelin LZ-130,
the world's first
airborne electronic
intelligence
platform, which
failed to discover
the secrets of
British radar.

the Luftwaffe believed those towers were connected with newly-developed radar. It was imperative to find out if they were in fact radar transmission towers, what frequencies they used and the range of their signals. Hitler had forbidden any intelligence operations in Britain, especially during the time of the Munich Pact, but in 1939, believing the British were in fact enemies, he authorized German intelligence to begin operations in Great Britain.

What Hitler did not understand was that intelligence was not a faucet that could be turned on and off at will. Forbidden to develop any assets in Britain, German intelligence now faced the task of somehow creating a presence there virtually overnight. An impossibility, so the Luftwaffe sought a quick, unconventional way of gathering intelligence on those towers, one that would not require assets on the ground. The solution: the world's first elint (electronic intelligence) platform.

The platform was an airship, the LZ-130, to the ill-fated Hindenberg. Built in 1938, it was originally designed as a passenger liner, but when the Americans refused to sell Germany helium (a much safer gas than the highly flammable hydrogen aboard the Hindenberg), the Luftwaffe got the bright idea of using it as an electronic intelligence platform. LZ-130 was jammed with electronics detection gear and in May 1939, was sent on 'demonstration' and 'test' flights whose routes somehow always included the eastern coast of Britain.

This curious flight path attracted the attention of the British Air Ministry, which logically concluded that the Germans were snooping on their greatest technological secret – radar. The suspicion was confirmed by further 'test' flights, all of which at some point skirted the British coast. There was a simple countermeasure: the British shut down the tower transmissions every time LZ-130 approached. As a result, the LZ-130 operation failed utterly, a failure that would prove costly to the Luftwaffe a year later, during the Battle of Britain, when those radars were able to pick up German formations at long range, allowing the numerically inferior British fighter force to be vectored with maximum effect.

The British assumed the LZ-130 had some sort of elint gear aboard, but it had to be an assumption because British intelligence had no insight into the state of Germany's own radar program. Nor did it have much in the way of information on Germany's military electronics in general. That was only part of a general British intelligence myopia before World War II, a myopia that had everything to do with official neglect, mostly budgetary.

MI6, Britain's chief foreign intelligence agency, had ended its service in World War I on something of a high note. This was due in large part to the drive and strong personality of its first chief, Mansfield Smith-Cumming. He had been

BELOW: Mansfield Smith-Cumming (left), the first chief of MI6, with his sailing cronies in 1907.

intelligence establishment of any decent size. In 1921, the budget for the entire British intelligence structure was only about £100,000; in 1935, it was £180,000. The effect on that structure was not immediately obvious. British intelligence in the inter-war period to a large extent was living on its reputation. To the people who actually worked in intelligence, the real state of affairs was clear: things, as Claude M. Dansey could attest, were in a bad way.

Dansey, an ex-army officer who had served in British intelligence during World War I, was typical of many members of the postwar MI6 who had gotten a taste of the espionage life and found they were addicted to it. Like a number of other postwar recruits to British intelligence, Dansey found himself bored with corporate life, which paled in comparison with the excitement and intrigue he had experienced in the war. However, Dansey was not impressed by what he saw of the postwar MI6. All its chiefs

selected for the job largely because he had dabbled in some amateur spying before World War I, carefully disguising himself as a heavyset German, then wandering around the German countryside as a hiker. However, there was no way he could have collected much in the way of useful intelligence, given the fact that he did not speak a single word of German. He also had a reputation as a man of extraordinary self-discipline. Addicted to speed, one day he lost control of his car, which overturned. Smith-Cumming found himself pinned under the wreckage, the wreck atop his mangled leg. He pulled a pen knife from his pocket, then amputated his own leg to remove himself from the wreck.

He could legitimately claim credit for MI6's brilliant successes in America and the Middle East, along with much more modest wartime successes in the Netherlands and Belgium. However, those successes could not alter the realities of postwar economics, when there was simply not enough money available to adequately fund an

of station, attached to British embassies, were given the cover of passport control officers. Since that had been the standard cover for years, it was a matter of common knowledge that the diplomat with the title in any embassy was invariably the MI6 chief of station. When he was assigned to Rome in 1929, Dansey learned that even the lowliest taxi driver seemed to know who the MI6 station chief was.

Even worse, there was little or no training for MI6 agents, save for a brief, basic course on espionage fundamentals. New agents showed up at their assignments and were given the vague instructions to collect intelligence on the political, military, industrial, economic and 'social scandal in high places' of the target country. If they asked how they were supposed to go about accomplishing that, they were told that they would figure it out, somehow. No agent could expect to get rich in MI6's service as pay rates were notoriously penurious and those assigned to overseas stations were expected to pay at least some of their expenses out of their own pockets. For that reason, MI6 preferred to recruit ex-military officers, who were expected to live mostly on their pensions. Vetting of new agents was almost non-existent, a process that relied mostly on old-boy connections to determine if a potential agent was 'right'.

Dansey was so alarmed by what he saw that as he began to rise in the MI6 hierarchy (by World War II, he was the agency's deputy director), he formed what amounted to a parallel MI6, an organization that would replace a disaster he was certain was just waiting to happen. In the event of a war, he concluded, the MI6 chiefs of station, along with their generally mediocre agents, would be rolled up in an instant. The solution he devised involved recruiting sources with no known connection with British intelligence who had access to information of interest. Dansey called the group Z Organization. It was eventually to enlist nearly 300 non-MI6 assets with access to various kinds of intelligence.

THE COST OF ESPIONAGE

The roster of amateur spies included sources ranging from industrialists who had contacts with foreign industries to newspaper correspondents. Their involvement was conditional on Dansey's strict instructions: keep your eyes and ears open, and collect whatever interesting intelligence came your way, no matter how trivial it might appear; never write anything down while in foreign territory and do not take any photographs. Those recruited to Dansey's private network met his two key standards: deep patriotism and a fondness for the thrill of dabbling in espionage.

Like MI6, Britain's internal security agency MI5 suffered from a lack of money. Consequently, its roster was pretty thin. In 1930, it had a total of 13 full-time officers responsible for combating foreign espionage and such domestic threats as the Communist Party. MI5 personnel were mostly ex-military, and were expected to live on their military pensions, supplemented with modest MI5 funds. Consequently, the quality of the MI5 officers was low. They tended to fixate on military aspects of counterespionage – such as their obsession with the effect of 'Communist propaganda' on the armed forces. Meanwhile, they were totally unaware that the NKVD and the GRU had honeycombed the country with a

ABOVE: The border checkpoint between Estonia and the Soviet Union before World War II, where unalerted Soviet border troops were overwhelmed in 1941.

RIGHT: Cells at Moscow's Lubyanka Prison, where scores of Soviet intelligence agents were imprisoned, charged with being 'Western spies' during Stalin's purges.

number of espionage networks that were already leaking Britain's secrets to Moscow.

Both agencies might have been able to rally official support for more funds and better personnel, but they made the bad mistake of dabbling in politics, precisely where intelligence agencies should never tread. The most serious incident came in 1924, when the country was rocked by blaring newspaper headlines revealing something called the 'Zinoviev letter'. It was allegedly a letter written by Gregory Zinoviev, head of the Comintern, to the Communist Party of Great Britain directing them to conduct subversion to destroy the British army. The letter, which reportedly had been intercepted by British intelligence, was pure political dynamite. It ultimately played a key role in the downfall of the Labour government of Ramsay MacDonald, which had begun delicate negotiations with the Russians on trade relations. There is still a great deal of dispute whether the letter was genuine (Zinoviev denied ever writing it), but the weight of evidence is that it was a forgery by Russian exiles encouraged by senior MI6 and MI5 officers who sought to elect a Conservative government.

In the late 1930s, MI6 again became ensnared in politics, this time involving its intelligence judgments about Nazi Germany. The official policy of Neville Chamberlain's government was appeasement – the belief that Hitler's aggression could be handled best by negotiation. That policy had an important intelligence implication: the belief that Germany's mighty military power made coming to an understanding with Hitler imperative. The most important aspect of that belief was the assumption that the Luftwaffe had a great fleet of bombers capable of reducing Britain to a smoking ruin in a matter of hours. The belief was already firmly rooted in popular opinion. For years it had been subjected to wildly exaggerated popular press accounts of devastating attacks by modern bombers and a very popular futuristic movie based on H.G. Wells' Things to Come, which featured scenes of bombers dropping gas bombs to wipe out entire populations.

MI6 had very little insight into the Luftwaffe, but did find it politically convenient to tell the government what it wanted to hear: the Lufwaffe's bomber force could inflict terrible damage on Britain in the event of war, since the Royal Air Force lacked the resources to stop them. In fact, the Luftwaffe had nowhere that capability, but wanted everybody to think it did, so they exerted every effort to spread inflated accounts of great fleets of German bombers. It was those exaggerated accounts that MI6 passed on as fact.

The same exaggerations were planted on another

intelligence service, the American Army's Military Information Division (MID). The conveyer was a very unlikely spy, Charles Lindbergh, the famed 'Lone Eagle' (first to fly solo across the Atlantic). Invited in 1938 to Germany by Reichsmarschall Hermann Goering, chief of the Luftwaffe, to visit the resurgent German air industry, Lindbergh volunteered his services to Colonel Truman Smith, the U.S. military attaché in Berlin. Smith was eager to gather intelligence on the growing power of the Luftwaffe and Lindbergh was in an ideal position to get it. Eager to impress the famous hero (and influence U.S. public opinion), the Germans would show Lindbergh just about everything they had. Lindbergh succeeded far beyond Smith's expectations. With the shy, modest charm that had endeared him to millions of people, Lindbergh seduced the Germans into giving him extraordinary access, including letting him actually take the controls of their latest planes.

It was a nearly unbelievable intelligence opportunity, but what Lindbergh saw he filtered through a political prism. A committed isolationist intent on keeping the United States out of a European war, Lindbergh accepted at face value all the exaggerations the Germans planted on him, especially boasts about a huge bomber fleet. Lindbergh finally concluded that Britain would have no chance against so mighty a force in the event of war, so there was no point in America intervening in a war the British would lose in a few hours.

Smith passed on Lindbergh's intelligence uncritically to the MID, which in turn passed it on with equal lack of analysis to the Army Air Corps. It was eagerly received there as confirmation of their conviction that the next war could be won by strategic bombing – American strategic bombing. Such narrow parochialism was fairly typical in America's pre-WW II establishment, which was small, fragmented and underfunded.

The MID had a total of only 66 men assigned to it during the 1930s, almost all of them largely untrained. They spent most of their time collating information from U.S. military attaches around the world. However, the attaches were also largely untrained in intelligence and suffered from a similar budgetary constriction. Most of them were assigned as military attachés only because they came from independently wealthy families and so could pay much of the cost of their assignment out of their own pockets. The U.S. Navy's Office of Naval Intelligence (ONI) also relied on attaches. Like the Army, most had been assigned for their ability to pay their own way, not because they knew much about intelligence-gathering. State Department Intelligence, the third leg of the U.S. intelligence triad, relied on the reports of ambassadors sent to various 'desks', each one representing a particular area of the world. The sole bright spot in U.S. intelligence was its cryptanalytic capability, split between the Army and Navy. The Americans had come late to cryptanalysis, in World War I, but thanks to the efforts of its dedicated staff, after the war had managed to keep the U.S. in cryptology's first rank, despite tight funding and penurious salaries.

In 1939, as the dark clouds of approaching war appeared in Europe and the Far East, American intelligence looked blindly at the cataclysm certain to come. With few eyes and ears abroad, it had no insight into the dangers lurking everywhere. The British situation was not much better. Meanwhile, there were more than 36,000 Soviet intelligence agents and their assets pumping information to Moscow while German intelligence had deployed 7,500 agents and assets.

Judged strictly in terms of numbers, the intelligence struggle appeared to be unequal, but there was another, more subtle factor at work, one that would prove decisive. On 17 May 1939, NKVD agents forwarded to Moscow a major intelligence coup: news of a secret briefing Hitler had given to his senior military commanders, in which he had announced his long-term objective of invading the Soviet Union. The report was immediately forwarded to Stalin, who returned it after contemptuously scrawling on the bottom, "English provocation! Investigate!"

No more morale-shattering reaction can be imagined, yet, with a few exceptions, the men and women of Soviet intelligence soldiered on, continuing to gather intelligence. Only deep-seated dedication to the Communist cause can explain the loyalty of thousands of Soviet intelligence agents and assets, who carried on devoting their lives to a system that seemed to be in the grip of some sort of insanity.

That devotion took forms that are incomprehensible. The friends and colleagues of the nearly 5,000 agents arrested during Stalin's purge of Soviet intelligence in the 1930s were perfectly aware that the victims were not "long-time agents of British intelligence" or "fascist wreckers" or "disgusting imperialist worms" as Stalin claimed. Yet, they remained silent as their fellow agents were dragged away to the Lubyanka to undergo the horrors of Beria's 'conveyor belt' of torture, at the end of which they confessed to whatever crimes Beria decided upon. They knew that none of the 153 agents executed as Brtish, American and German spies were guilty, nor were any of the 6,000 agents removed from the rolls of Soviet intelligence and banished to the Russian hinterlands, because they were suspected of being 'foreign agents'.

As things turned out, the slavish devotion of Soviet intelligence to the regime would prove decisive in saving the Soviet Union from the gravest threat in its history: World War II.

THE CATCHER WHO SPIED: AMATEURS

EVEN AMONG THE NOTORIOUS SECRET POLICE AGENCIES OF THE 1930S, THE JAPANESE KEMPEI TAI OCCUPIED A SPECIAL NICHE FOR ODIOUSNESS.

Notorious for its brutality, torture dungeons, pervasive spying on Japanese society and strict security measures, the agency had turned Japan into a police state. The Kempei Tai was especially noted for dogged thoroughness; not even the faintest wisp of espionage escaped the attention of its 10,000 agents and thousands of informers.

All the more surprising then, that in 1934, the Kempei Tai was outwitted by a decidedly amateur American spy. In November of that year, among the agency's tasks was checking entry visas submitted by Major League Baseball for a team of all-stars scheduled to play in a tour of Japan. Unfortunately for the Kempei Tai, the agents assigned weren't baseball fans. Thus, they did not wonder why Morris (Moe) Berg, a so-so catcher for the Washington Senators, was on a team of superstars that included Babe Ruth and Lou Gehrig. Because the Kempei Tai agents did not wonder, they had no idea that Berg was on the team for only one reason – the U.S. Navy's Office of Naval Intelligence (ONI) had secretly approached the major leagues to include him on the roster. Berg was a spy for ONI.

On 29 November, Berg told his teammates he was feeling ill and begged off joining them that afternoon for an exhibition game. After they departed, Berg left his Tokyo hotel and walked to the nearby St. Luke's International Hospital. Bearing a bouquet of flowers, he asked in near-perfect Japanese for the room number of his "close friend," the wife of a U.S. diplomat, who was in the hospital having a baby. Directed to the seventh floor, Berg entered an elevator, but did not stop at that floor. Instead, he got out at the top floor, then went through a fire exit door to the roof of the hospital, at that time among the tallest buildings in Tokyo. There, he took out a small movie camera from under his coat and, for the next hour, slowly panned that camera around the city, concentrating on industrial installations and Japanese warships anchored in Tokyo Bay. Then he left the hospital, the camera and flowers concealed under his coat. Later, while the American all-stars were defeating a team of Japanese all-stars, 23–5 (including a gargantuan home run by Ruth), Berg passed the film to an American diplomat in a brush contact on a busy Tokyo street.

Pictures from that film proved invaluable eight years later as essential intelligence for the surprise American bombing of Tokyo, a raid that severely rattled Japanese

morale. The pictures were later part of the target folders for the devastating fire-bombing raids that destroyed more than half the city and killed more than 100,000 people.

THE STORY TOLD

It was not until some years after his death in 1972 that this hidden part of Berg's life became public knowledge. First recruited in 1932, his espionage in Tokyo was just one of a number of such operations carried out by a man who never received any formal espionage training and whose efforts were conducted solely out of patriotism. That put him in a special category of agent known as 'amateurs'.

The 1930s were something of a golden age for such spies. In an era of economic troubles that meant sharply reduced intelligence agency budgets in many countries, patriotic amateurs helped fill the gaps. Their ranks included an interesting assortment of human beings – industrialists, famous novelists, movie producers, businessmen, clergymen, fashion models, athletes – who shared patriotic motives and a willingness to undergo the risks inherent in the dangerous world of espionage.

In this rich variety of amateurs, there were few more intriguing than Berg, who was by any standard a rather odd duck. A *magna cum laude* graduate of Princeton, Berg was a star college baseball player later recruited to play in the majors. He was an unremarkable journeyman player, but was the endless subject of gossip in the baseball world. In a profession not noted for intellectualism, Berg spoke 12 languages fluently, and spent every spare moment during travel to away games devouring books, journals and newspapers. He even occasionally addressed mystified teammates in Latin or Sanskrit. They had no clue that this oddball had been recruited in 1932 as an amateur spy.

Berg, ultimately became an official spy after Pearl Harbor, when he joined the OSS (in 1952, he joined the OSS' successor agency, the CIA). Most amateurs, however, preferred either to remain amateurs or stopped spying altogether as wartime expansion of intelligence agencies reduced the need for amateur help. One of the more famous American amateur spies, Ernest Hemingway, decided to remain one during the war.

By 1941, Hemingway, who had served as an amateur spy for ONI during his world travels in the late 1930s, was

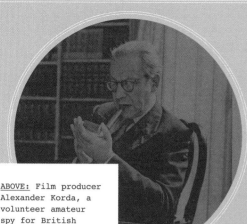

ABOVE: Film producer Alexander Korda, a volunteer amateur spy for British intelligence.

financial institutions, with branches all over the world and deep connections to foreign banks. Aldrich had only to pick up a phone to tap into Chase's vast resources and track German and Japanese finances. Another member of The Room was Roosevelt's closest friend, Vincent Astor. Roosevelt enjoyed cruising aboard the financier's oceangoing yacht, although the President did not join Astor's longer voyages to the Pacific. On these, Astor would sail among the Japanese mandates, snooping for evidence of a military buildup. Astor's real value as an amateur spy was connected to his directorship of the Western Union Telegraph Company, whose facilities were used by foreign embassies in the U.S. to transmit diplomatic messages. Astor arranged for Western Union to turn over copies of those communications to American codebreaking agencies.

Members of The Room tended to be Anglophiles, so it was not surprising they established a covert link with British intelligence, which had its own stable of amateur spies. Those spies worked for either of two separate organizations. One, informally known as 'Winston's Circle', was a group of prominent businessmen who shared Winston Churchill's fear that Britain's appeasement policies were certain to lead to the disaster of an unprepared Great Britain at war with Nazi Germany. The second, larger, group worked for Z Organization, the parallel espionage group designed to serve as a backstop for the established MI6 network. Claude Dansey, the MI6 deputy director who created it, firmly believed that amateur spies would accomplish more than MI6's regular agents, since they were unknown to counterintelligence agencies. He wound up with a disparate collection of amateur spies, among them a most unlikely agent who would earn a knighthood.

His name was Alexander Korda (real name Kellner), an émigré Hungarian movie director and producer whom Dansey recruited in 1932. With covert MI6 financing, Korda established London Films, a production company he used to travel all over the world 'scouting locations'. German counterintelligence failed to wonder why so many of those trips seemed to involve sensitive areas along Germany's borders. However, Korda's real contribution was to make movies that enhanced Britain's image among American moviegoers and chip away at isolationism. In late 1940, in part underwritten by covert MI6 funds, Korda produced *That Hamilton Woman*, a romance about Admiral Horatio Nelson and his mistress Lady Hamilton starring Laurence Olivier and Vivien Leigh. It was a box office smash, but, more importantly, the movie carried a subtle, but unmistakable, propaganda message, summed up in a speech delivered by Olivier: "You cannot make peace with dictators; you have to destroy them, wipe them out!" In the movie, he was referring to Napoleon, but no one in the audience could have missed the obvious parallel with Adolf Hitler.

living in Cuba, where he became close friends with the U.S. ambassador, Spruille Braden. Cuba had a large colony of Spanish Republican exiles, a number of whom were close drinking and fishing buddies of the famous novelist. Braden, who should have known better, agreed to a bizarre proposal by Hemingway: to use some of his Spanish friends to ferret out what he claimed was a large "fifth column" of Axis spies on the island who were providing intelligence on ship convoys to German U-boats lurking offshore. That was bad enough, but Hemingway went on to get Braden's approval for a plan to sail his fishing boat out into the allegedly submarine-infested waters, where some ageing former jai-alai players aboard the boat would hurl dynamite charges into the conning tower of a surfaced U-boat. After learning of this nonsense, an appalled FBI Director J. Edgar Hoover, who loathed Hemingway, pressured the State Department to bring his amateur operation to an end.

Hoover was also aware of some other amateur American spies, but those were gathered in a shadowy organization with close links to President Franklin D. Roosevelt and Hoover was not about to get too deeply involved in that sensitive area. The organization was called simply 'The Room' – named for the luxury Manhattan apartment in which a group of amateur spies met regularly to exchange intelligence. The men were the very cream of the American corporate establishment, all of whom shared a common conviction: Nazi Germany and Imperial Japan represented grave dangers certain at some time to become involved in a war with the United States. Thus, it was vital to collect as much intelligence as possible about these threats, so America would be prepared. All were friends of Roosevelt, who was desperate for intelligence which his nation's fragmented espionage structure was not providing.

This group of amateur spies included several men whose corporate positions provided access to top-grade intelligence. Among them was Winthrop Aldrich, chairman of the Chase Bank, one of the world's largest

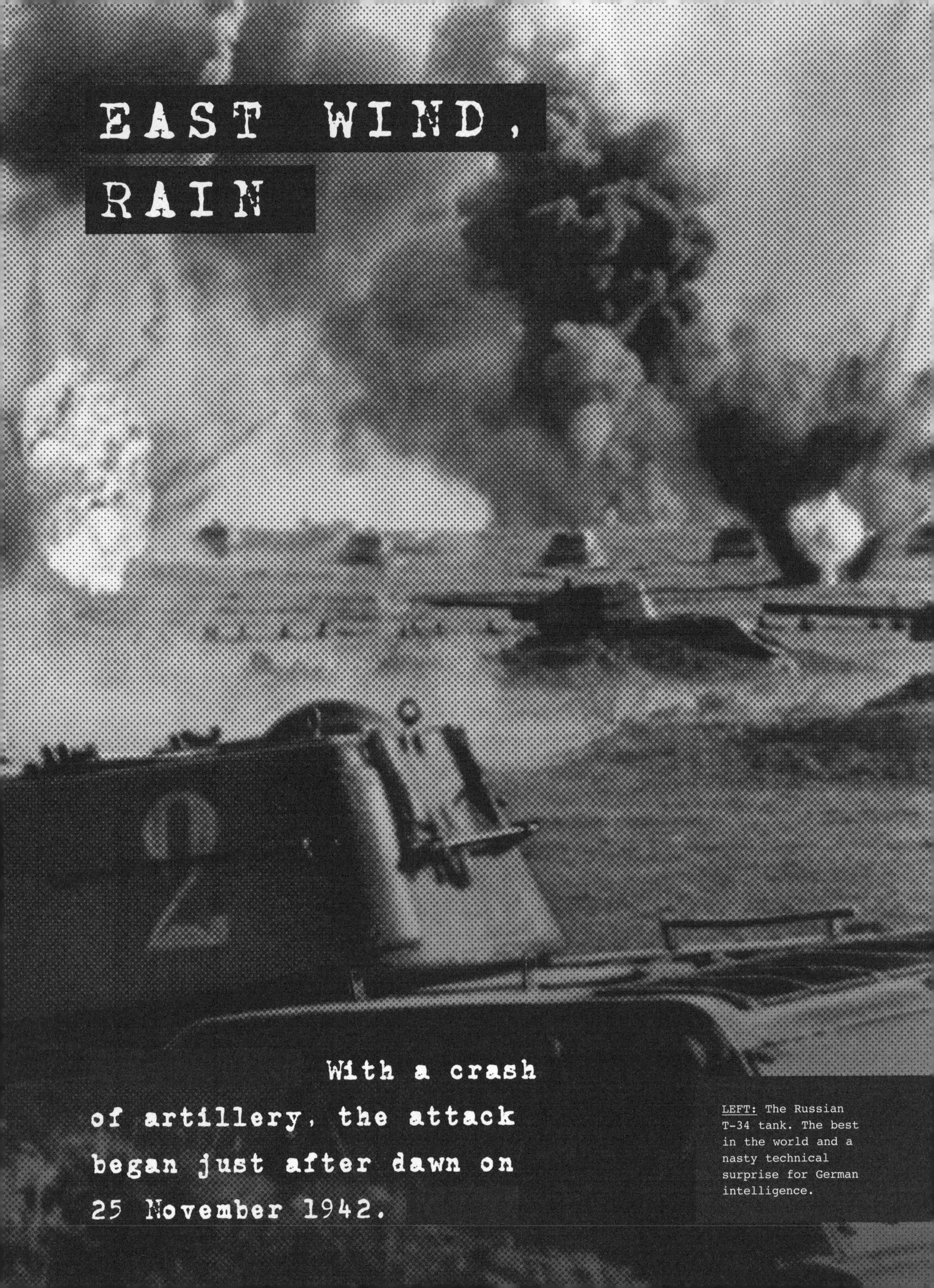

EAST WIND, RAIN

With a crash of artillery, the attack began just after dawn on 25 November 1942.

LEFT: The Russian T-34 tank. The best in the world and a nasty technical surprise for German intelligence.

Across more than a hundred miles of front, 2,352 Soviet tanks and 817,000 men charged into the salient held by the Germans near the town of Rzhev, in central Russia. Code-named Operation Mars, it was the northern part of a huge, ambitious pincer operation designed to break the back of the Wehrmacht in Russia. The southern pincer, Operation Uranus, aimed to destroy the German Sixth Army at Stalingrad. In the north the objective was destruction of the Ninth Army.

Marshal Georgi Zhukov, the Red Army's best commander, who had defeated the Germans at the gates of Moscow a year before, was confident that the operation he had conceived would succeed, largely because there was no way the Germans would learn about it beforehand. Like all Red Army operations, Operation Mars was wrapped in a cocoon of operational security to an extent unmatched by any other army in the world.

Special NKVD squads prowled the rear areas, on the alert for enemy spies while rounding up deserters, who were usually shot on the spot. More specialized NKVD detachments oversaw all radio traffic, imposing strict security standards to ensure that not even the smallest error would aid enemy listeners. Keys for enciphered communications were changed daily to balk enemy cryptanalysts. Still another special NKVD unit carefully monitored the enemy's radio traffic, searching for clues that the Germans might have detected signs of the approaching storm. There was no doubt, his intelligence officers finally told Zhukov, that not a whisper of Operation Mars had escaped. When the blow fell, the Germans would be totally surprised.

Given that level of security, Zhukov was all the more shocked when, some 48 hours into the operation, he began to receive unsettling news from his front-line commanders. The Germans, they reported, clearly knew the Russians were coming. Their anti-tank guns were concentrated against the main axes of advance for Soviet tanks and extensive field fortifications were constructed in sectors of major infantry advances. The German artillery hit Soviet troop concentrations with pinpoint accuracy, indicating

prior intelligence. Indeed, the Germans seemed to know just about everything about the Russian operational plan.

As the battle wore on, Zhukov got even more disturbing news. Despite a big Soviet advantage in numbers of men and material, the Germans were holding their positions and inflicting terrible casualties. In just one four-mile sector, more than 400 Russian tanks were knocked out in only two days. Undaunted, Zhukov ordered further attacks, but everything his forces tried failed, largely because the Germans uncannily anticipated every move. Finally, after suffering more than 350,000 casualties and the loss of over 1,700 tanks, Zhukov gave up. What remained of the Operation Mars force retreated back to Soviet lines.

Zhukov convened his staff to conduct a post-mortem on why the operation had gone so badly wrong, especially how the Germans had apparently learned so much about it. While he did this, far to the west the champagne was broken out in the Eastern Front headquarters of the Abwehr to toast its greatest intelligence victory of the war – and their spy in the Soviet high command whose information made the Rzhev victory possible. Glass after glass of the finest French wine was drunk in honour of that spy, the man the Abwehr code-named 'HEINE'.

Zhukov never did find out how the Germans knew he was coming and the Rzhev disaster remained a bloody blot on the record of one of World War II's greatest generals. A military disaster of that magnitude might have had a significant impact on his career, except that the brilliant success of the southern half of his grand pincer manoeuvre, the victory at Stalingrad, deflected attention from the defeat further north. Moreover, to Zhukov's puzzlement, neither Stalin nor other members of the Stavka, the Soviet high command, reproached him for what had happened at Rzhev. They seemed oddly disinterested in finding out how the Germans had learned about it.

There was a very good reason for that disinterest. In fact, Operation Mars had been deliberately betrayed to the Germans by the NKVD, with Stalin's full knowledge. HEINE was a Soviet agent, his bona fides carefully built on the thousands of corpses of his nation's soldiers. It was the prelude to a gigantic intelligence sting that would later shatter the German military on the Eastern Front.

HEINE was Alexander Demyanov, one of the great unheralded and underpublicized spies of World War II. A scion of a prominent White Russian family who in his youth became a fervent Communist, Demyanov joined the OGPU in 1929. Given his background, several years later he was assigned the task of infiltrating White Russian exiles to uncover any connections they might have to German intelligence. The Germans were known to favour recruiting such exiles as native-speaking assets who could infiltrate the Soviet Union. The OGPU carefully deployed Demyanov for the mission, getting him a job as an electrical engineer with a Moscow film studio, a job that allowed him to begin moving in Soviet cultural circles. As the OGPU was aware, the Germans liked to look for possible intelligence recruits there.

Demyanov was a classic dangle, dropping hints whenever he thought the Germans were listening about his White Russian sympathies and distaste for Stalin's oppressive regime. Within weeks, the bait was taken. He was invited to an Abwehr safe house, where he spoke with much greater frankness about his hatred of the Soviet government and his desire to overthrow that regime. He went even further. He was a member of something called 'Throne', a very secret underground organization of White Russians, which needed only some outside support to achieve its objective – a coup to drive the Communists from power. The listening Germans came fully awake, apparently never having heard of the infamous Trust operation of only two decades before. Demyanov was immediately recruited as an asset, after extracting a promise that in the event of a White Russian coup, he and his friends would be given high posts in the new government – which, of course, would be strongly pro-German.

Nothing came of this discussion, since only a few weeks after it took place, in June 1941, Germany invaded the Soviet Union. The Abwehr, preoccupied with other matters, forgot about their White Russian asset until December of that year, when a strange event took place. Just outside Moscow, a Red Army private named Alexander Demyanov crossed the front line one morning and announced he was a deserter. He claimed to have "important information" he wanted to impart to German intelligence. Aware that the Russians had been sending fake deserters across the lines to volunteer as intelligence assets (only to redesert when sent back to Soviet lines with any intelligence they had managed to pick up while in German hands), Demyanov was at first treated sceptically. However, his persistence finally got him sent up the chain of command to the main Abwehr outpost. There, the Germans ran a check on Demyanov and discovered he was the very same Demyanov who had been recruited just six months before.

ABOVE: Red Army assault teams attack German positions in Stalingrad, a crucial Soviet victory aided by a large-scale deception operation by Soviet intelligence.

Just to make sure he was still the anti-Soviet White Russian he claimed he was, Demyanov was subjected to a brutal test of his loyalty. He was taken to an apartment and seated beside an open window while he was questioned about his future work as a German intelligence asset operating behind Soviet lines. Outside, the Germans had arranged for four captured partisans to be stripped naked, strung up and then beaten with iron bars. The Germans carefully watched Demyanov for any reaction to the sound of the victims' screams as they were beaten to death. He showed not a flicker of interest. Having passed the test, Demyanov was told he would be parachuted deep behind Soviet lines with a radio, over which he would report any intelligence he could gather about Soviet troop dispositions and units being moved up to the front. He enthusiastically agreed and, a week later, was dropped some 200 miles deep into Soviet territory.

As Demyanov landed, what the Russians code-named Operation Monastery now moved into high gear. He was taken in hand by his real masters, the NKVD (the Cheka's latest acronymic descendant), to begin a double agent game that the Russians would play with consummate skill. Within a few days, HEINE began radioing detailed tactical information about Red Army units, which, the Germans were pleased to discover, was unfailingly accurate. Based on that information, the Germans were able to inflict a number of defeats on Red Army units. Thousands of Red Army soldiers were deliberately sacrificed to convince the Germans that their asset could be totally relied on. Completely convinced, the Germans never considered the possibility that the Russians were setting them up, sacrificing thousands of men for the sole purpose of boosting a double agent's bona fides. As representatives of a ruthless totalitarian regime, they should have known that such regimes were perfectly capable of sacrificing thousands of lives to advance an intelligence operation.

Over several months, the accuracy of the reports from HEINE elevated him in the eyes of German intelligence to their greatest asset on the Eastern Front. The NKVD then moved to the next, critical move, setting HEINE in motion to catch much bigger game. In late 1942, Demyanov radioed exciting news to his controllers. Due to his background as an electrical engineer, he had been enrolled in the Red Army's communications school and informed he would become the chief radio operator for the Stavka. The near-ecstasy with which the Germans greeted this news was understandable, for they now had an unparalleled source, one who handled every important message broadcast by the Soviet high command to its forces.

Sure enough, HEINE quickly offered a blockbuster, providing complete details of the Soviet plan for the offensive against the Rzhev salient. The resulting German victory solidified total Abwehr trust in their star asset. Still, a few Abwehr officers began to wonder. How was it possible that the NKVD counterintelligence, renowned for its thoroughness and radio detection operations, failed to spot all those transmissions from HEINE? Then there was the matter of the single event that had made him so completely trusted, the Rzhev salient operation. True, HEINE's information had cost the Red Army 350,000 casualties, but it was odd that while he had access to all that high-level information, he somehow failed to hear anything about the Russian plans for the Stalingrad operation. These doubts were pooh-poohed and HEINE continued to provide what his handlers considered pure gold.

However, in the summer of 1943, even his most fervid supporters in the Abwehr felt some uneasiness after he reported that Red Army reserves assigned to the Kursk salient – the target of a major planned German offensive – were almost entirely infantry, with little mobility. In fact, those reserves turned out to be tank divisions that destroyed German armour, inflicting a major defeat that spelled the end of German offensive capabilities on the Eastern Front. Still, despite growing doubts, faith in HEINE persisted and the Germans paid the penalty. Early in 1944, he radioed details of a huge Soviet offensive planned against Army Group South, toward the Balkans. The Germans stripped other army groups of units to shore up

RIGHT: A German supply column under attack by Soviet planes during the crucial battle of Kursk, a disastrous German defeat largely attributable to Soviet spies.

LEFT: Some of the nearly four million Soviet prisoners of war captured by the Germans in the early months of World War II. Stalin's refusal to believe his own intelligence about the impending invasion left the Soviet military unprepared.

the southern defences. When the blow fell in July 1944, it fell not in the south, but against Army Group Center. The Red Army ripped a 250-mile-wide gap in the German lines, inflicting 450,000 casualties.

The Germans finally realized that their superspy HEINE had been an NKVD plant all along, but by then it was too late. The damage had been done. German intelligence's credulity and failure to take a hard, objective look at Demanyov when the first indications arose that he might be a double agent can be blamed at least in part for the disaster. However, it is also true to say that the NKVD demonstrated great patience and skill in achieving one of the greatest double agent operations in World War II.

There was a terrible irony in that triumph, for it took place in the wake of what still ranks as one of the worst intelligence disasters in history – one for which the vast Russian espionage networks were blameless. What their bosses did, however, is another matter. It remains one of history's enduring mysteries why Josef Stalin, when handed detailed, specific intelligence that Nazi Germany was about to invade the Soviet Union, refused to believe it.

On 22 June 1941, when over a million German troops and thousands of planes and tanks smashed into the Soviet Union, the planes of the Red Air Force were not camouflaged, troops were not in defensive positions and Russian troops were under explicit orders not to fire on any invading forces without direct orders from Moscow. This unpreparedness had been personally ordered by Stalin. It came despite intelligence from Leopold Trepper reporting on the mass movement of German troops from France toward the Polish–Soviet border; a report from Richard Sorge in Tokyo that Hitler had decided on an invasion of the Soviet Union in the latter half of June and a report on 19 June by a key NKVD asset in Germany that the German invasion would begin on 22 June at 3 a.m. (he was off by only a half hour).

Finally, there was a strong hint from Winston Churchill. He had been told by his ULTRA codebreaking operation on 29 March 1941 that three German panzer divisions and two motorized divisions had been moved to Cracow, Poland – obviously not intended for an invasion of Great Britain. Without revealing the great ULTRA secret, Churchill told Stalin that an "unimpeachable source" had revealed the German troop movements, which had obvious implications for the Soviet Union. Stalin dismissed Churchill's message as a "provocation".

That was mild compared to his reactions to the intelligence he was receiving from his own intelligence organizations. He sneered that Sorge's intelligence was useless because, "He's spending too much time in brothels," insisted that Trepper "should be sent to his fucking mother," and demanded that the sources for NKVD intelligence reporting German intentions to invade the Soviet Union be "hunted down and punished" for sending "doubtful and misleading information" to Moscow. His blind dismissiveness was aided by the chiefs of the GRU and the NKVD, who slavishly pandered to his prejudices by telling him what he wanted to hear. The GRU reports from Trepper and Sorge were accompanied by a cover memo which noted that while the reports were interesting, they probably were "British provocations". NKVD reports had a similar caveat and Beria went so far as to congratulate Stalin on the eve of the German invasion that the Russian people would be eternally grateful for his refusal to be taken in by "disinformation".

Soviet agents received a string of rebukes from Moscow Center for these "false reports". Much like their willingness years before to soldier on despite the purges that slaughtered so many of their friends and colleagues, they were not discouraged by the blind rejection of intelligence they knew to be true. When the German invasion, code-named Barbarossa, fell upon a totally unprepared country, their agony can only be imagined. They and their assets had risked their lives to collect the intelligence that would have saved the Soviet Union, only to have it ignored. However, their rock-hard faith in the cause remained and they immediately set to work, redoubling their efforts to collect intelligence that now was more vital than ever. All the while, they were aware that the effort was putting a noose around their necks. The more intelligence they collected, the longer their radios had to stay on the air, exposing them to German counterintelligence's efficient radio location operation.

The first to fall was Trepper's operation. His radios were on the air for hours at a time, broadcasting the huge volume of intelligence his agents were collecting. That made the efforts of the German radio location experts that much easier. The end came in 1942, when the Germans located his main transmitter in Brussels. They raided the house, capturing four members of Trepper's ring in the process, including the radio operator. Trepper himself showed up at the house just as the raid took place. Thinking fast, he passed himself off as a dimwitted seller of rabbits and was shooed away. He went underground, but was later caught in Paris. Meanwhile, those arrested in Brussels were savagely tortured to reveal other spies and over the next several months, the Germans rolled up the network, ultimately arresting hundreds.

The NKVD networks were also picked off, one by one, for the same reason – radios on the air for hours at a time. Specially equipped detection vans with technicians roamed the areas where clandestine radio signals had been located, triangulating the signals until they were pinpointed to a particular area or apartment building. From there, it was a simple matter of searching house by house or apartment by apartment until the transmitter was located. Success in tracking down transmitters was almost wholly dependent on those transmitters staying on the air for relatively long periods of time. Aware of that, GRU and NKVD radio operators had been trained to remain on the air for as short a period of time as possible – short 'bursts' of just a few minutes – to balk radio location efforts. The procedure defeated radio location operations for years, but after Barbarossa, when the radio operators had to transmit reams of intelligence, they had no choice but to say on the air for long periods, often for hours at a time.

Like Trepper, Richard Sorge and his ring were ensnared by lengthy transmissions. As did other networks, after Barbarossa, Sorge's operation began pumping large volumes of material toward Moscow. His transmitter was mobile, but it had to remain at a fixed site when actually transmitting, ultimately leading the radio location experts of the Japanese Kempei Tai counterintelligence agency to a general area where the transmitter was operating. While they were trying to pinpoint the radio's exact location, they got a lucky break. They arrested the leader of the underground Japanese Communist Party. Under torture, he revealed that several Japanese Communists had been recruited for a major Soviet spy ring. Arrested and tortured in turn, they led the Kempei Tai to Sorge. He was arrested in late 1941, but not before he was able to transmit one of the most significant pieces of intelligence in the history of espionage.

It reported to Moscow that the Japanese government had decided not to attack the Soviet Union, as Hitler wanted them to do, but instead move southward to obtain raw materials. Fortunately for the future of the Soviet Union, Stalin finally chose to believe what his star spy was telling him. The Soviet far eastern provinces were stripped of several hundred thousand Siberian troops that had been deployed to block a possible Japanese invasion. They were rapidly shipped westward, just in time to save Moscow from imminent capture by the Germans.

By 1943, the only surviving major Soviet intelligence network in Europe was the Red Orchestra's Swiss outstation. German counterintelligence, which called it 'Rote Drei' (Red Three) because of its three radios, correctly assumed that the Swiss-based operation had gathered a small mountain of intelligence for Moscow, given the fact that their radios were pumping out signals for up to 13 hours a day. Strong diplomatic pressure was exerted on the Swiss to close down the radios and arrest the ring. The Swiss promised to do so, but never seemed to quite get around to it. The lassitude convinced the Germans they were playing a double-faced game, allowing Nazi Germany easy access to Swiss banks and other un-neutral benefits, while at the same time working for a German defeat by such acts as allowing a Soviet espionage ring to transfer a lot of intelligence to Moscow.

The Germans might have been even more upset about Rote Drei if they knew that the ring had been blessed with a walk-in, a quiet, scholarly man who said he had access to Nazi Germany's innermost secrets, including all its military operational plans. Alexander Rado, the veteran GRU agent in charge of the ring, code-named him 'LUCY', the name by which he passed into espionage history as one of its legendary spies – or perhaps he was not.

The real name of LUCY was Rudolf Roessler, an anti-Nazi émigré who had fled to Switzerland in 1933 after the Nazis came to power. In Lucerne, he ran a liberal Catholic magazine whose columns were filled with dense, nearly obtuse, ecclesiastical and political arguments. Not much of a good source of intelligence for a spy, but when Roessler approached one of the key assets in Rote Drei and offered to provide information, he claimed to have unbelievable access to the uppermost levels of the German high command. According to Roessler, anti-Nazi Germans who remained in top-level military posts were secretly providing him with high-grade intelligence. He described those sources only as 'WERTHER' (a source in the German armed forces command), 'TEDDY' (a source in the army high command), 'OLGA' (a source in the Foreign Ministry) and 'FERDINAND' (a source in the Luftwaffe high command). These sources, Roessler claimed, radioed him topflight intelligence via messages 'piggybacked' atop their regular traffic.

Alexander Foote, the British asset who worked as chief radio operator for Rote Drei, realized that Roessler's 'piggyback' explanation was technically impossible. That raised the question: how then was Roessler really receiving his intelligence? Rado was also puzzled, but since he was desperate for anything he could get at that moment of the Soviet Union's greatest crisis, he decided to take a chance on Roessler. So did the GRU, despite Roessler's condition for providing intelligence to the Rote Drei that he would never reveal his sources. Under normal tradecraft practices, such a condition would have been unacceptable. Not knowing the identities of sources (especially ones at the level Roessler was claiming) would make the GRU vulnerable to disinformation planted by the Germans via Roessler, perhaps their agent. However, the GRU was desperate. Therefore, Moscow Center ordered Rado to enlist Roessler on a trial basis to determine if his information would prove accurate.

Both Rado and the GRU were stunned by what Roessler began handing over: detailed, sensationally revealing intelligence that clearly came from the highest levels of the German high command. The material included actual operational orders sent to major units, often before the units had received the actual messages. All of Roessler's intelligence was current, meaning he was receiving it hot off the press, so to speak. He provided Rote Drei with Hitler's actual orders to his formations on the Eastern Front and copies of Abwehr intelligence reports on the Soviet military. Subjected to the most detailed cross-checking, all of Roessler's material proved correct. Eager to keep this golden goose laying eggs, the GRU did not press him on the identity of his sources.

In 1943, the Swiss finally cracked down on Rote Drei, closing down its transmitters and throwing Rado, Foote and the others into prison. Roessler fled underground. Perhaps coincidentally, the crackdown occurred just at the time when the Soviets had achieved dominance on the Eastern Front, thus obviating the need for the kind of high-level intelligence Roessler was providing. In any event, the end of Rote Drei left in its wake a tantalizing espionage mystery. Just who were Roessler's sources? The mystery remains because Roessler, who died in 1962, went to his grave without every revealing them – or if in fact they ever existed. One theory is that he was merely a cutout, passing on British ULTRA decrypts in a form the Russians would accept.

LUCY represented the capstone of a remarkable recovery by the Soviet Union from an initial military disaster, a recovery that owed much to its intelligence services. Two

BELOW: The stricken battleship *U.S.S. Arizona* burns in Pearl Harbor after attack by Japanese warplanes on 7 December 7 1941. A series of errors by American intelligence agencies led to the near destruction of the U.S. Pacific Fleet.

other nations, the United States and Great Britain, also owed much to their intelligence services in recovering from initial military disasters. One of those disasters remains espionage's prototypical failure – Pearl Harbor.

From the moment its construction began in 1919, the U.S. naval base at Pearl Harbor in Hawaii existed on a fundamental assumption: war between the United States and its Pacific rival Japan was inevitable. Although the base was intended as the site for an advanced naval force to deter Japanese aggression, the U.S. Navy was never happy with it. Pearl Harbor was dependent on a 3,000-mile-long supply line; had only one narrow entrance channel (easily blocked in the event of attack), and its ships, fuel storage and repair facilities were all squeezed together in a relatively small area. That meant an attack could catch the Pacific Fleet's ships conveniently at anchor in what amounted to a fish bowl. The operating presumption was that the fleet, alerted to the approach of an enemy, would be able to sail from its restricted anchorage and engage the enemy forces on the open ocean.

However, that mandated good intelligence on threats against the base, precisely what the Americans did not have. The fragmented and small American intelligence establishment, perennially starved for funds, had no insight into Japan. More importantly, it was blind to what the Japanese intended doing with the mighty military machine they were building. The Japanese invasion of Manchuria in 1931 and the attack on China several years later provided part of the answer, but that still left a very large question: what did the Japanese intend to do about the United States, the chief rival to Japanese imperial ambitions in the Pacific?

Unable to penetrate the tight security in Japan itself, the Americans were reduced to watching and listening from the periphery. The Office of Naval Intelligence (ONI) used 'hypo' radio detection stations to hunt for Japanese naval radio signals to plot locations of naval forces. The Army Military Information Division (MID) used wiretapping operations against Japanese installations in Hawaii and elsewhere, while an ONI unit, Op-20-G, worked to crack Imperial Japanese Navy operational codes. The final strand was America's greatest intelligence resource – an Army codebreaking operation that had mastered PURPLE, Japan's top diplomatic code. Unfortunately, PURPLE had limited value as an insight into Japan's military, since only diplomatic communications were decrypted.

In late November 1941, this fragmented intelligence system broke down altogether, a breakdown that could not have occurred at a worse time. Japan had decided to seize the natural resources it desperately needed by conquest in the south Pacific. The drive would be initiated by a surprise attack on the U.S. Pacific Fleet at Pearl Harbor, carried out by a four-carrier task force. One by one, the components

of U.S. intelligence failed to spot it, largely because the Japanese had anticipated what each of them would do.

The ONI 'hypo' listening stations detected nothing because the Japanese attack force sailed across the Pacific under strict radio silence. Op-20-G could not read JN-25, the main Japanese naval code used to deploy warships, because the Japanese suddenly changed the code some time before the sailing of the Pearl Harbor attack force. The decrypted PURPLE messages, which the Americans assumed would always give them advance warning of any major Japanese military move, contained no mention of Pearl Harbor because the Japanese high command kept knowledge of it from Japan's diplomats. The MID bugging of Japanese businessmen and diplomats revealed nothing, since none of them were told about the impending attack.

Finally, the sole American intelligence eyes in Japan itself, the U.S. military attachés working out of the U.S. embassy, were blinded – or more accurately, fooled. As the Japanese were aware, the American attachés, unable to develop any assets in Japan, had only their own eyes as intelligence resources, meaning what they could actually see. The Japanese were further aware that the attachés relied on a simple technique to determine if any components of the Japanese fleet had sailed – they simply counted the number of sailors they saw at liberty around the main Japanese naval bases.

If large numbers of sailors were seen, that meant the ships were in port, while just a few sailors meant ships had sailed. The Japanese dressed thousands of their soldiers in naval uniforms and set them loose in major ports. The attachés concluded that the Japanese fleet, especially its attack carriers, were in port. Even interception of the phrase the Japanese broadcast in the clear to alert their forces that war with America was imminent – "East Wind, Rain" – was useless, since nobody had any idea what that phrase meant.

Added to all these failures were a number of gaffes at Pearl Harbor itself, including the ambiguous warning from Washington, the failure by the Navy and Army commanders to send out reconnaissance patrols, and the failure to put up torpedo nets to protect the anchored fleet in the mistaken belief torpedoes could not be launched in the harbor's shallow depths. When all the errors came together, the inevitable result was what entered the history books as the 'perfect intelligence failure'.

In all the post mortems after the Pearl Harbor disaster, the shortcomings of American intelligence were mercilessly exposed. With the exception of the MAGIC codebreaking operation, the U.S. espionage establishment before the war was revealed as wholly inadequate. It knew next to nothing about the looming threats from Nazi Germany and Imperial Japan. That blindness extended to military technology, a failing that in the early days of the war caused the shedding of a lot of American blood – German tanks impervious to American anti-tank shells, Japanese 'Long Lance' torpedoes more advanced than anything the U.S. Navy had, superior Japanese navy night-fighting capabilities, superior German submarine technology, to name just a few. The most dangerous failure involved a Japanese plane, the Mitsubishi A6M – christened the 'Zero' by U.S. pilots because they knew nothing about it. A brilliantly designed agile fighter plane, for the first 18 months of the war the Zero outflew and outmanoeuvred every fighter it came up against, exacting a terrible toll.

There was no excuse for American intelligence not knowing about the Zero. A year before its appearance at Pearl Harbor, the first Zero models operated in China, where volunteer American pilots flying for the Chinese encountered them. The Americans sent back alarmed reports to Washington, warning that the Japanese had deployed a fighter plane that was years ahead of the best America could put in the sky. Somehow, their reports got lost in the byways of bureaucracy and the appearance of the Zero at Pearl Harbor came as a great technological shock. British intelligence did no better. Unaware of the Zero, on 12 April 1942, 60 Royal Air Force fighters overflying Ceylon took on a flight of 36 Japanese fighters the British pilots knew nothing about. The planes were Zeros and shot down 27 of the British fighters in less than 20 minutes.

The hard lesson American intelligence learned was that it had to get into the technical intelligence business, something it had not bothered to do, even while the pace of new military technology quickened as war approached. Quickly, teams of technical experts and scientists were enlisted for special intelligence teams that operated on the battlefields. They collected captured enemy equipment and took it apart for analysis, looking for weak points or anything that could be borrowed to improve American military technology. One of the technical intelligence teams solved the problem of the Zero. In June 1942, they learned that a Zero attacking Dutch Harbor in the Aleutians had been hit by a single bullet from American ground fire that severed its oil supply line. As the plane haemorrhaged oil, the pilot sought to land it on a nearby island. He managed to land the plane on what appeared to be a grassy meadow, but was in fact a bog. On landing, the plane flipped over, killing the pilot. However, the plane was virtually undamaged.

A U.S. technical intelligence team pulled the Zero out of the bog, put it back in flying shape and subjected the plane to an exhaustive analysis through a series of flight tests. Among other things, they learned the Zero had two crucial weaknesses: no self-sealing gas tanks (a special rubber shield which softened in contact with petrol, closing bullet-holes) and no armour around the cockpit – a sacrifice of pilot survivability to save weight. The results of the technical team's analysis were rushed to the drawing boards of the Grumman Aircraft Corporation, builder of U.S. Navy aircraft. Its designers set to work to adapt and improve their F6F Hellcat – then still in development – as a fighter to beat the A6M. After only a few months in combat, it swept the Zero from the skies. Thousands of Japanese pilots died when American tracer bullets punctured the gas tanks of the Zeros, turning them into fireballs.

The British learned the same lesson, although it followed a more difficult path. In 1939, at the outbreak of war, Group Captain F.W. Winterbotham, head of MI6's Air Section, concluded that the agency was seriously deficient in scientific intelligence. This was a grave mistake in a struggle against Germany, then the world's leading scientific power. To rectify it, he recruited a bright 23-year-old physicist named R.V. Jones and gave him a mandate to organize the collection

BELOW: Nazi Germany's secret 'vengeance weapon', the V-2 rocket, revealed by the scientific intelligence section of MI6.

ABOVE: William 'Wild Bill' Donovan, director of America's first quasi-central intelligence organization, the OSS.

of scientific intelligence, analyze it and come up with recommendations on British countermeasures.

The energetic Jones went to work, but encountered resistance from MI6's old guard, which had little interest in scientific intelligence. "Scientific illiterates" Jones called them, but he pressed on, finally achieving a breakthrough of sorts when one of his reports on German military electronics crossed Winston Churchill's desk. Impressed, Churchill asked for more, a clear political signal that Jones enjoyed high-level favour. Jones finally got his wish when every scrap of intelligence that might be related to German technology and science was routed to him. Putting together clues in those reports, Jones scored a number of technical triumphs. Amongst them was the discovery of a secret electronic beam the Germans were using to guide their bombers over Britain (he devised a counter-beam that diverted the German beam) and an advanced German magnetic sea mine (balked by a system Jones devised to demagnetize ships).

Jones' most significant triumph came in March 1943, when his attention was called to the transcript of conversations recorded by a bug planted by MI5 inside one of the barracks housing senior German officers at a British POW camp. Two

generals captured in North Africa were passing the time discussing their families in Germany and the future course of the war. Suddenly, one of them mentioned a "miracle weapon". The other general asked why "the weapon" was taking so long and was told it would be ready the following year adding, "Then the fun will start... there's no limit on the range." Jones put that clue together with some other intelligence scraps and was finally able to deduce that the Germans had developed a long-range bombardment rocket (which turned out to be the V-2).

Both the Americans and the British had learned a hard lesson about the necessity for technical and scientific intelligence. However, the British insisted that there was a subsidiary lesson the Americans had yet to learn: such intelligence had to be part of a centralized intelligence organization. As the British never tired of pointing out, the chief reason for the Pearl Harbor disaster was the fragmented American foreign intelligence structure. In the British view, there were plenty of clues to the impending attack – if only there had been a central American intelligence agency able to pull them all together.

There were many American government officials – notably President Franklin D. Roosevelt – who had come to the same conclusion, even before Pearl Harbor. However, it was not that simple. As the politically astute Roosevelt understood, there was a traditional suspicion, rooted deep in the American character, about centralized federal power. In American public opinion, centralized intelligence meant 'Gestapo', a dirty word in American politics. Nevertheless, Roosevelt wanted a new American central intelligence organization, although to achieve it he had to proceed very carefully.

Roosevelt's first move in 1940 was to enlist William O. Donovan, a World War I hero and prominent attorney as his special representative for a 'fact-finding' visit to Britain. Donovan was a prominent Republican, which protected Roosevelt's political flank, but his appointment stirred uneasiness among the military intelligence agencies. They suspected the President was setting the stage for making him his intelligence czar. The suspicion was correct, but Roosevelt's more immediate goal was to get an answer to a critical intelligence question: could the British hold out against the Nazi onslaught?

The American intelligence establishment – State Department intelligence and the military intelligence agencies – were divided on the question. His ambassador in London, Joseph Kennedy, was of even less help. Kennedy, a defeatist and appeaser whose reports portrayed a Britain on the edge of collapse, was just one step short of being an outright Nazi apologist who hectored Roosevelt to make a "deal" with Hitler.

Acutely aware of what was at stake in Donovan's visit to Britain, Churchill ordered his intelligence and military establishments to cooperate fully with Donovan, holding nothing back. During his three-week tour of Britain in July and August of 1940, Donovan saw everything worth seeing, especially the full scope of British military capabilities. The tour's highlight came one day when Donovan was handed the holy of holies, an ULTRA decrypt of orders by Hitler to his military high command to complete preparations for Operation Sealion, the German invasion of Britain. As Churchill hoped, Donovan could come to only one conclusion: with that kind of intelligence capability, how could Britain lose?

Donovan's report to Roosevelt was unequivocal. The British would hold out, provided they got some material help from the "arsenal of democracy". Two weeks after Donovan's visit, Roosevelt announced a deal under which the Americans would give Britain 50 destroyers in exchange for leasing rights to British military bases in the Caribbean and the western Atlantic. Several months later, he convinced Congress to pass the 1941 Lend–Lease Act.

Pearl Harbor and the German declaration of war against America made Great Britain and the United States full-fledged allies, including in the area of intelligence.

Donovan was the main point of contact in a new position Roosevelt created for him, Coordinator of Information. The deliberately bland title was meant to conceal Roosevelt's real intention, to create America's first centralized intelligence organization under the direction of Donovan. However, strong pressure by the military intelligence agencies and J. Edgar Hoover of the FBI (who had created an intelligence section within the Bureau) compelled Roosevelt to withhold any real power from Donovan.

Nevertheless, Roosevelt was still determined to get his way. In early 1942, he came up with a compromise that all concerned could live with. First, a new intelligence agency, the Organization of Strategic Services (OSS) was created, with Donovan as director. It would be a semi-independent military organization under loose, overall control of the U.S. military. The military intelligence organizations would retain their functions and responsibilities, while the FBI's intelligence organization would be restricted to operations in Latin America.

The American political system's ability to arrive at such compromises represented the real genius of that system, but it was not very helpful in organizing intelligence. As the exasperated British never tired of pointing out, the compromise that created the OSS did nothing to solve the problem of America's fragmented intelligence. Events proved them right, for the OSS record in the war was spotty, at best. Donovan, armed with the big budget Roosevelt arranged for him, recruited thousands of agents, concentrating his efforts in the world he knew best – the Eastern Establishment. The enlistment of so many of the socially prominent led some military intelligence agencies to sneeringly refer to the OSS as the 'Oh So Social'. The quality of Donovan's recruits varied widely. They ranged from scions of wealthy families whose interest in intelligence was restricted to the officer's commissions they were awarded and military service away from the dangers of front-line combat, to genuinely talented agents, including three future directors of the CIA in William Casey, Richard Helms and William Colby.

Another future CIA director, Allen Dulles, ran one of OSS's real success stories, the agency's outpost in Berne, Switzerland. Dulles, who had had some intelligence experience in World War I while working as a junior diplomat in the country, established connections with the anti-Nazi underground in Germany for intelligence sources. His prize recruits included Fritz Kolbe, a German Foreign Ministry official who provided copies of top-level German diplomatic documents.

In other theaters of war, however, the OSS had very little impact. General Douglas MacArthur, commander of U.S. forces in the southwest Pacific, flatly banned the OSS from any intelligence operations in his theater, preferring

ABOVE: One of the prize women recruits to the OSS, Julia Child, later famous as television's 'the French Chef'.

very rarely as actual agents on the roster of an intelligence service. Donovan not only recruited women as agents, he made it clear that in the OSS women were to be regarded as the equal of men. The policy attracted a large number of bright female college graduates who ordinarily would have had no chance of joining more traditional-minded intelligence agencies.

Among the bright young women attracted to the OSS was Julia Child, a Smith College graduate assigned to an OSS outpost in China. Her talents did not include cooking, as she later recalled, when she was given the assignment of solving an apparently intractable problem. It involved OSS underwater explosives, used in sabotage operations against enemy shipping. In shark-infested waters, too many of the explosives were being set off by curious sharks. Child's solution was to experiment with cooking various concoctions as a shark repellent, finally emerging with one so vile she could barely stay in the same room with it. However, the concoction worked; sprinkled in the water near the explosives, it repelled sharks. Still in use to this day, it marked Child's first foray into the world of cooking, ultimately leading to her later fame as the 'French Chef'.

Among Donovan's other female agents were two remarkable women who demonstrated that when it came to bravery and brains, women were the equal of men in the dangerous world of espionage. One was Virginia Hall, daughter of a wealthy Baltimore family. In 1938 she applied to join the U.S. Foreign Service. Her application was rejected because the State Department as a matter of policy did not hire amputees (Hall's left leg had been amputated at the knee after being shattered in a hunting accident some years before). By 1940, she was living in Paris. Eager to help in some way, she volunteered for the ambulance corps and fled to London after France collapsed.

Hall's fluency in French led to her recruitment by MI6's Special Operations Executive (SOE), as its first female operative. She was sent to German-occupied Lyon, where she organized French Resistance units and arranged the arrival of other SOE agents. The tireless work of the 'lady with the limp' inevitably came to the attention of the Lyons Gestapo, headed by the infamous Klaus Barbie. She managed to stay one step ahead of Barbie and his thugs for months, until the Gestapo began plastering every surface in the area with wanted posters containing her picture. Finally, she realized it was time to flee. She headed for Spain, walking several hundred miles and across the Pyrenees to safety despite severe pain from a prosthetic leg that was giving her severe trouble. Once there, she radioed London that 'Cuthbert' (her pet name for her prosthetic leg) was giving her terrible trouble. Assuming 'Cuthbert' meant a French Resistance fighter, SOE headquarters cabled the following reply: 'IF CUTHBERT TROUBLESOME ELIMINATE HIM.'

to use his own intelligence organization. American military commanders in Europe tended to regard the OSS as a hindrance, rather than a resource. The overall American commander, General Dwight D. Eisenhower, was at best neutral toward an organization he felt was insufficiently disciplined and did not provide much in the way of useful intelligence. The OSS encountered complex political problems in other operating areas, particularly Burma and India, where the British were very nervous about the threat to their colonial empire from OSS agents' open encouragement of anti-colonial nationalists. In Indochina, the French became upset when they learned the OSS had recruited a Vietnamese nationalist named Ho Chi Minh, the colonial regime's most dangerous enemy.

Donovan, a dynamic and energetic spymaster, was a man who disdained formality and made it clear he paid little attention to organization charts. Regarded affectionately throughout the ranks, he spent much of his time visiting his troops in far-flung outposts to buck up their morale. If someone had an idea, however crackpot it might seem to be, Donovan was certain to make the time to listen to it.

Donovan also had a reputation for open-mindedness, most prominently demonstrated in his policy of enlisting many women for the organization. That represented quite a departure from traditional espionage practice where women were occasionally recruited as assets, but only

ABOVE: French Resistance fighters are instructed in use of the Sten gun, supplied by the British SOE.

ABOVE: Sefton Delmer, the brilliant propaganda expert who ran British Intelligence's black propaganda operations during World War II.

With America in the war, Hall returned to London and enlisted in the OSS. She was parachuted into southern France. Disguised as an elderly peasant woman, she worked with local Resistance forces, organizing weapons drop zones and fighting with units that destroyed bridges, derailed freight trains and killed scores of German soldiers. At the end of the war, she returned to Baltimore and quietly lived out the rest of her life until her death in 1982 at the age of 78, never discussing her career in espionage, even with her own family. After her death, the family was astounded to find in her safe deposit box an OBE she had been awarded by the British, along with medals for valour from the OSS.

While Hall was eluding the Gestapo in France, another of Donovan's female recruits was involved in an even bigger espionage game, guaranteeing that the projected Allied invasion of North Africa would succeed. Amy Thorpe Pack, the American-born wife of a British diplomat, was a beautiful, restless woman who yearned for adventure. She was unfulfilled in her husband's dull diplomatic postings (although she did try to enliven one such posting in Santiago, Chile, by using the embassy grounds for target shooting after talking the naval attaché into teaching her

how to fire a pistol). In 1937, she discovered espionage as an outlet for her love of danger and excitement, volunteering her services to MI6.

After Pearl Harbor, she switched her services to Donovan, who had just the mission in mind for her. It involved penetrating the Vichy French embassy in Washington, D.C., to get a look at the Vichy military ciphers. The Americans planned an invasion of Vichy French territory in North Africa, which meant that intelligence on the Vichy military forces guarding the project landing sites was vital.

Pack's approach was direct. Posing as a pro-Vichy journalist, she seduced the embassy's press attaché into helping her. He revealed that the ciphers were kept in a large vault in the embassy, which led to a daring plan. Pack and her lover would conduct a presumed tryst in the embassy one night, during which they would unlock a window. A team of OSS safecrackers would enter, deduce the vault's combination, and then remove the cipher books for a waiting team that would rush them to a nearby safe house equipped with a photo studio. The books would be photographed, then replaced before embassy employees returned the next morning.

On the appointed night, Pack and her lover showed up at the embassy. A wink from her lover to the nightwatchman signalled an affaire d'amour about to take place. They entered the room and opened the window. The OSS team was just about to enter through the open window when Pack heard the watchman approaching. Thinking fast, she stripped naked and stood by the door. As the light from the watchman's flashlight illuminated her, she heard him murmur his apologies and quickly retreat, mortified that, as a Frenchman, he had interrupted a session of lovemaking. After he left, the OSS team entered, took the books away and six hours later replaced them. At dawn, an appropriately dishevelled Pack and her lover left the embassy under the bemused gaze of the watchman. Several months later, armed with decryptions of those ciphers by British codebreakers, American forces landing in North Africa neutralized the Vichy forces in less than an hour.

Donovan's greatest contribution to intelligence was an innovation that did not involve any spies. He created a separate branch of the OSS called Research and Analysis, which enlisted every expert he could find on a wide range of subjects. The concept, now standard in modern intelligence organizations, involved submitting intelligence to experts for evaluation on what it all meant. They would also focus their expertise to spot important intelligence clues that agents might miss.

One of the branch's more notable triumphs was locating Germany's synthetic oil plants, which had been carefully hidden and camouflaged to protect them from American bombers. The Air Force, unable to find them, turned to the OSS for help. Infiltrating agents into Nazi Germany for the task would not have worked in a police state of tight controls, so Donovan gave the job to several of the top experts he recruited from the U.S. petroleum industry for his Research and Analysis Branch. In just a month, they were able to pinpoint every German synthetic oil production facility.

It turned out that the experts were aware that German railroads charged a special freight tariff to carry the oil produced by those plants. The tariff was assessed on a sliding scale, depending on distance. An examination of the railroad industry's prewar profit statements found that they included revenue from the tariffs. Those figures allowed them to calculate precisely the distance the railroads had travelled from pick-up to oil storage facility, pinpointing the locations of the plants. Armed with that intelligence, American bombers began taking them out, eventually starving Germany's tanks and planes of fuel.

The British were impressed with Donovan's Research and Analysis Branch, but were much less impressed with the OSS overall. In the British view, too many OSS agents

were hopeless amateurs whose overzealousness caused no end of problems. For their part, many OSS agents who came into close contact with MI6 were not very impressed with what they saw. They were especially critical of MI6's SOE operations in occupied Europe, which had an ambiguous record.

The fundamental problem was that operations to "set Europe ablaze," in Churchill's famous phrase, committed the fatal blunder of combining sabotage and intelligence collection, which are mutually antithetical. Blowing up a bridge instantly alerts enemy counterintelligence that agents are operating in the area, hardly the right atmosphere for intelligence collection. Moreover, too many brave men and women, ill-trained, were sent to their deaths. The Germans penetrated several SOE networks, largely because of sloppy tradecraft and poor radio security.

Donovan and the OSS upper echelon tended to be much less critical of British intelligence. This was largely because, unlike the lower ranks, they were aware of several brilliant British operations that only a restricted number of people knew about. One of them was run by a plump, owlish German émigré whose life was changed one day when he met the KGB's legendary propaganda master, Willi Muenzenberg.

A journalist in the years before the war, Sefton Delmer had struck up a friendship with Muenzenberg, who one day ushered him into one of his greatest operations – black propaganda. Muenzenberg had virtually invented this technique, which involved creating what appeared to be a genuine radio service operated by 'political exiles' – although in fact it was controlled by an intelligence agency to spread dissension and unrest in the target country.

Muenzenberg's masterpiece was called 'Freedom Radio', a powerful transmitter operated by anti-Nazi Germans at a secret location somewhere in Germany (actually, it was located in Paris). Using colloquial German speakers, Freedom Radio broadcast a mixture of gossip and commentary that focused on assorted corruption and sexual peccadilloes of high-ranking Nazi officials. Its credibility was enhanced by highly accurate inside information (provided by the NKVD) and the commentators' down-to-earth approach, along with bitter denunciations of world leaders (among them references to President Roosevelt as a "half-Jew moron".)

Delmer was struck by how many Germans, convinced that the station and its commentators were genuine, would privately repeat choice tidbits they heard on the station. In the event of war, Delmer realized, such black propaganda could prove to be a powerful weapon in the hands of his country. He got his chance at the outbreak of war, when he joined the Political Warfare Executive (PWE), British intelligence's propaganda arm that hoped to repeat the success of British World War I propaganda.

However, Delmer discovered that the people now running the organization had a poor grasp of how the new art of radio propaganda operations should be run. For broadcasts beamed at Germany, it was using émigrés who were ex-academics. Their formal German did not establish a connection with ordinary Germans, who spoke so-called 'low German' full of slang. Further eroding any credibility was the fact that it was clearly an arm of the British government and its basic message – Germany should lose the war – was not one most Germans could embrace. Ordinary Germans did not want to lose the war; they wanted the war to end.

Delmer's criticisms of how the operation was working did not win him any friends in the PWE, but he was lucky enough to attract the attention of one of the more unconventional minds in British intelligence, Ian Fleming. The restless scion of a prominent family who had become bored with a career in the family banking business, Fleming took up journalism, much to the dismay of his family. They would have been further dismayed had they learned Fleming began moonlighting as an amateur spy for MI6. It was a sideline that made him realize he had found his true calling in life: espionage.

Like so many others who had drifted into espionage, Fleming found himself addicted to the excitement and danger of the secret world. Several months before the outbreak of war, Admiral John Godfrey, head of the Naval Intelligence Division (NID), an old friend of the Fleming family, recruited Fleming for his organization. He selected Fleming mainly because he fit the profile of the kind of men Godfrey wanted: bright, young (Fleming was 31) and able to think unconventionally. Godfrey named Fleming as his 'special assistant', in which post he was to think up unconventional ideas for NID operations – the wilder the better.

Fleming would spend the next six years pulling ideas out of his active imagination (a talent useful for his postwar career as the author of the James Bond novels). Among his ideas were a special commando unit made up of misfits that conducted daring espionage missions deep in German-occupied territory, the recruitment of professional thieves to steal advanced German aircraft engines and the enlistment of a team of safecrackers to break into foreign consulates and steal codes and ciphers. When Fleming met Delmer and heard about his ideas for black propaganda operations, he was immediately enthralled. So in turn was Godfrey, who used his considerable influence to pressure PWE into giving Delmer a trial of his ideas.

The traditionalists in PWE were not quite prepared for what happened next. In May 1941, using a super-powerful transmitter hooked into the same wavelength as the official German government radio service, 'Gustav Siegfried Eins'

began broadcasting. Listeners heard a man called 'Der Chef', who described himself as a diehard Prussian officer who loved Germany, but hated the Nazis. He had set up a clandestine radio somewhere in Germany, he said, from which he intended to "tell Germany the truth about the Nazis". Der Chef, who spoke caustically in colloquial German, had equal contempt for Nazis and the leaders of the democracies, especially Churchill, described as "that fat, syphilitic Jew".

Such rhetoric convinced many ordinary Germans that Gustav Siegfried Eins was undoubtedly genuine. Despite the best efforts of the Gestapo to suppress it by decreeing death for anyone caught listening, they continued to do so until late 1944, when Delmer finally closed it down. By then, Gustav Siegfried Eins had played a significant role in undermining German morale through Der Chef's accounts of Nazi corruption and incompetence.

What made Delmer's broadcasts especially effective was the coordination with the other arms of British intelligence. Every scrap of intelligence about conditions inside Germany – from POW debriefings, photo reconnaissance, tidbits from neutral diplomats and businessmen – was integrated into the broadcasts to make them absolutely credible and buttress the fiction that the transmitters were operating from somewhere inside Germany.

Intelligence was particularly important for Delmer's greatest propaganda success – Radio Atlantic. This claimed to be a clandestine short-wave station run by German naval personnel disgusted by what they saw of the Nazi regime's corruption. Beamed on the wavelength used for communications with U-boats, Radio Atlantic's commentators used the most salacious intelligence tidbits to attack the Nazi regime. U-boat crews later taken prisoners by the British reported that Radio Atlantic had a devastating impact on their morale by recounting such stories as the senior German general buying a mink coat for his mistress as his troops were freezing to death in Russia and the lavish seven-course dinner senior Nazi officials attended after ordering still another cut in the daily food rations of ordinary German citizens.

Delmer was occasionally given highly sanitized information from ULTRA for his black propaganda operation, but another operation of British intelligence made much greater use of the golden river of decrypts. Indeed, they were the keys to the most successful counterespionage operation in the history of espionage. Appropriately enough, it was code-named 'DOUBLE CROSS'.

It all began shortly after the outbreak of war in 1939 when a young Oxford academic named Hugh Trevor-Roper joined MI5. He was assigned to a branch known as MI8-C on the organization chart, which was tasked with intercepting and decoding communications used by German intelligence.

RIGHT: Ian Fleming, British intelligence's 'dirty tricks' mastermind during World War II. He later used his experiences for his James Bond series of spy novels.

ABOVE: Identity papers for Dusko Popov, code-named 'TRICYCLE', star agent in MI5's Double Cross operation.

Fluent in German, Trevor-Roper devoted up to 18 hours a day working on intercepted German messages. On Christmas day 1939, he finally made a breakthrough when he discovered that the Germans were using a book code based on the popular novel *Our Hearts Were Young and Gay*.

This knowledge provided MI5 with the perfect counterintelligence weapon. It meant German spies could be pinpointed, then rounded up and executed. However, Trevor-Roper questioned this traditional approach. He argued that reading German intelligence communications presented an unparalleled opportunity to double German agents when they were caught, using them to feed back disinformation. MI5's old guard instantly rejected the idea, noting that a turned agent operation carried the seeds of its own destruction. To make it work, the Germans would have to believe that their spy was sending genuine intelligence – which meant he would have to be given intelligence whose veracity the Germans could check for genuineness. The moment they encountered any cooked material, they would know their spy had been doubled and was now working for

the enemy. Moreover, sending secrets to Germany would defeat the very purpose of arresting and executing the spy in the first place.

This was a shortsighted view, Trevor-Roper insisted. What if, he wondered, British intelligence had some sort of coordinating organization involving all arms of the intelligence and military establishments that would carefully cook a blend of truth and half-truth to be fed back to Germany? Since MI5 was reading German intelligence communications, it could monitor how well that cooked intelligence played and allow the British to fine tune what they were sending. That advantage would also let MI5 know the identities of German spies being sent to Britain.

Fortuitously, a few other MI5 officers – including Dick White, who would later become director of MI5 and eventually MI6 – had arrived at the same conclusion. By sheer dint of effort, they were finally able to talk the MI5 senior leadership into a daring experiment – a committee of key intelligence and military officials to cook intelligence for the purpose of feeding it into captured spies and their radios. Because the committee was so highly secret, it could not be given a formal bureaucratic title, so its participants simply referred to it as 'the XX committee', usually shortened to 'Double Cross', the name by which the overall operation became known.

The Double Cross system had no sooner been set up in early 1940 when there was a sudden influx of German spies. Some were parachuted into the country, others came in the guise of refugees. However they arrived, MI5 was aware of their existence and their assigned missions from the first moment, thanks to the cracking of the Abwehr codes and, subsequently, ULTRA decrypts. A standard processing system evolved: the spy would be immediately taken into custody upon arriving in Britain and shipped to Camp 020, an interrogation center not too far from London. There the spy received the bad news that his interrogators knew exactly who he was and what mission he had been assigned. He was then given a choice: co-operate with us and be spared your life; refuse and expect a firing squad. Unsurprisingly, almost all the spies caught up in the net agreed to co-operate, defined as telling MI5 everything about themselves, their Abwehr recruiters, the codes and radios they would be using and anything else of interest.

Now the real game began. The doubled spy was put into the hands of teams of MI5 radio experts so that they could learn his 'fist', the distinctly different way each human being operates a Morse code key. Once an MI5 radio operator could duplicate the spy's fist perfectly, the next critical step was to establish contact with the Abwehr's main espionage communication center just outside Hamburg. They would report that agent so-and-so had safely landed in England and was now beginning his mission. When Hamburg acknowledged the message and pronounced itself ready to begin receiving the spy's reports, the trap was sprung. Cooked material began to flow to Germany.

Over the next four years, 140 German spies were dispatched to Britain, all of whom fell into the Double Cross net. Not only were German intelligence operations completely balked, but the British also got an unexpected bonus when it turned out that some of the double agents could be used for deception operations, including several German spies detected operating in other countries. Among the early such agents was a hedonistic Yugoslavian banker named Dusko Popov, whom the Abwehr recruited in Lisbon to spy on the British. MI5 quickly detected him, whereupon he agreed to become a double agent.

Popov was carefully built up in German eyes as a man with access to high-level sources in the British establishment and thus the highest levels of the British military. Code-named 'TRICYCLE' by MI5 (a subtle reference to his habit of taking two women to bed at once), the high-living Popov began feeding the Germans cooked material on British military strength after the fall of France. It was sufficient to convince them that an invasion of Britain would be much more difficult than they had supposed.

Another Lisbon-based German spy MI5 turned, a Spaniard named Juan Pujol (code-named 'GARBO'), played a crucial role in the deception plan for the Normandy invasion in 1944. Over a period of several years, the Double Cross system built him up as German intelligence's best agent in Britain, a man who had recruited an entire sub-group of sources within the British military. At the crucial moment on 6 June 1944, GARBO told the Germans that the Normandy landing was actually a feint for the actual invasion, which would take place at Pas de Calais. That cooked intelligence was an important factor in Hitler's decision to withhold reinforcements from the beachhead for a crucial 48 hours.

The dazzling success of the double cross system was attributable, in no small measure, to the nearly unbelievable incompetence of German intelligence. Partially, the incompetence could be explained by Nazi Germany's organizational chaos, particularly in intelligence. However, the leading cause was Hitler himself, who subjected intelligence to his bad habit of making important decisions on the basis of instinct rather than analysis or information. German intelligence in Britain fell victim to this process. In 1937, Hitler expressly forbade his intelligence establishment from undertaking any spy operations in Great Britain. Hitler at that point was convinced he could come to some sort of political accommodation with the British.

By 1940, having changed his mind and concluded that such an accommodation was no longer possible, Hitler summoned his Abwehr chief, Wilhelm Canaris, and ordered him to begin an espionage offensive against Great Britain. Canaris' reaction can only be imagined. Barred from recruiting a single agent in the country for years, he was now expected to materialize an intelligence presence out of thin air. The result was a crash program to recruit dozens of willing volunteers, rush them through a rapid training program that barely covered the basics of espionage and then send them off to Britain – either under cover as alleged refugees or parachuted into the countryside. Even under the best circumstances, it is difficult to see how these ill-trained agents could have accomplished much.

The same kind of incompetence plagued German intelligence operations in the United States and for much the same root cause: Hitler's vacillation. As with the British, Hitler blew hot and cold about the Americans. For years he forbade German intelligence from conducting any espionage in the United States of America, no doubt remembering World War I, when German intelligence's sabotage operations helped draw the Americans into the war. However, as the Americans drew closer to Great Britain, Hitler began to realize he did not know much about the vast U.S. industrial capacity. In the event of war, how long would it take American industry to convert to a total war footing? Once it did, how much war material could be produced? To answer those questions, in the spring of 1940, Hitler ordered an all-out intelligence offensive in America.

BELOW: An aerial view of the Normandy beachhead on D-Day, 6 June 1944. An elaborate deception by Allied intelligence left the Germans unprepared for the invasion.

Once again, German intelligence had to resort to a crash program, which amounted to the only place it could think of for recruits – America's huge German immigrant community. The Abwehr managed to recruit 33 German-Americans, most of them with low-ranking jobs in defence industries. It was not an especially impressive feat, considering that the FBI's counterintelligence capabilities were not very good at that point. In fact, the Bureau believed the Gestapo handled all German intelligence and it had never heard of the Abwehr or the Sicherheitsdienst. However, there remained the problem of transmitting all that intelligence back to Germany. At that point, the Germans committed a monumental intelligence blunder.

The blunder was named William Sebold, a German immigrant living in the United States. His real name was Dembowski; some years before, as a petty criminal, he had served some jail time in Germany. Determined to build a new life, he obtained false papers in the name of Sebold and then emigrated to the United States where he became a naturalized U.S. citizen, beginning a middle class life as an airplane mechanic.

In 1939, on a visit to his ailing mother in Hamburg, the Gestapo picked him up. They offered him a choice: either agree to become a spy for Germany or the Gestapo would inform U.S. authorities that he had obtained his citizenship under a false name which was immediate grounds for deportation. Sebold agreed and found himself whisked off to an Abwehr training school, whose course of instruction included radio communications, at which he excelled. The training completed, Sebold returned to the United States with instructions to provide any intelligence he might encounter in the aircraft industry.

Sebold had no intention of doing anything of the kind. He contacted the FBI, which got the bright idea of using him to infiltrate German intelligence operations in the U.S., a subject it knew little about. The FBI succeeded far beyond its wildest dreams because one day Sebold received in the mail a letter enclosing a strip of microfilm. It announced the

Abwehr was drastically overhauling its system for conveying intelligence collected in the U.S. to Germany. The current system, which used couriers aboard German liners on the New York–Bremen run, was much too slow. Instead, Sebold was informed, he would serve as the collector of that intelligence, which he would radio to Germany via a powerful transmitter the Germans had already set up in New York. The collection would be carried out by means of a front office in a New York City office building, to which the assets would travel and deliver whatever intelligence they had to give Sebold for transmission.

RIGHT: William Sebold (right) and Federick Duquesne, chief German Abwehr agent in the U.S., covertly photographed by an FBI surveillance team in 1940.

It is hard to imagine a graver violation of all the elementary rules of espionage tradecraft, especially compartmentalization. Sebold would meet all the Abwehr assets in the United States, which meant he could reveal them all in the event he was arrested, to say nothing of what he knew about the intelligence they had collected. For the FBI, it was a counterintelligence agency's dream. Sebold dutifully opened the front operation, called Diesel Research Corporation. Day after day, the assets strolled into the office, turning over their material, all the while photographed and recorded by an FBI movie camera behind a mirror on one wall.

The FBI took the reports in hand. With the co-operation of the military services, they reworked them into a melange of truth and half-truth and sent them on via Sebold's radio. The Bureau kept the game going for 16 months, until growing German suspicions about the material it was receiving from Sebold meant it was time to close down the operation. In January 1942, the FBI struck, arresting all 33 of the Abwehr assets and decapitating German intelligence in America in one blow, from which the Germans never recovered.

If the record of the Abwehr was poor, the performance of its chief competitor, the SD, was even worse. From the moment of its creation by Reinhard Heydrich, the SD was an organization dominated by Nazi ideology and a relentless campaign to eliminate its rival, the Abwehr. As part of the Nazi security establishment, the SD was deeply involved in the genocide against Europe's Jews. It was staffed largely by men Canaris bitterly called "gentlemen killers" – university graduates who believed that slaughtering millions of people was justified in the cause of advancing Nazi ideology. Its intelligence product tended to be dominated by Nazi racism, such as the report which solemnly informed Hitler that Roosevelt's real name was 'Rosenfeld'.

SD's foreign intelligence operations were run by Walter Schellenberg, a committed Nazi who had no intelligence experience, but nevertheless considered himself a spymaster of genius. To prove it, he undertook a number of bizarre operations which proved only that he had a vivid imagination. One involved recruiting the famous French fashion designer Coco Chanel, apparently hoping she would gather intelligence from her wide contacts in the fashion world. Predictably, the recruitment was a failure, since the possibility that anyone in that world would ever have any contact with important intelligence was remote, at best.

Another operation Schellenberg conceived demonstrated even less judgment. Known as Operation Willi, the idea behind it was to capitalize on the Duke of Windsor's pro-Nazi sympathies by kidnapping him while he was on a trip to Spain and taking him to Germany, where he would denounce his own country and urge his former subjects to surrender. Even assuming that the Duke would agree to urge Britain to surrender, Schellenberg failed to understand that there was no possibility that a million Britons would lay down their arms simply because an ex-monarch asked them to do so.

No one was more delighted by this record of German intelligence ineptitude than William Stephenson, the chief British spy in the United States. He had more than enough to worry about without having to be concerned with cunning German spies. Officially, Stephenson was head of the innocuous-sounding British Security Coordination, based in New York City. He had arrived there in May 1940, with a broad mission that amounted to repeating the World War I success of William Wiseman, especially getting the United States into the war.

counterespionage, the guarding of British installations from German sabotage, propaganda and the conduct of covert operations. However, he concentrated most of his efforts on his chief task of getting America into the war. To achieve it, he would eventually recruit nearly 3,000 assets and agents for a covert operation that dwarfed anything like it in the history of espionage.

A tireless spymaster, Stephenson recruited anyone whom he thought would be of help, including the mystery writer Rex Stout, who wrote propaganda material that Stephenson planted in the columns of another asset he recruited, Walter Winchell. Stephenson's reach extended into Hollywood, where he talked Cary Grant out of enlisting for military service. Instead he persuaded the British-born star to serve as his eyes and ears in the film world, keeping watch for any movie stars who were sufficiently right wing to be lured into aiding the Nazi cause.

Pearl Harbor – and Hitler's ill-considered decision to declare war on the United States four days later – finally accomplished Stephenson's prime objective in America. However, before that, his covert political action operation had succeeded in seriously undercutting the isolationist movement and snuffing out any attempt by Nazi Germany to win influence or sympathy in the United States, even among the more than ten million Americans of German ancestry. Perhaps more importantly, Stephenson forged a strong Anglo-American intelligence alliance that remains to this day. His influence on the future structure and course of American intelligence was profound. That accomplishment earned him the Medal of Merit, the United States' highest civilian decoration. He was the first non-American ever to win it.

This task, as Stephenson was the first to realize, would be a lot harder to accomplish in 1940 than it was in 1917. According to the public opinion polls, over 80 per cent of Americans wanted no part of a European war, a sentiment that had spawned a very powerful anti-intervention movement called America First. Although German intelligence was inept, it had not repeated its World War I mistake of antagonizing Americans by blowing up their factories and sabotaging their ships.

To accomplish his main goal, Stephenson's mandate was very wide. It included all British intelligence operations,

However, there was another honour he received that spoke volumes of his service to British intelligence: a knighthood. "This one," Churchill said as he wrote out his recommendation for it, "is near and dear to my heart."

And with that, Stephenson's British Security Coordination operation – immortalized by its communications code name of 'INTREPID' – was closed down, its mission accomplished.

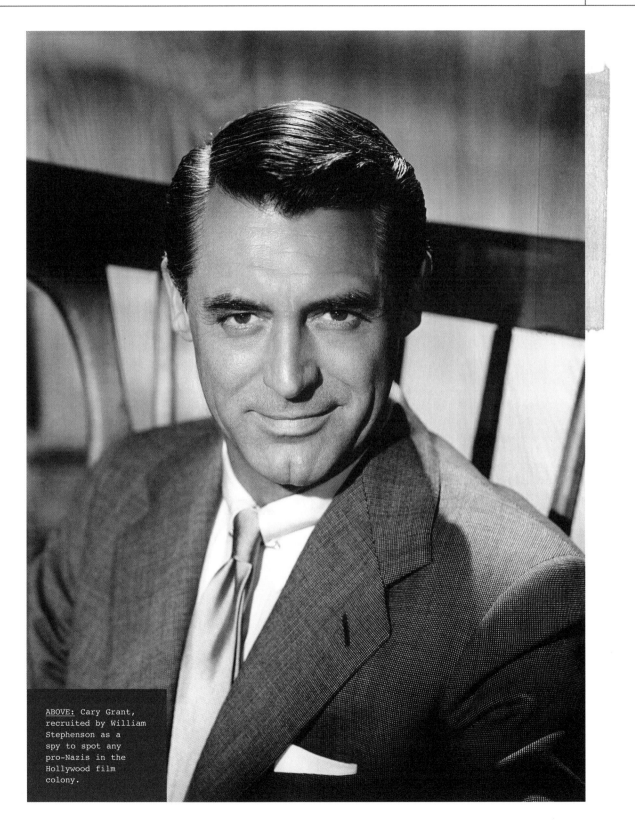

ABOVE: Cary Grant, recruited by William Stephenson as a spy to spot any pro-Nazis in the Hollywood film colony.

DEUS EX MACHINA:
CRACKING THE ULTRA CODE

EVEN THE WORLDLY-WISE MEN OF THE DEUXIÈME BUREAU, FRANCE'S MILITARY INTELLIGENCE AGENCY, HAD NEVER SEEN ANYTHING QUITE LIKE IT.

The plump, heavyset German who was their prize asset had an appetite for the high life that defied belief – lavish, champagne-fueled dinners with up to four prostitutes at ritzy hotels, followed by wild sex marathons with them that lasted until dawn. As Frenchmen, they admired that kind amatory energy, but as intelligence agents, they were appalled. Such flashy behavior, they counseled him, tends to attract the attention of counterintelligence and was certain to get him arrested sooner or later.

Characteristically, Hans Thilo-Schmidt paid no attention. As the men of the Deuxième Bureau were aware, Thilo-Schmidt, a completely amoral creature dedicated solely to making a lot of money, was a man who marched only to the sound of his own drummer. It was a characteristic that was obvious from the first moment he became a Deuxième Bureau asset on a summer day in 1931, when he walked into the office of the French military attaché in Berlin and offered to betray his country. After outlining what he had to offer, Thilo-Schmidt then laid down his non-negotiable conditions. He would never meet with the French on German soil, would initiate contact only at times of his own choosing, would only deliver his material in face-to-face meetings with senior Deuxième Bureau officials on weekends and holidays (to explain his absences) and, above all, would be paid a lot of money.

The French happily assented to all these conditions, even the last, because Thilo-Schmidt was that rarity in espionage – pure gold. A cipher clerk in the OKW (the German military high command), Thilo-Schmidt had access to something the French considered beyond price – Enigma, the code machine that enciphered all of Germany's most secret communications. Two years before, the Deuxième Bureau had learned that Germany, heeding the lessons of its cryptographic disasters in World War I, had completely overhauled German secret communications. The Germans bought the rights to a Swiss-produced code machine originally intended for commercial use, drastically overhauled and upgraded it, finally producing a technical marvel that could produce up to 26 million possible word combinations with each keystroke. The first intercepted Enigma

signals confirmed the worst French fears – the messages produced by the machine were absolutely unbreakable. The only hope was for the Deuxième Bureau somehow to get its hands on the technical secrets of those machines.

This was not a simple task. The Germans guarded their Enigmas like crown jewels. Just as the French despaired of ever getting an insight into Enigma, Thilo-Schmidt walked into their lives. At his first covert meeting with the French at a small village in Belgium, he handed over an instructional manual for Enigma, along with some technical papers on the machine's enciphering system. The stunned French intelligence agents then handed over, in cash, the first payment he demanded – $10,000 in American money (somewhere around £200,000 in today's currency. Thilo-Schmidt immediately spent some of the money on a night of wine, women, and song.

This French intelligence coup, which would soon give them the first inroads into Enigma, was a small rivulet. In time it would merge with rivulets from three other countries – Poland, Great Britain and the United States – to become the most extraordinary story in the history of espionage.

THE BIGGEST CODE OF ALL

The common thread that ran through the developments in those three countries was an insight which occurred to several brilliant men at the same time: a revolution in cryptanalysis was at hand. No longer could cryptanalysis use the traditional pencil and paper methods of nimble minds relying mostly on intuition. Enigma signified the dominance of code machines, a technology whose ability to generate millions of possible ciphered combinations with the tap of one key made attack by conventional methods useless. The solution – cryptanalytic establishments must recruit mathematicians who could divine the spin of the machine rotors and various electrical connections from the signals they generated, which would then be used to replicate the machines.

In Poland, the Biro Szyfrow 4, Polish military intelligence's cipher section, quietly began poring through the records of mathematical students at the University of Poznan. They finally emerged with 20

ABOVE: German soldiers dispatch a message enciphered by the Enigma machine in 1942, unaware that every word was being read by the British.

of the most brilliant. These were recruited for work described as so secret they would not be permitted to tell their wives or families. The glittering star among them was Marian Rejewski, among the world's leading experts on permutation theory, an esoteric branch of mathematics that led him to deduce the electric wiring of each of the rotors on the Enigma machine.

In the United States, meanwhile, the leading American codebreaker, William F. Friedman of the Army Security Agency, was recruiting the country's best mathematicians for what he described as an "interesting adventure". That turned out to be an attack against 'PURPLE', the codename for the main cryptographic machine of Japan, America's perceived enemy.

What would prove to be the most significant development came in Great Britain, where the Government Code and Cipher School, the country's cryptographic agency, went trawling among the best mathematicians at Oxford and Cambridge for the British assault against Enigma. Their prize recruit was a young Cambridge graduate student, Alan Turing, whose early work on "computing machines" had already put him in the first rank of the world's mathematicians.

The outbreak of World War II merged these four streams into one mighty river. Both the Polish and French efforts were melded into the British program after the collapse of Poland and the fall of France. In 1941, the covert intelligence relationship between the United States and Great Britain extended into cryptography. The British let the Americans in on their work against Enigma, while Friedman's operation turned over a copy of the Japanese PURPLE machine they had managed to construct by deducing its interior electrical system (an amazing

LEFT: The cipher machine Enigma. Nazi Germany was convinced it was unbreakable, but Polish and British codebreakers proved otherwise.

feat, codenamed MAGIC, that was the cryptographic equivalent of cloning a human being without ever seeing the twin).

The enhanced British effort, codenamed ULTRA, was termed "the geese who laid the golden eggs," by Winston Churchill. It was no exaggeration. In 1940, ULTRA began to read high-level messages transmitted over a machine the Germans trusted totally. No wonder, as Turing calculated the theoretical number of possible configurations an Enigma machine could generate was 3 x 10 to the 114th power, a mind-boggling number. However large it was, Turing deduced that the number was finite. To get a handle on it, he would need to come up with some sort of technology capable of sorting through all those possible combinations to spot the machine's settings. His solution borrowed an idea first formulated by Rejewski – a large-scale calculating machine that sorted through all the possible machine settings for any given message. Rejewski called his device a bombe, named after a popular brand of Polish ice cream.

In honor of Rejewski's efforts, Turing adopted the same name for a refined and much larger device of his own design. It was a monster some seven feet long and six feet high, weighing more than a ton. When turned on, its thousands of vacuum tubes, pulleys and electromagnetic connections rattled into action, sounding like some sort of contraption out of science fiction. In fact, it was the world's first computer, a machine whose basic operating system functioned just the way a modern computer does. It had a vast memory that stored all the possible Enigma combinations and was activated by a program that ordered the memory to search an intercepted message for its cipher key.

By late 1941, ULTRA was reading German messages almost as fast as they were transmitted. In some cases, the British decrypted messages before their intended recipients received them. Special attention was focused on German U-boats, the single greatest threat to the long seaborne supply line from America to Europe. Fortunately for the ULTRA cryptanalysts, they had a lot of U-boat traffic to work with, since directing boats to patrol areas and co-ordinating attacks by wolf packs (groups of submarines directed to a common target) generated a lot of messages. By 1943, the priceless intelligence from ULTRA made Germany's U-boat force an open book. ULTRA proved to be the decisive factor that won the Battle of the Atlantic, a secret the Allies took the greatest pains to conceal. As long as the Germans believed their naval communications via Enigma were safe, they would not change the system.

The Allies' uncanny ability to detect and destroy his U-boats caused Admiral Karl Doenitz, head of the U-boat force, to wonder if his communications had been compromised. He ordered a full-scale review, which emerged with the judgment that since the Enigma's mathematical possibilities were somewhere in the stratosphere, there was no possibility that German naval messages were being read. Much the same conclusion was reached by Japanese cryptographers, who concluded that since PURPLE, used for high-level diplomatic traffic, had so many mathematical possibilities, no known cryptanalytical method could crack it. They also noted that, if the Americans had cracked PURPLE, then why were they so unprepared at Pearl Harbor?

Fate was not kind to the four men who played the key roles in this cryptanalytical saga. Marian Rejewski returned to Poland after the war, but discovered the new Communist government did not trust him. He was shuffled off to a boring job overseeing an industrial enterprise and never worked on a code or cipher the rest of his life. William F. Friedman, who had suffered a nervous breakdown during the intense work cracking PURPLE, spent the rest of his life haunted by the question of why his government failed to use his great achievement to anticipate Pearl Harbor. As his French handlers predicted, a flamboyant lifestyle led the Gestapo to Hans Thilo-Schmidt in 1942. When they finished wringing from him everything he knew, he was shot.

Alan Turing's fate was the saddest. After the war, he returned to Cambridge and a private life as a homosexual, when that was a serious crime in Great Britain. In 1952, he was arrested for having sex with a 19-year-old man and offered a choice – either go to jail or agree to undergo experimental hormone treatments designed to 'cure' homosexuality. He decided on the treatments, which caused him agonizing pain and greatly enlarged his breasts.

Unable to bear the pain and embarrassment any longer, one morning in 1954 Turing prepared a cyanide concoction in his home laboratory, injected it into an apple and then took a bite. He was dead within minutes. Only four people, one of them his mother, attended the funeral. Almost four years to the day after his death, homosexuality was decriminalized in Great Britain.

Turing would come to be immortalized, not for his role in ULTRA, but for his greater contribution to the machine that created the Information Age. Some 20 years after his death, two 19-year-old American college students, working in their parents' garage, put together the first complete home computer. The machine, as well as their new company, was called Apple. Only a few people understood the significance of the company's logo – a once-bitten apple.

THE MOLE WARS

As dawn broke
that April morning in 1967,
Colonel Tran van Trung of the
B1 Intelligence Service of the
Democratic Republic of Vietnam
began his mission.

LEFT: During the Vietnam War, the North Vietnamese used the extensive network of underground tunnels they had built as communications and supply routes, as well as to conceal troops and escape from heavy U.S. bombardments.

After carefully checking to see if there was any possible surveillance (there was none, he concluded), he climbed into his rickety old sedan and began driving north. As he drove out of the city of Saigon, he passed the large U.S. embassy building. On the building's second floor, Tran van Trung knew, the CIA had been working all night processing the latest raw intelligence gathered from throughout north and south Vietnam. All the data was fed into their computers – body counts, number of villages under South Vietnamese government control, percentage of the countryside dominated by the Viet Cong and amount of enemy supplies captured.

Outside the city limits, Trung passed the sprawling Bien Hoa air base, from which American air reconnaissance flights were taking off on missions over North Vietnam, Laos and Cambodia. Their advanced cameras were able to take long strips of photographs that would later be put together in large mosaics showing objects on the ground measuring just a few inches in diameter. Meanwhile, U.S. spy satellites were flying far overhead, some of them with cameras to snap pictures of North Vietnamese industrial installations, others with advanced electronics to vacuum up radio and telephone transmissions that would be sent to the National Security Agency for processing. Inside a nondescript building on the base, bristling with antennas, technicians were combing the airwaves for any signals from North Vietnamese tactical radios.

Twenty miles northwest of Saigon, Trung reached a small village. He parked his car out of sight, behind a house. As he got out of the car, two men suddenly materialized. Without a word, he followed them on a path through rice paddies to the edge of the Ho Bo Woods. There, one of the men accompanying him rapped sharply on a tree with a stick. In response, two Viet Cong guerrillas with AK-47s appeared and, with a brief nod of recognition, led Trung deep into the woods. After walking some distance, they stopped at a tree stump. Behind it, one of the guerrillas reached into a pile of leaves and lifted a trapdoor, revealing the entrance to a tunnel. Trung entered it, switching on a small flashlight. After walking quite some distance, he emerged into a large,

well-lighted room filled with a dozen men. They talked a brief while and then Trung handed over a roll of film.

His mission completed, Trung retraced his steps and headed back to Saigon. Meanwhile, the roll of film began a complex journey to Hanoi. Couriers took it to a Viet Cong post on the Cambodian border, where armed guards carried the film to Phnom Penh and turned it over to contacts from Chinese intelligence. In turn, they flew the film to Guangzhou, in southern China, from which it was rushed to B1 headquarters. The film was then developed to reveal some 100 pages of intelligence that Trung had typed on a battered Hermes machine and then transferred to film. Those pages contained a month's work of intelligence Trung had collected, a wide range of information on the internal doings of the South Vietnamese government, American military plans and what American diplomats were reporting to the State Department.

Back in Saigon, Trung went to work at his job in the press center as interpreter, legman and highly informed source for a dozen news organizations. They knew him as Pham Xuan An, a smiling, charming man noted for a mind capable of absorbing and retaining huge amounts of detail – a perfect attribute for a journalist and a spy. Since 1963, he had been the indispensable assistant to newspaper and television journalists, who hired him to draw on his unparalleled sources within the South Vietnamese government and his in-depth knowledge of the country. He became a fixture at the Vietnam war's nexus, around which diplomats, soldiers and journalists freely exchanged gossip and assorted tidbits of information. Like a camera, the mind of Pham Xuan An recorded everything he heard. Later, he emptied whatever was in that photographic memory into an intelligence report. Each month, when the report was ready, he would follow an unfailing routine: a drive out of Saigon to the small village, allegedly to visit his aged mother, a hike into the woods and a rendezvous with fellow officers of B1 to turn over his film.

Completely unsuspected, An would follow this routine for 12 years. It only stopped when one day in 1975, when North Vietnamese tanks rumbled into the grounds of the

Presidential Palace, marking the end of South Vietnam and the long war. An showed up for work, as usual, but this time dressed in the uniform of a colonel in the North Vietnamese Army. His chest was bedecked with medals awarded for his work as spy, the most valuable his country ever had.

The cost to North Vietnam of An's intelligence operation was exactly $1.19 a week, the expense of a roll of ordinary film. No reliable estimate is possible on how much American intelligence spent in Vietnam during the time of An's service, but a safe guess would be somewhere in the low billions for all those spy satellites, computers, analysts, agents and thousands of South Vietnamese assets. It was money wasted. American intelligence in Vietnam was a colossal failure. It never developed any sources in North Vietnam and consistently underestimated that country's willingness to fight on against the world's mightiest industrial power. It was also inevitably surprised by major Communist military offensives and politicized what intelligence it did collect to boost the preconceptions of policymakers.

In 1967, while An was telling the North Vietnamese just about everything they needed to know, U.S. President Lyndon B. Johnson was demanding that the U.S. military and intelligence establishments show him "real progress" in the war. Dutifully, military intelligence concluded that there were then about 250,000 enemy forces – Viet Cong and North Vietnamese regulars – fighting in South Vietnam, a significant reduction in the total from the previous year. That meant the American military effort was approaching the fabled 'crossover point', when the rate of enemy casualties would outpace their ability to replace them.

CIA analysts were appalled; they did not know much about Vietnam, but they could count. They counted somewhere around 580,000 enemy forces, actually an increase over the previous year. However, CIA Director Richard Helms, reluctant to bear Johnson's wrath if he presented him with such a figure, ordered the analysts to compromise. The result: an intelligence report to Johnson concluding there were 290,000 enemy forces, representing real progress – the basis for Johnson's optimistic pronouncements about real progress and the famous "light at the end of the tunnel".

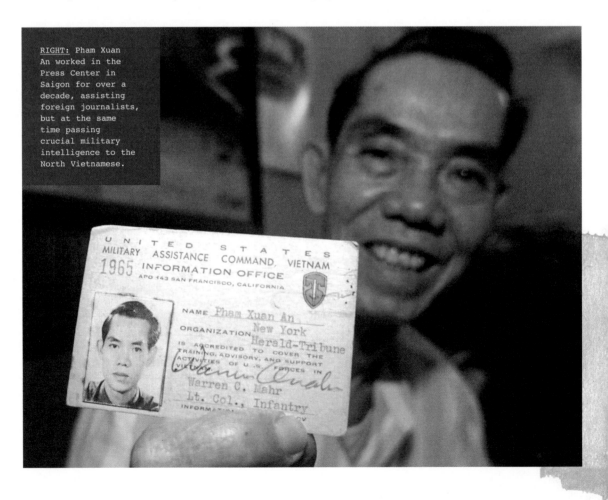

RIGHT: Pham Xuan An worked in the Press Center in Saigon for over a decade, assisting foreign journalists, but at the same time passing crucial military intelligence to the North Vietnamese.

UNITED STATES MILITARY ASSISTANCE COMMAND, VIETNAM
1965 INFORMATION OFFICE
APO 143 SAN FRANCISCO, CALIFORNIA

NAME Pham Xuan An
ORGANIZATION New York Herald-Tribune
IS ACCREDITED TO COVER THE TRAINING, ADVISORY, AND SUPPORT ACTIVITIES OF U.S. FORCES IN VI...

Warren C. Mahr
Lt. Col., Infantry
INFORMAT...

Several months later, the Communist Tet offensive erupted, belying all the optimism, proving the intelligence wrong and destroying public support for the war. On 26 March 1968, Johnson asked for a private briefing by the CIA's analysts on what he called "the reality" of Vietnam. He gave them exactly 15 minutes. Unfettered at last, the analysts delivered the unvarnished truth: Communist forces had been underestimated by one half; the pacification program was a shambles; the bombing of North Vietnam was a failure and the North Vietnamese, no matter their losses, would fight on for another one hundred years, if necessary. Johnson listened quietly, then left the room without saying a word. Five days later, he announced a halt to the U.S. bombing of North Vietnam and his intention not to seek re-election.

What happened in Vietnam stands as a perfect example of how, after World War II, espionage became very much a function of size – big and small. The 'big' meant the vast, sprawling intelligence establishments of the industrialized powers, mainly the United States and the Soviet Union. Drawing on the hard lessons of World War II and the intelligence disasters they had suffered, large nations concluded that the key to avoiding future such disasters was centralized intelligence. This meant a single government espionage agency responsible for coordinating the production of all intelligence. To that end, they invested huge sums to construct an intelligence apparatus they believed would give them insight into the plans of their enemies and provide warning of potential and approaching danger. These structures covered every possible aspect of intelligence – scientific and technical experts to evaluate the latest advances in military technology; teams of analysts to process raw intelligence into finished estimates; thousands of agents operating everywhere in the world; training schools capable of turning out a hundred agents at a time; large-scale cryptological units utilizing the most advanced technology and round-the-clock reconnaissance operations.

The largest espionage establishment was built by the Soviet Union, which by the end of World War II had more than 150,000 employees. It also had an equivalent number of border guards (a task traditionally assigned to Soviet Intelligence) and thousands of local informers. That structure was constantly expanded, until by the 1980s, the KGB – successor agency to the NKVD – had some 500,000 employees, plus 220,000 men in its border security forces. The GRU, Soviet military intelligence, had some 10,000 employees by war's end. The espionage establishment of the Soviet Union's greatest rival, the United States, had far fewer employees – the exact number is classified, but is unofficially estimated to be around 50,000. However, it had much larger components devoted to cryptological operations and reconnaissance.

Judged strictly in terms of size and breadth, it would seem that such large intelligence structures as the Soviet and American establishments would have a decisive advantage. However, as things turned out, it was the espionage agencies of the 'smalls' that conducted the most successful operations. Largely, that was because without the kind of resources that a superpower could invest in intelligence, they were forced to concentrate on the most affordable basic weapon of espionage – people. Their efforts focused on developing the most suitable human beings they could find into agents capable of operating independently, comfortable in deep cover and willing to work in conditions of great danger. The operating philosophy was simple: the greatest espionage instrument ever invented was not the computer, spy satellite or a tiny electronic bug; it was a human being. No nation demonstrated that truth better than one of the world's smallest nations, Israel.

Israeli intelligence was born in the perfect environment for espionage, the underground struggle of the Zionists in Palestine, where Jewish settlers had to deal with both the British Mandate authorities and the sea of largely hostile Arabs around them. It was a situation further complicated by the Zionists' attempts to move European Jews threatened by the Holocaust to safety in Palestine – attempts the British were working hard to defeat, since they would upset the delicate balance between Jew and Arab in the Mandate. To keep track of it all, the Zionist movement created an intelligence service called Sherut Yediot (commonly called Shai) that actively recruited among Jewish civil servants of the Mandate administration.

In one recruitment operation that would have far-reaching consequences for the future, Shai recruited a network of young, native-born Palestinian Jews and put them through an intensive espionage training course run by veteran operatives from the Zionist underground movements in Europe. Known as 'the Arab boys' within Shai for their fluency in Arabic, they were trained not only to operate within Palestine, but also to serve as deep-cover agents in Arab countries. Shai's greatest moment came in 1948, when it ran a worldwide series of covert arms acquisitions which proved vital for the Jewish forces in the war that led to the creation of the state of Israel. Tons of arms were obtained from a myriad of sources (including gangsters Mickey Cohen and Meyer Lansky in the United States) and smuggled through a British blockade.

When the state of Israel decided to create a new foreign intelligence service called Mossad, it could draw on the large number of sources and trained agents Shai had developed. The leaders of the new agency were all veterans of underground work, sometimes extending back for decades. They never had a lot of money to work with, so they built the ranks by carefully developing agents who could meet very high standards of independent thinking, meticulous attention to tradecraft and ability to operate seamlessly in a foreign (and often dangerous) environment. The agency's senior leadership tended to operate like high-stakes gamblers, taking great risks in daring operations very few other intelligence agencies would attempt. Not all of them succeeded, but many of the successes were spectacular – kidnapping Nazi war criminal Adolph Eichmann, rescuing terrorist captives in Uganda, stealing a seven-ton radar station in Egypt and infiltrating the Syrian high command. The Mossad would come to acquire a reputation as the best human intelligence service in the world and the reputation was well-deserved.

Even the Russians, who fancied themselves the premier human intelligence practitioners, ruefully admitted that the Israelis often outclassed them. They had in mind, among other examples, the case of Viktor Grayevsky, a prominent journalist with many high-level sources in the Polish Communist Party and government. He was recruited in 1955 as a KGB asset, but Grayevsky didn't bother telling the KGB that his real name was Spielman and that he had already been a Mossad asset for several years. Angered by the Soviet Union's growing anti-Semitism, Grayevsky sought a way to take it out on the KGB. He got his chance in 1956, when one of his sources in the Polish Communist Party returned to Warsaw from the Twentieth Party Congress in Moscow and gave Grayevsky a blockbuster. It was the text of a secret speech by then-Soviet Premier Nikita Khrushchev delivered to the Congress, in which he denounced Stalin, complete with a full bill of particulars of his crimes. Grayevsky rushed the text to his Mossad contact in Warsaw (an Israeli diplomat), who in turn sped it off to Tel Aviv.

The Mossad, instantly recognizing its potential as a propaganda weapon to disrupt Communist parties all over the world, turned over the text to the CIA, which made it public. The KGB frantically tried to track down the source of the leak, but never succeeded. Several years later, Grayevsky emigrated to Israel, where he was re-recruited by an unsuspecting KGB, this time to provide intelligence on the Israeli government. He immediately informed Mossad, which used him as a conduit for disinformation until 1971, when the KGB finally learned that Grayevsky/Spielman was the man who had caused them so much damage years before.

Israeli intelligence's finest hour came in 1967, when the nightmare of a war on three fronts loomed on the borders of Jordan, Egypt and Syria. The situation mandated not just good intelligence, but perfect intelligence. Even one error might mean defeat for the vastly outnumbered Israelis. As Aharon Yariv, head of Aman (Israeli military intelligence) told his chief subordinates, it was not enough for Israel to know the numbers and capabilities of the Egyptian Air Force, "I want to know what menus are in the goddam Egyptian sergeants' mess!"

That is precisely what his agents were able to tell him and a lot more besides. They were able to provide: the operating schedules of Egyptian air units, the quality of maintenance on their planes and even the names of individual pilots (on the day the war broke out, they were astounded to receive personal radio messages from Israel advising them not to attempt to fly, since they would almost certainly die). Armed with precise intelligence, the Israeli Air Force wiped out its Egyptian counterpart in just over two hours, destroying almost all its planes on the ground. The Egyptian Army fared no better. The Israelis had very precise intelligence on its strength and operational plans, a major reason why it was so decisively defeated when it encountered the Israeli Army in the Sinai.

The man who made that possible was a Mossad spy named Wolfgang Lotz, who had worked in Egypt for several years under cover of a rich German businessman passionately interested in raising horses. This part of his cover was designed to lure a number of Egyptian Army officers, ex-cavalrymen, who shared the same passion. Lotz, armed with lavish Mossad funds (agency auditors called him 'Champagne Spy' for all the money he needed to maintain his luxurious cover), bought a large horse farm to which he invited Egyptian officers. Lotz patiently worked himself into their confidence, using his alleged World War II service with the legendary 'Desert Fox' General Erwin Rommel, a sainted figure to the Egyptians. Lotz also made sure to work anti-Semitism and anti-Israel comments into his social conversation, further strengthening the bond. Before long, the officers were consulting this presumed expert on desert warfare about what he thought of their plans to fight the Israelis in the deserts of Sinai.

A similar disaster struck the Syrian Army and, again, it was a Mossad spy who was largely responsible. The spy's name was Eli Cohen, an Egyptian-born Jew fluent in Arabic. The Mossad targeted him against Syria, a dangerous military threat. The Israelis were especially concerned about the Golan Heights that overlooked northern Israel, which the Syrians were busy fortifying with bunkers and protected artillery positions. Under cover as a rich Syrian businessman and playboy, Cohen's lavish parties attracted the elite of the Syrian government and military, whom Cohen seduced with expensive gifts and beautiful women. He became fast friends with a number of senior Syrian military officers, who took him to the Golan Heights and proudly showed off the 'impregnable' line of fortifications they were building. Cohen made some appropriately admiring comments, but then added a suggestion. The heat was often oppressive on the heights, he told the officers, causing undue suffering among the crews manning the bunkers and dug-in artillery. He suggested that eucalyptus trees should be planted around the positions, to provide shade from the hot sun. A brilliant

suggestion, the Syrians decided and trees were soon planted around the positions.

When war broke out shortly afterward, Israeli pilots and artillery gunners had no trouble pinpointing just where those positions were located. Tragically, Cohen did not live to see his great triumph. Two days before the war broke out, a team of Russian radio-detection experts requested by the Syrians to track down a clandestine radio they had detected located his radio. He was horribly tortured, then hanged in a public square in Damascus.

Another of the 'smalls' that racked up an impressive record for its size was the Hauptverwaltung Aufklarung (HVA), East Germany's foreign intelligence service. Its success was largely attributable to its director, one the century's great spymasters. His name was Markus Wolf, a dedicated German Communist who had spent most of his early life in the Soviet Union, where his Communist parents fled to escape the rise of Hitler and the Nazis. He had followed the standard KGB career path: recruitment by the KGB from the Comintern school, where he was being trained for underground work, intensive instruction in the KGB's own training school and a first assignment to test his suitability. In Wolf's case, that first assignment was in occupied Germany in 1946, under cover as a journalist covering the Nuremberg Trials. He did well enough to attract the attention of the KGB's upper echelon. However, before he could be assigned to another mission, Wolf convinced them that he was the right man to head up the foreign intelligence agency the Russians were creating for the new state of East Germany. In 1952, he went to work and quickly demonstrated his singular talent for espionage.

Long considered the model for the character of 'Karla', the Soviet spymaster in John le Carré's espionage novels, Wolf's forte was patience. He often spent years inserting long-term penetration agents into NATO and the government, military and intelligence structures of West Germany – his favourite target. At one point, he had nearly 4,000 agents in that country and several other NATO countries. All of them maintained ordinary lives until Wolf decided they had reached the point where they were ready to be switched on. He also had a hand in East Germany's pervasive surveillance of its citizens, particularly the more famous – such as Olympic skater Katerina Witt, whom he was determined to prevent from defecting.

Wolf's most famous mole was Gunther Guillaume, a low-ranking employee of an East German publishing house in 1955 when Wolf decided he would be the perfect man to infiltrate the West German government. What about Guillaume convinced Wolf he would be a good penetration agent remains unknown, but he turned out to be a spectacular success. In 1956, Guillaume 'escaped' to Germany with his wife, opened a small copying business and joined the local branch of the Social Democrats, volunteering for a number of party duties. That work was rewarded in 1969 with an appointment as junior assistant to the newly-elected Social Democrat chancellor, Willy Brandt.

Finally, 14 years after Wolf had set him in motion, he was in a position to return dividends on the investment. Guillaume came to be Brandt's senior aide, in which position he began to see many classified documents, all of which he shipped eastward. Even better, Brandt began to confide in him, sharing even more secrets. To Wolf's distress, Guillaume was tripped up in 1974, when the U.S. National Security Agency cracked the codes Wolf was using to keep in contact with his moles in West Germany. One of the messages mentioned a high-level spy in the chancellory with a newborn son – a perfect profile of Guillaume. However, by that point, Guillaume had forwarded a lot of high-level intelligence eastward.

Wolf shared that intelligence with the KGB, as he did the material gathered from many of his other, more important, sources. These included 'TOPAZ', a French asset who worked in NATO headquarters in Brussels and the deputy head of the Soviet Bloc Division of the BND, West Germany's foreign intelligence service. The KGB was very grateful for Wolf's sources. This was because, beginning in 1945, it began to encounter some serious problems with its human sources – for many years the bedrock of Soviet intelligence's espionage operations.

The networks of both the KGB and the GRU in Europe had suffered extensive damage during the war. At the war's end, the Russians were attempting to rebuild them, while at the same time working to build new intelligence agencies in the Eastern European nations in the Soviet orbit. No rebuilding was necessary in Great Britain and the United States, where the large networks Soviet intelligence had built before the war remained intact – and very productive, especially the British 'Ring of Five'. In the United States, more than 300 assets were still at work, including several members of the OSS, two State Department officials, an assistant to the President and an assistant Secretary of the Treasury. The network had proven invaluable for Soviet intelligence's most successful World War II operation, obtaining the secrets of the U.S. atomic bomb project.

The Soviets had every reason to expect that this espionage empire, composed of a series of rings, would continue to produce valuable intelligence, since both British and American intelligence seemed unaware of their existence. However, on the morning of 2 September 1945, Igor Gouzenko, a 24-year-old GRU code clerk at the Soviet embassy in Ottawa, Canada, picked up a newspaper and read a short article that absolutely stunned him. To Gouzenko, already afflicted by doubts about life in his own country, as contrasted by what he saw of the freedoms enjoyed by the people of Canada, the story was something of an epiphany. A Greek fruit merchant was suing the city for constructing a new road in such a way that it was destroying his business.

Gouzenko clipped out the story and showed it to his co-workers. Was this not the most amazing thing they had ever seen, he asked, a lowly citizen actually suing his own government? This was a mistake. One of his co-workers reported him to the embassy's security unit. Within 24 hours, Gouzenko was ordered to return to Moscow a week hence for 'reassignment'. Gouzenko knew what that meant and on 5 September 1945, he stashed hundreds of decrypted GRU telegrams inside his clothes and walked out of the embassy, never to return.

Gouzenko's defection provided the first peek into the huge espionage apparatus the KGB and the GRU had constructed over a period of 30 years in North America. The documents he brought with him also provided the initial clues into the scope of the Soviet espionage effort against the atomic bomb project. It revealed a ring operating in Canada, along with hints that the Canadian operation was only one component in a much larger operation centered in the United States.

Both the KGB and GRU frantically tried to save what they could, pulling their officers out of Canada and beginning arrangements to evacuate their best assets. However, like a man trying to put out a brush fire with a bucket of water, the Soviets discovered they could not extinguish all the blazes that now seemed to break out everywhere. Just two months after Gouzenko's defection, a woman named Elizabeth Bentley walked into an FBI office in New York and dropped a bombshell. She was a courier for a large ring of Soviet intelligence assets in the U.S. government. Her motives for turning herself into the FBI were complicated, but they apparently centered on her unhappiness with the way the

ABOVE: East German champion skater Katerina Witt, subject of a pervasive spying operation by the regime's infamous secret police.

The Russians had managed to accomplish some successful damage control, but another fire broke out, one they did not know about. The fire was lit by the Army Security Agency (ASA), at the time America's leading codebreaking organization. In 1944 it had been ordered to take a look at Soviet diplomatic communications for any clue that the Soviet Union was conducting secret negotiations with Nazi Germany for a separate peace. In the view of President Franklin D. Roosevelt, such a separate peace raised the spectre of a million German troops, along with their planes and armour, suddenly unleashed on Allied forces in the West. It would be enough for the Germans to achieve at least a military stalemate – a repeat of the 1918 peace deal between Germany and the Bolsheviks that allowed the Germans to send hundreds of thousands of troops to the Western Front.

The American concern had been touched off by a report from State Department intelligence in late 1943, reporting that Soviet and German diplomats had opened highly secret talks in neutral Sweden about a possible peace deal . Those talks had come to nothing, but the possibility existed they might restart at any moment. American interception stations that plucked out German and Japanese messages from the ether had also picked up Soviet traffic. That traffic had been laid aside, since there had been no reason for an attempt to crack it. Now, in an operation code-named 'VENONA', the ASA went on the attack.

ASA cryptanalysts got a surprise when they took a first look at the traffic between Moscow and the Soviet embassy in Washington, D.C., and consulates in New York and San Francisco during the war. There was a huge volume of it, far beyond the normal traffic of diplomatic installations, even in wartime. The only possible explanation was that the Russians had been transmitting a massive amount of

KGB had dealt with her after the death of her lover, who had served as co-ordinator of the collection of intelligence from the ring.

The KGB learned of Bentley's defection because the FBI, in the interests of maintaining good relations with British intelligence, routinely informed the newly assigned head of the MI6 station in Washington, H.A.R. Philby. The FBI did not know that Philby was the KGB's prize British asset, nor did they learn, until many years later, that he passed the bad news to Moscow. The Russians immediately ordered all assets ever in contact with Bentley to cease spying. It was a measure that they believed (correctly, as it turned out) would prevent any legal prosecution of them, since all the authorities had was the unsubstantiated word of an alleged co-conspirator. More importantly, the quick reaction defeated a FBI plan to roll up the entire network by using Bentley as a double agent.

LEFT: Four of the infamous 'Ring of Five' — British spies that were recruited by the Soviet government and, over a period of many years, secretly passed vast amounts of confidential information from their positions inside the British establishment. Clockwise from top-left: Anthony Blunt, Donald Maclean, Kim Philby and Guy Burgess.

intelligence information, which meant there were a lot of sources providing it. As the cryptanalysts began working on the intercepted messages, they encountered a huge, apparently insurmountable, roadblock – the Russians had super-enciphered those messages with one-time pads. Theoretically, that meant the traffic was indecipherable, but several ASA analysts persevered. They noticed there were a number of repetitions in some of the messages. An impossibility, since the whole point of one-time pads was to make the ciphers truly random.

They delved further into the messages and in a remarkable feat of decryption, using only paper and pencil, they finally realized that Russian code clerks had committed an error of truly monumental proportions. They had used the same one-time pads twice. Apparently, wartime shortages, a delay in shipping new pads or perhaps simple laziness had compelled them to commit this lapse in security. The Russians now paid the penalty for such sloppiness, as the ASA cryptanalysts, armed with the cryptological equivalent of a can opener, began to decipher thousands of messages.

The decryptions revealed that Soviet intelligence had recruited hundreds of Americans, almost all of them Communists, to provide information. They also made clear, to the shock of the American government, that the atomic bomb project had been completely penetrated by Soviet intelligence, revealing every one of its scientific and technical secrets. Working with the FBI, the cryptanalysts began putting together clues to determine the identities behind code names of assets named in the messages. Among the first was the identity behind Soviet intelligence's most important asset inside the Manhattan Project, an émigré German physicist named Klaus Fuchs. Convinced during an MI5 interrogation that someone in Soviet intelligence (perhaps a defector) had given him up, Fuchs confessed. In the process he revealed that while he worked at Los Alamos, he passed his intelligence to a Soviet intelligence courier, subsequently identified as an American Communist and longtime KGB asset, Harry Gold.

Fuchs' identification provided the FBI with an unexpected bonus when Gold, confronted with it, confessed that he had served as courier for another Soviet intelligence asset working on the Manhattan Project, a machinist named David Greenglass. At that point, the FBI realized that the Soviets had committed a grave violation of tradecraft: using the same courier for two different assets.

Again, Soviet intelligence paid a severe penalty for a mistake. Greenglass confessed, revealing the name of another Soviet asset who had recruited him, his brother in law, Julius Rosenberg (whose name had already turned up in VENONA decrypts). In turn, the FBI learned that Rosenberg, aided by his wife, Ethel, was running a ring that specialized in stealing technological secrets of the U.S. military. The KGB was able to extricate two members of the ring before the FBI rounded up all its members. However, the Rosenbergs were arrested just as they had made arrangements to slip into Mexico, the preliminary step for a KGB extrication to the Soviet Union. They were convicted and, in 1953, executed.

In espionage terms, the real significance of the Rosenberg case and a number of other, equally shocking cases was its major role in touching off a full-fledged anti-Communist hysteria in the United States. Loyalty oaths, congressional investigations and the 1940 Smith Act (which declared the U.S. Communist Party an illegal organization) swept all Communists and accused 'fellow travelers' from every nook and cranny of American life. By 1954, at the height of the hysteria, the hundreds of sources the KGB had recruited and nurtured over several decades were gone, with no prospect of replacing them from the decimated ranks of American Communists.

Soviet intelligence suffered a second body blow when its most prized assets, the 'Ring of Five' in Great Britain, were lost. As with Fuchs and the Rosenbergs, VENONA provided the critical attack point. A number of decrypted measures concerned what obviously was a highly valued agent, code-named 'HOMER', a source both the FBI and MI5 deduced was working somewhere at the higher levels of the Foreign Office. Finally, the cryptanalysts decrypted a message reporting that HOMER had traveled from his post at the British embassy in Washington to New York to be with his pregnant wife as she prepared to give birth. Those details fit only one person – Donald Maclean, a junior diplomat at the Washington embassy.

Plans were made to arrest Maclean, but before that could happen, Philby again intervened to balk a promising counterespionage operation. In his position as MI6 chief in the United States, Philby had been brought into the great VENONA secret, since a number of the names in the decrypts were British citizens. He was able to keep the KGB informed of the progress of the VENONA decryption efforts, especially the tightening net around Maclean. The KGB was alarmed at the prospect of Maclean's arrest, since he was in rough psychological shape and drinking heavily, almost certainly from the strain of living a double life. A Maclean in such a condition, the KGB feared, would reveal the other members of the Ring of Five while under interrogation.

Determined to keep Philby as an asset (there was talk of him becoming the chief of MI6), the KGB decided on a drastic solution. Maclean would be swiftly exfiltrated to the Soviet Union before he could be arrested. The plan was to have Guy Burgess, a fellow Ring of Five asset, shepherd the increasingly unstable Maclean on a 'vacation' to the continent, where they would make their way to Prague, from which Maclean would leave for Moscow.

The plan worked perfectly, except for one detail: unaccountably, Burgess suddenly decided to go to Moscow with Maclean. The KGB now confronted a major intelligence disaster, for American and British intelligence could only ponder who could have warned Maclean of his impending arrest. Worse, Burgess' rash action inevitably pointed the finger of suspicion at Philby. As the British were aware, Burgess had lived in Philby's Washington home for a while and the two men were known as close friends. The Americans began to think along the same line, noting that all the assets revealed by Bentley had suddenly gone to ground after Philby was informed of her defection. Maclean had fled to Moscow one step ahead of an arrest after Philby was informed of the identification of HOMER in the VENONA decrypts. Not legally solid proof of treachery, obviously, but there were too many coincidences to explain away. They were enough to move General Walter Bedell Smith, director of the CIA, to send a cable to his MI6 counterpart: 'RECALL PHILBY OR WE BREAK OFF THE RELATIONSHIP.'

With that, the career of the greatest asset Soviet intelligence ever produced was at an end. The KGB had come within a hair's breadth of achieving the mind-boggling feat of having its asset as head of MI6, with consequences that can only be imagined. Philby talked his way out of serious legal trouble, but in 1962, a senior KGB officer with firsthand knowledge of Philby's many years of service as an asset defected to the CIA. Questioned by MI6, Philby gave a limited confession, then fled to the Soviet Union. Some years after he reappeared in Moscow, the two remaining assets of the Ring of Five – Anthony Blunt and John Cairncross – were ensnared by the revelations of other defectors. They confessed in exchange for immunity. To a large extent this was an empty legal exercise, since both men had stopped working for the KGB after 1945.

Soviet intelligence now faced the task of reconstituting those shattered networks. Not an easy task, for in addition to the postwar internal security purges of Communists, the Russians no longer had what they called 'the great illegals', the master spy recruiters of the 1920s and 1930s who had put the pre-World War II networks together. Men like Deutsch and Maly, who had recruited the Ring of Five, perished in Stalin's purges. They had been replaced by an entirely new generation of KGB and GRU agent runners, apparatchiks perfectly schooled in espionage techniques, but without the daring and imagination of their predecessors. The new generation of Soviet intelligence plodded on, but was meeting only limited success in establishing new networks. Its was a task made even harder by their bosses' decision that they should avoid, if possible, recruiting from Communist organizations which were extensively penetrated by counterintelligence (at one point, close to a third of the dwindling membership of the U.S. Communist Party were FBI informants).

While the Russians were trying to build new networks, American intelligence was wandering around in some confusion. General Donovan, head of the OSS, had drawn up a plan in 1945 for a new central American intelligence service. It very much reflected the ideas of Donovan's two closest friends in British intelligence, Admiral Godfrey, head of NID, and William Stephenson, chief of MI6's British Security Coordination in the U.S. Drawing on the British experience, Donovan proposed a central agency with responsibility for all foreign intelligence and a separate domestic security agency with exclusive responsibility for counterintelligence. Donovan's plan went over like the proverbial lead balloon in the rest of the American intelligence establishment. J. Edgar Hoover of the FBI, who was trying to expand the Bureau's intelligence, hated it, as did the military intelligence agencies, also seeking to become the dominant force in foreign intelligence.

The knives were out and they found a willing executioner in President Harry S. Truman, a Missouri populist who had a deep, abiding suspicion of large, centralized government organizations. Besides, he saw British fingerprints all over Donovan's plan, which in Truman's view made it all the more unacceptable. Truman distrusted the British, a sentiment he also felt about Donovan. Therefore no one was surprised when he not only rejected Donovan's plan, but also unceremoniously fired the OSS chief and ordered his organization disbanded, replacing it was something called the Strategic Studies Unit (SSU). It was a small organization of a few dozen ex-OSS officers with a vague mandate, very little money and not much in the way of support from the White House. It was supposed to be collecting foreign intelligence, but spent most of its time dealing with the depredations of intelligence empire-builders in the FBI and military intelligence. The result, inevitably, was that there was not much in the way of useful intelligence being collected.

As time went on, however, it became clear that this half-cocked system was not going to work, especially in the context of a grave new threat to the United States that arose. The wartime alliance with the Soviet Union had come apart and the two nations were embarked on a course of conflict that would become the Cold War. From the American standpoint, the new struggle created an acute and immediate need for intelligence about the world's largest nation, intelligence the Americans did not have.

The extent of that ignorance was summarized by an encounter in 1947 between an Air Force general and an ex-OSS agent then working for the SSU. The Air Force was concerned about the Soviet Union's fleet of intercontinental bombers. It was vital to learn when those bombers took off from their airfields in Russian territory, so that the U.S. could prepare its defences in event those planes were headed for the United States. What the Air Force needed, the general told the SSU agent, were American spies on the ground, each one equipped with long-range radios and assigned to watch one Soviet military airfield. When a spy spotted bombers taking off, he would immediately radio the news. "How many bomber-capable airfields are we talking about?" the agent asked. "Oh, about 22,000," the general replied.

ABOVE: John Cairncross's identity as a Soviet spy was only publicly confirmed in 1990, when he was named by KGB defector Oleg Gordievsky.

Finally, in 1947, a radical solution was devised – the National Security Act. This amounted to a complete overhaul of the American national security structure to put it on a war footing for the struggle against the Soviet Union. Among other things, the new law created the country's first real centralized intelligence organization. The Central Intelligence Agency (CIA) was to be exclusively responsible for foreign intelligence and forbidden a domestic role. That function was assigned to the FBI, which also had exclusive responsibility for counterintelligence. The CIA would be headed by a Director of Central Intelligence (DCI). All foreign intelligence was to come through his hands and he was to serve as the President's chief adviser on intelligence matters.

The new CIA began its existence with a recruiting drive to fill the ranks, attracting hundreds of ex-OSS types. After the war, many of them had gone into prosperous business careers, but in a pattern that has been repeated often in the world of espionage, wartime service as spies addicted them to the secret world. However delighted they were to be back in a dark world they loved, the men and women in the new intelligence agency faced the daunting task of filling in the large blank that was the Soviet Union. U.S. intelligence had no agents operating inside that country, no assets, no insight into the size and capability of the Soviet military, no idea of Soviet intentions and not even a vague idea of what was going on inside the Kremlin.

The answer to that vast pool of ignorance, of course, was either infiltrating agents into the Soviet Union or recruiting assets there. But either method faced near-insurmountable obstacles. Stalinist Russia was the most oppressive police state the world had ever seen. It had an internal security apparatus that controlled every possible aspect of Soviet life. In a country where even the Moscow telephone directory was considered a classified document, all Soviet citizens existed in a network of informers, both on the job and where they lived. Russians had to be very careful about what they said, since even the mildest criticism of the government might result in years in the gulag, the Soviet Union's vast prison labour system. The USSR did not encourage foreign tourism and any foreigner in the country could expect pervasive surveillance. It was the perfect environment for counterintelligence and a deadly atmosphere for foreign intelligence.

LEFT: A U.S. Air Force 'weather research' balloon. Outfitted with cameras and detection gear, the balloons flew over the Soviet Union on pre-U-2 spy flights.

Clearly, developing a CIA foothold in the Soviet Union was not going to be easy and certainly not something that could be accomplished in a short period of time. However, the need for intelligence was acute. What at the time was presumed to be an interim solution was devised – technology. If the CIA could not spy from inside the Soviet Union, it would spy on the behemoth from the outside.

The first attempt involved a very old technology, balloons. Post-War astrophysical research revealed that there existed something called the jet stream, a high-altitude wind that blew west to east above a height of about 45,000 feet during the winter months, at speeds of over one hundred MPH. The newly created Directorate of Science and Technology of the CIA arrived at a bright idea. What if a balloon could be designed to operate at that altitude and under those conditions? What if the balloon could also be outfitted with cameras or other sensor technology? Such balloons could be launched into the jet stream across the Soviet Union, taking

pictures by means of a camera operated by an automatic shutter system. The CIA let out a number of secret contracts to develop a new generation of spy balloons, an effort that finally resulted in a two-storey-high balloon constructed of lightweight plastic material that could operate at altitudes up to 80,000 feet. Some of the new balloons were equipped with sensors to measure the radioactivity from an aboveground nuclear weapons test, others with cameras configured to snap pictures as the balloons overflew the Soviet Union.

In late 1947, the first test flights of the secret spy balloons were conducted from the White Sands Proving Ground in New Mexico. The tests proved the concept would work, although there was an unanticipated side-effect. Once in the upper atmosphere, the balloons' gas bags were violently flattened by the violent winds, often assuming a saucer shape. Since the plastic material of the balloons was coated in a special silver finish to reflect sunlight, the result was the 'flying saucer' scare. One test flight balloon crashed on a ranch near Roswell, New Mexico. Eager to cover up the existence of the secret project, an Air Force officer made the ill-advised decision to describe it as a "crashed flying saucer", an assertion he later withdrew, igniting a conspiracy theory that persists to this day.

When launched into the jet stream over the Soviet Union, the spy balloons proved to be a mixed success. Since they could not be controlled and were subject to the vagaries of high-altitude wind currents, the balloons could not be targeted to photograph specific sites on the ground. A number of them crashed on Soviet territory before they could finish their flight near Japan (where they were 'hooked' by planes and their sensor packages recovered). However, to the surprise of the CIA, the pictures the balloons took were amazingly clear, even from very high altitudes. The results proved that if the CIA could devise some sort of piloted platform capable of operating at high altitude, they would achieve the perfect reconnaissance device out of the range of air defences. The solution was provided by the brilliant aircraft designer, Clarence (Kelly) Johnson of Lockheed. He came up with an odd plane that was something like the technological equivalent of a dragonfly, a lightweight craft with extraordinarily long wings. It was called the Utility Two, more commonly known as U-2.

Beginning with its first flight in 1955, the U-2 was a glittering success. Armed with advanced cameras designed by Edwin Land of Polaroid, the U-2s were launched from a secret bases on the periphery of the Soviet Union on flight paths that took them on missions crossing the entire country. At certain points along that flight path, the pilot switched on the cameras to snap overhead pictures of air bases, nuclear testing sites, missile facilities, naval anchorages and just about anything else of intelligence interest. It was the greatest achievement in technical espionage in history to that point.

Although Soviet radars had detected the U-2s as they entered Russian airspace, no existing surface-to-air missile or fighter could reach the spy plane's 85,000-foot operating altitude. However, President Dwight D. Eisenhower understood it was only a matter of time before advances in radar and missile technology doomed the U-2 flights. "Someday," Eisenhower said prophetically, when approving the program, "one of these machines is going to get caught and we're going to have a hell of a storm." He turned out to be right. On 5 May 1960, one of Johnson's U-2s, piloted by Francis Gary Powers was struck by a new, advanced Soviet surface-to-air missile. Powers managed to parachute to safety, but was captured and subjected to a show trial.

Years later, Johnson came up with another innovative spy plane design, the SR-71 Blackbird. It was capable of operating at altitudes above 90,000 feet and speeds near Mach 3 (about 2,300 MPH). The Blackbird would zoom in and out of sensitive areas, sucking up radar and electronic signals with its detection gear and snapping pictures with its advanced cameras. The fastest plane in the world in the 1970s and 1980s, it could outrun anything in the air.

By the time of Powers' downing, the U-2 had already been scheduled for replacement by the next step in espionage technology, the spy satellite. The Soviet Union had orbited the world's first earth-orbiting satellite in 1957 and the technology advanced in quantum leaps over the next decade. The first spy satellites were outfitted with cameras programmed to snap pictures; at a certain point in their flight paths, a signal was sent, ordering the satellites to eject their film packages, which were retrieved by planes that snagged the packages with special nets. As the technology continued to advance, spy satellites could send the pictures they took back to ground stations in real time.

ABOVE: U-2 pilot Gary Powers, shot down over the Soviet Union in 1960. He was jailed for spying, but repatriated to the U.S. in 1962 as part of a 'spy swap'.

At the same time, a series of highly specialized satellites were developed, designed for specific missions – detection of flame exhausts from missile tests, electromagnetic pulses of nuclear explosions, radar frequencies and sigint 'ferret' satellites to pluck electronic signals from 200 miles up in space. Development of the sigint satellites ended one of the most dangerous technical intelligence operations. Up until then, a series of U.S. Air Force and Royal Air Force flights by jet bombers deliberately violated Soviet air space to record ground-based electronics. They then raced for safety as Soviet air defence fighters bored in. The flights were very costly. Scores of pilots and crewmen were killed when their unarmed planes were shot down before they could make it to safety.

The shift to satellites as the primary means of collecting technical intelligence, an espionage process prettied up with the formal term 'national technical means', had the unanticipated effect of levelling the espionage playing field between the Soviet Union and the United States. During the time of the U-2 and border-crossing 'ferret' flights, the Russians had no equivalent, since they lacked bases on the American periphery. Satellites ended that advantage. Soviet spy satellites, while they never matched the technical sophistication of their American counterparts, nevertheless were perfectly adequate for obtaining what the Russians needed to know about American military dispositions, bases, nuclear weapons tests and missile launching facilities.

Although the original idea behind spy satellites was to collect intelligence, both sides came to realize that they also fulfilled the basic objective of all modern intelligence – early warning. A satellite programmed to monitor an ICBM launching site could provide almost instantaneous warning of a launch. In a time when ICBMs needed only 15 minutes to reach their targets on the other side of the world and create thermonuclear Armageddon, that kind of early warning was critical – and remains so.

For the technical wizards on both sides who had come up with such marvels as satellites capable of picking up even local phone calls hundreds of miles below, there was no end of clever devices to conduct espionage. Given free rein and lavish budgets, they came up with an Aladdin's Cave of wonders to steal a march. Among these were a Soviet miniature electronic bug concealed in the olive of a martini (discovered when the drinker decided to nibble on the olive in his drink) and a CIA operation that bugged the private radiotelephone conversations of high Soviet officials as they rode to work in their limousines (the charms of Olga the masseuse seemed to be a favourite topic of conversation). Another KGB operation bugged the typewriters in the U.S. Moscow embassy, transmitting every keyboard stroke, while an ONI operation used specially outfitted U.S. nuclear submarines to tap into underwater communications cables

RIGHT: The SR-71 Blackbird, another innovative, high-speed spy plane from the drawing board of American Clarence Johnson, who also designed the U-2.

in the Sea of Okhotsk. There was also a pistol concealed in a lipstick to give KGB spies the ultimate in concealed firepower; innocent-appearing Soviet fishing trawlers jammed with electronic gear to intercept U.S. Navy communications; a large tunnel dug from West to East Berlin to tap into Soviet land lines and miniature cameras concealed in Xerox machines used by the Soviet consulate in San Francisco that transmitted each page as it was put into the machine for copying.

Infamously, there was also a KGB bug concealed in a large wooden replica of the U.S. Great Seal – a gift by Russian schoolchildren to the U.S. embassy in Moscow. An entire sub-specialty of such operations involved planting bugs in embassies. They often involved striking ingenuity, such as the MI5 operation in 1970 that planted bugs in the still-wet cement of pillars under construction for expansion of the Soviet trade mission in London. The CIA went them one better just a few years later, when it managed to plant super-miniaturized bugs in the cinder blocks of the new Soviet embassy being constructed in Washington, D.C., using tiny drills only one hundredth of an inch in diameter.

The emphasis on technology, which swallowed the bulk of intelligence agency budgets, became the subject of a running argument between two very different approaches to intelligence – 'humanoids' and 'techies'. The argument, which still rages to this day, centers on which is the best method to obtain intelligence, humans or machines. The techies have long argued that humans are inherently unreliable, since they are subject to bias, make mistakes and, above all, it is difficult to determine when an intelligence source has been compromised or doubled.

The techies often cite the Cuban Missile Crisis as an example of the superiority of technology over human sources. The crisis began in 1961, when Cubans fleeing the island reported that when they were living in Cuba, in towns near major ports, they were often awakened at night by the sounds of heavy trucks rolling past their homes. The trucks were described as carrying large, long, cylinder-type objects covered in tarpaulins, descriptions that precisely matched the dimensions and shapes of Soviet intermediate range nuclear missiles.

These accounts were recorded by teams of CIA debriefers at refugee centers in Florida, assigned the task of interviewing refugees in depth for any scraps of intelligence they might know. The debriefers became alarmed as they heard consistent stories about people seeing strange shipments at night from Cuban ports into the countryside. The similarity

RIGHT: Soviet fishing boats trawled not just for fish, but for U.S. Navy communications, which were intercepted using high-tech surveillance equipment.

RIGHT: Assiduous
in its efforts to
eavesdrop, the KGB
concealed a bug
inside a copy of
the U.S. Great Seal,
presented to the
American embassy in
Moscow by Russian
schoolchildren.

of the accounts convinced the debriefers that Russian missiles were being moved into Cuba. That conclusion was rejected at the upper levels of the CIA. The refugees, bitterly anti-Castro, were probably making it up. Besides, installing nuclear missiles in Cuba would be an insane act for the Soviet Union, which was perfectly aware of how the Americans would react to such a threat only 90 miles from their shores.

Incontrovertible proof that the Soviets had indeed installed missiles in Cuba, the techies noted, came not from spies on the ground or unverified refugee reports, but U-2 overflights. The Soviets consistently denied that they had shipped nuclear missiles to Cuba – until pictures from the

U-2s proved them liars. When they also denied shipping fighter jets to Cuba, technology also proved then liars – U-2 photographs of Soviet cargo ships docked at Cuban ports showed large crates being unloaded. 'Craterologists' at the CIA, experts on how the Soviet military crated sections of disassembled planes for shipment, were able to determine that those crates contained sections of jet warplanes. Finally, when the Soviet Union agreed to withdraw the missiles, it was technology – overhead photo reconnaissance – that confirmed those missiles had in fact been removed and shipped back to the Soviet Union aboard merchant ships.

True enough, argued the humanoids, but the fact was that American intelligence was mobilized to divine the

MRBM LAUNCH SITE 2
SAN CRISTOBAL
1 NOVEMBER 1962

MISSILE-READY TENT

FUEL TRAILERS

FORMER LAUNCH POSITIONS

FORMER LOCATION OF MISSILE-READY TENTS

ABOVE: A U.S. air
reconnaissance
photograph that
proved the
installation of
Soviet medium-range
missiles in Cuba.

truth about reports of Russian missiles in Cuba by a human spy, Colonel Oleg Penkovsky. More than a year before the crisis, Penkovsky, a GRU expert on missiles, had offered his services to MI6 and the CIA, citing his estrangement from the Soviet system. Penkovsky, one of the greatest assets Western intelligence ever had behind the Iron Curtain, provided two crucial pieces of intelligence. Firstly, technical details on how the missiles were deployed, allowing the CIA to spot distinctive patterns that revealed a missile firing site. Secondly, he gave the precise size and technical capabilities of Soviet missiles. In this latter category, Penkovsky revealed that the Soviet missiles were plagued with technical problems and that there were far fewer of them than the Russians boasted of having. Those revelations were crucial for the resolution of the crisis, since the Americans knew they could make the Russians back down. In the nuclear poker game, they were aware of the weak cards Moscow was holding.

Generally, the Americans preferred a technical approach to intelligence. Not a surprise, since intelligence organizations tend to reflect their nations' particular strength and the United States certainly reigned supreme in technology. The Russians, on the other hand, had always demonstrated superiority in human intelligence operations and its intelligence establishment concentrated its efforts in that area. Determined to replicate their success in recruiting the Ring of Five, the Russians concentrated much of their recruitment efforts among a generation of college students, hoping for a future Philby and Maclean. Those efforts focused on the foreign students attending Patrice Lumumba University in Moscow, recruiting students who would eventually enter government service, rising to positions where they would have access to valuable intelligence. The CIA had the same idea, recruiting among the large numbers of foreign students enrolled in American colleges and universities. The agency relied on sympathetic professors as spotters to tip them about promising students who would welcome a recruiting pitch.

Another category of human intelligence operations involved attempts to recruit assets who could be of more immediate benefit. All the major intelligence agencies mounted major efforts to penetrate their competitors, carefully watching for any clues suggesting political disenchantment, severe money troubles, sexual obsessions (preferably paedophilia) and career troubles that could be exploited. The KGB was particularly adept at so-called 'honeypot' operations. These used specially trained male agents (called 'ravens') and female agents ('swallows') to lure targets into sexual encounters the KGB would photograph or film. The subjects would then be confronted with a choice: work with us or suffer the consequences of what we have photographed. This technique had only limited utility, since people do not like being blackmailed into betraying

their country. Moreover, it occasionally backfired – such as the married French diplomat who, informed that he had been photographed romping with some swallows, requested copies of the pictures to show off his sexual prowess to his apparently very understanding wife.

Judged overall, most of the Cold War recruitments did not justify all the effort put into them, since few of the assets were never in a position to provide much in the way of high-grade intelligence. There were exceptions, such as the assets the U.S. National Security Agency recruited in the late 1980s among the executives of a Swiss manufacturer of cryptographic machines, whose customers included the government of Iraq. The very pro-American executives agreed to an American operation that planted 'trap doors' – concealed entry points in the machines' computer chips – in devices shipped to Baghdad. From that moment, the NSA had access to the cryptographic machines' inner workings, making the cracking of its ciphers child's play.

While the Americans were reading every high-level military message sent by Saddam Hussein and the Iraqi high command, they got an unexpected bonus. They learned from the decrypted messages that the Russians had secretly given Iraq advanced electronics to jam U.S. Global Positioning Satellites (GPS), a critical technology for U.S. military targeting and troop deployments. Using the decrypted messages, military technicians were able to pinpoint the location of the GPS jammers and on the first night of the assault on Iraq during Desert Storm in 1991, U.S. planes took them out with laser-guided bombs. The unjammed GPS system then served as guidance for an air campaign that smashed Iraq's military machine to pieces.

As things turned out, the most valuable assets were almost all walk-ins, people who decided to betray their countries, usually for money or because of political disenchantment. Intelligence agencies always had to be careful that a volunteer was not a dangle, an agent sent with the specific mission to pose as a willing asset, but in fact part of an operation to plant disinformation. Dangles represented an especially tricky problem, since no agency wanted to turn away potentially valuable assets by prematurely deciding they were not genuine.

The solution: teams of specially trained agent-runners specifically detailed to handle walk-ins. The usual procedure was to set up a number of 'genuineness tests', meaning requests that the walk-in submit secret documents or information that were forwarded to experts to determine genuineness. If the experts pronounced the material the real thing, then the handlers moved to the next phase, setting up a secure system for the asset to convey further material. Soviet intelligence liked to set up very elaborate and detailed such systems, often involving dead

'My dear friends:

I write this in some haste on Tues evening, 1 September. I am afraid that the signal HILL is not well-thought-out; the wooden post is often damp and mildewed -- discolored -- and the pencil mark I made on the morning of 19 August does not appear to have been observed. After making the signal at HILL with pencil at about 0700 on 19 August, I placed the drop at GROUND about 1600 that same day. I was worried about the visibility of the signal and waited until daylight of 20 August to check to see if it had been erased -- it did not appear to have been erased, and I retrieved my package (which included documents!) later that day. Unfortunately, I left Washington for a vacation trip to California on 21 August, returning on 30 August. I will signal HILL on Weds morning, 2 September, but this time using chalk instead of pencil. If my package is not retrieved during the evening of 2 September, I will return to the old, SMILE, signal site to mark it on 4 September and put my package down that afternoon. In any case, I'll keep trying until you get it. Given the shortness of time before our next meeting, I am putting a note on the package which I hope will cause the people here to send you a telegram confirming my intent to make our scheduled meeting on 5/6 October. Best regards, K

ABOVE: Messages sent by Aldrich Ames, the KGB's traitor inside the CIA, to his controllers. FBI counterintelligence agents recovered them from dead drops when Ames came under suspicion.

drops with multiple security checks.

Prize walk-ins for the KGB included CIA agent Aldrich Ames, who betrayed nearly two dozen CIA assets in the Soviet Union and NSA analyst Ronald Pelton, who betrayed the agency's submarine cable tapping operation. They also included Geoffrey Prime, an employee of the Government Communications Headquarters (GCHQ), the British codebreaking agency, who betrayed the extent of the agency's success in cracking Soviet ciphers and Robert Hansson, a supervisory agent in FBI counterintelligence, who provided the KGB with the names of the CIA's assets working in the Soviet Union. CIA successes included, besides Penkovsky, a senior GRU official, General Dimitri Polyakov, who for 26 years provided the identities of GRU agents and Russian military secrets. MI6 had an especially spectacular walk-in, a top KGB official named Oleg Gordievsky, who at one point was a resident in Great Britain.

The greatest danger to walk-ins was another category of asset, the defector. Like other kinds of assets, motives of defectors vary. Sometimes, it is simply career stagnation, such as KGB officer Anatoli Golitsin, who in 1962 defected to the CIA after learning his inflated opinion of his abilities was not shared by his superiors. Others defected because of political disillusionment, such as the Soviet diplomat Arkady Shevchenko, whose exposure to rampant corruption at the upper levels of the Soviet establishment convinced him that the Soviet system had to be destroyed in order to save Russia. Still others defected to save their lives, such as Walter Krivitsky, chief of GRU operations in Western Europe in the 1930s, who defected to the United States when he learned he was about to perish in Stalin's purges.

Most often, defectors work for an intelligence agency and they usually defect with a sufficient amount of material, either in written form or in their heads, they can use to secure a good position on the other side. Almost always, that involves the identities of assets they know about. These names amount to defectors' high cards, which they play out to enhance their own value to the new team. When Anatoli Golitisin defected to the CIA in 1962, he instantly played his best card – he had firsthand knowledge that Kim Philby was a KGB asset. Some time earlier, when a Polish intelligence agent named Mikhail Goleniewski defected, he told MI6 that one of its agents, George Blake, was a KGB asset. As Blake and dozens of other assets learned the hard way, an asset can never be sure that the agent he is working for will not some day defect to the other side and betray the betrayer.

These kinds of espionage games, despite all the new technology, involved the use of standard techniques that had been used in spying since the time of the Bible. The struggle between spies and counterespionage, the recruitment of assets and the time-honoured motives of money and sex would be as familiar to the king's spies of ancient Assyria as they are to the huge intelligence bureaucracies of modern industrial states. However, there is one difference, which arose during the Cold War – the use of intelligence agencies as foot soldiers in a covert war.

The covert struggle was a product of the reality of the Cold War. The nuclear stalemate made conventional war

RIGHT: 'Walk-ins' like Aldrich Ames were valuable sources of information for the KGB and CIA, but had to be handled carefully to ensure they were not 'dangles'.

unthinkable between the major powers, so the struggle shifted underground. It became a battle for influence and dominance throughout the world. The official U.S. policy was containment, which meant that communism was to be contained behind the Iron Curtain and, eventually, overthrown. Not by military action, the traditional solution to intractable political problems, but by all the weapons of subversion – propaganda, political destabilization, economic warfare, bribery and disinformation.

The model on how that war was to be fought was provided by the KGB in eastern Europe after World War II. Before the war, the Soviets had organized exiled Communists from eastern European countries into what amounted to shadow governments, ready to move in and take the reins of power. As the Red Army swept through eastern Europe, behind them came battalions of KGB officers, their shadow governments in tow. What happened next was a pattern repeated by the KGB in a half-dozen countries.

It would begin with a propaganda campaign aimed at convincing the populace that the postwar coalition government was honeycombed with 'traitors' and 'war criminals'. This was followed by a wave of strikes and 'spontaneous demonstrations' demanding that Communists be given key cabinet posts (especially the interior ministry). A gradual takeover of the internal security apparatus was achieved, followed by arrests of 'conspirators', 'Quislings' and 'war criminals' and the infiltration of other coalition government agencies, ultimately destroying the government from within, to be replaced by the Communist shadow government.

The CIA's covert action warriors borrowed some of these techniques for their own operations to destabilize governments their bosses decreed were inimical to U.S. national security – Guatemala, Iran (an operation run with British intelligence), Indonesia, Nicaragua and Chile. From the American government's standpoint,

ABOVE: FBI agent
Robert Hanssen was
one of the most
infamous double
agents in the
history of American
intelligence, where
he spied for the
Soviet Union, and
then Russia, from
1979 to 2001.

the virtue of such covert operations was that they achieved the desired result without overt involvement. The United States was in effect conducting war against another nation without having to bother with such constitutional requirements as asking Congress for a declaration of war.

The problem was that the covert war could not remain covert for very long; as CIA agents liked to say, "You can't hide a hippopotamus with a handkerchief." Moreover, early successes in covert action operations – notably in Guatemala and Iran – seduced the Americans into

thinking that covert action was the easy, cheap solution to all their difficult foreign policy problems. They learned that it was not quite so simple at the Bay of Pigs in Cuba, a disaster that began a long, gradual disengagement from covert action operations as Congress mandated oversight. The KGB, too, learned a hard lesson about covert action. Its disastrous failure in Afghanistan showed that the techniques that worked so well in countries like Hungary, Czechoslovakia and Romania would not work in a very different kind of society.

For both the American and Soviet intelligence establishments – the two giants who dominated post-World War II espionage – the gradual phaseout of covert action operations marked a trend toward traditional espionage. The Americans emphasized their strength in technical means of intelligence collection and the Russians focused on human intelligence. Overall, the record of success was very spotty, with both sides suffering a series of major intelligence disasters. Russian intelligence, using suspect sources, badly misread the situation in Afghanistan, leading the Soviet Union into a military intervention that failed ignominiously. The Americans suffered an intelligence failure of equal magnitude in Vietnam and later, another failure – this time in conjunction with British intelligence – in Iraq, with consequences that have created what can only be called a mess.

However, the supreme Cold War intelligence failure, ironically enough, involved a seminal event that neither American nor Soviet intelligence saw coming, despite a mountain of evidence that it was about to happen – the end of the Cold War itself. The end, including the collapse of the Soviet Union, somehow escaped the notice of Soviet intelligence's hundreds of thousands of agents and an internal security apparatus that was supposed to keep track of Russian popular opinion. The KGB failed to comprehend that the very system it worked so hard to support was imploding from within. Despite billion-dollar spy satellites, thousands of agents and an organization whose reach extended into every corner of the world, the CIA also failed to see the implosion coming.

In 1991, the Russian people rendered their final and decisive judgment on the KGB when they tore down the statue of Feliks Dzerzhinsky that stood in Lubyanka Square near KGB headquarters. For whatever it is worth, it should be noted that the American people did not tear down the statue of Nathan Hale that stands in front of CIA headquarters.

This is true enough, but the CIA and the rest of American intelligence have not enjoyed a vaunting reputation among the American public. To a certain extent, the public's low estimate of the agency stems from a peculiarly American tendency to judge intelligence as a function of investment. Throw enough money at any problem (education, welfare, the environment), many Americans believe, and good results should be guaranteed. If not, then it's a problem of the people spending the money. Thus, the billions of tax dollars invested in an agency like the CIA should produce excellent intelligence. However, the process doesn't work that way. Intelligence, especially in the American political context, is a complicated process in which all influences, ranging from human frailty to presidential politics, play important roles.

No incident better illustrates the process than the disaster in Iraq. The U.S. intelligence failure there stems from an earlier failure which took place in 1991, when both the CIA and the military intelligence agencies discovered that they had completely missed the true extent of Saddam Hussein's program to develop weapons of mass destruction (WMD).

Among other shocks, the CIA learned that it had no clue that Iraq's nuclear weapons program was only 18 months from testing an actual warhead. That largely accounts for American intelligence's conclusions, some 12 years later, that Hussein was busily reconstituting that program after it was dismantled following Desert Storm.

Politics also played an important role. The circle of President George W. Bush's closest advisors, led by Vice President Dick Cheney, were adamant that Iraq had managed to build an extensive arsenal of WMD. Their rock-hard conviction was impatient in the face of cautions by the CIA. Believing that the agency was deliberately sceptical of alarms about WMD from anti-Hussein Iraqi exiles, Cheney and the Secretary of Defence Donald Rumsfeld created their own intelligence unit, which told them what they wanted to hear: that Iraq had an active WMD program (this turned out to be wrong) and that Hussein and al Qaeda were allies (which also turned out to be wrong) – alarming intelligence justifying a preemptive U.S. attack.

As Benjamin Disraeli once said, in another context, "It was worse than a crime; it was a blunder."

RIGHT: Fake rock used by MI6 agents in Russia as an electronic dead drop to receive reports from the agency's assets.

THE GREAT PLUTONIUM HUNT: ATOMIC ESPIONAGE

ON 6 JANUARY 1939, AN EVENT TOOK PLACE IN THE RAREFIED WORLD OF NUCLEAR PHYSICS THAT WOULD SET OFF THE MOST DRAMATIC AND DEADLY DEVELOPMENT IN THE HISTORY OF SCIENCE.

On 6 January 1939, an event took place in the rarefied world of nuclear physics that would set off the most dramatic and deadly development in the history of science. It would also ignite a fire in the world of espionage, with implications that continue to this day.

On the surface, the event appeared prosaic. A paper by two prominent German chemists was published in *Naturwissenschaften*, the prestigious German physics journal, a must-read in the world scientific community. The paper reported an experiment in which they had bombarded a uranium nucleus with neutrons, causing mysterious results. The chemists did not quite understand what had happened, but nuclear physicists everywhere did – the Germans had split the atom. This news had momentous implications, because the rupture of forces holding the nucleus together releases tremendous energy. A series of such reactions, strung together in a chain, would create a destructive force on a scale the world had never seen. In other words, it could be the ultimate weapon.

For those familiar with the languid schedules of scientific journals, the appearance of the *Naturwissenschaften* article was odd. The experiment had taken place in late 1938 and the two scientists had submitted their paper to the journal on 22 December of that year. It was published only 15 days later, an unprecedented rush to publication. How was that possible? Because a spy arranged it. The spy was aware that it was only a matter of time before the Nazis grasped the real significance of that simple experiment and began a program to harness it into a nuclear weapon.

Rushing the chemists' paper into print would serve as a warning bell to the world: nuclear fission had been achieved in Nazi Germany, with all that implied. The spy's name was Paul Rosbaud. Scientific adviser to the Springer Verlag chain of scientific publications, including *Naturwissenschaften*, Rosbaud was friends with virtually every prominent scientist in Germany. He was also an anti-Nazi who had been recruited a year before by MI6 to keep tabs on German science's contribution to Hitler's

war effort. He went on to become one of World War II's greatest spies, over the next seven years providing MI6 with every scientific secret of Nazi Germany he could find, especially its atomic bomb program.

Rosbaud's first great service to MI6 was the quick publication of the atom-splitting experiment, one jump ahead of the inevitable suppression by the Nazis of all such public mention in Germany of science with military implications. His action helped set off a scientific race to build an atomic bomb. At the same time it also ignited a rush among the world's intelligence agencies to discover what they were convinced was 'The Great Secret' and, if possible, steal it.

Of the dozen intelligence establishments that went to work on atomic espionage, none devoted more people and resources to the effort than Soviet intelligence. Both the NKVD (predecessor of the KGB) and GRU (military intelligence) were reoriented to atomic espionage as their highest priority. Each agency was combed for top agents for the task, codenamed 'OPERATION ENORMOZ'. Most of them were assigned to Soviet intelligence's top target for atomic espionage – the United States of America. The Soviets correctly deduced this was the one nation most

ABOVE: German emigré scientist Lise Meitner (right) alerted the scientific world about Germany's discovery of fission.

likely to develop atomic weapons. They concentrated on trawling among Communists who had any role in the Manhattan Project, cover name for the vast American atomic bomb program.

The operation produced a number of sources, but, ironically enough, the most valuable asset turned out to be a walk-in. He was Klaus Fuchs, an émigré German physicist in Great Britain who also happened to be a fervent Communist. Somehow, that fact eluded security vetting when in 1941 Fuchs joined the Tube Alloys Project, cover name for Great Britain's early project to develop an atomic bomb. Fuchs volunteered his services to the GRU, which not only learned about the ultra-secret British project, but got a bonus when Fuchs was assigned to the Manhattan Project as the American and British atomic weapons programs were merged. Fuchs betrayed everything he learned about the American bomb, invaluable intelligence that saved the Soviets anything from five to ten years in the development of their own atomic bomb.

ENORMOZ was the crowning achievement of Soviet intelligence. Its success underscored just how bad America's own atomic intelligence was. Split among several different agencies, with little scientific input, it concluded that the Soviet Union would need another 60 years to develop a nuclear weapon (although Soviet nuclear physics was well advanced); that the United States could monopolize uranium sources (the Soviet Union actually had some 84,000 tons of uranium deposits); that there was a single 'atomic secret' that could be protected (there was no secret to nuclear fission) and that a Nazi atomic bomb was imminent (ignoring MI6's

RIGHT: The world's first atomic bomb explodes over a New Mexico desert on 16 July 1945. This was the climax of a top-secret project that was actually an open book to Soviet intelligence.

intelligence in 1943, obtained from Rosbaud, that the Germans had failed).

These grave intelligence failures led to a very different approach when the CIA was created in 1947. The new agency established a science and technology division, devoted exclusively to scientific intelligence and staffed with highly-trained, scientifically literate personnel. Its highest priority was nuclear weapons – who had them, where were they being developed, what was their technical level and a long list of other vital intelligence. To achieve it, the effort had access to the most advanced intelligence hardware, ultimately including special spy satellites bristling with electronic gear designed specifically to detect and measure the telltale signs of a nuclear weapons program.

As the CIA was to learn to its cost, however advanced the technology, there were significant limitations. In 1973, an SR-71 spy plane, dispatched to confirm rumors of a secret Israeli nuclear weapons program, overflew the main Israeli nuclear research facility in the Negev desert and from 80,000 feet took remarkably detailed reconnaissance pictures that clearly showed the numbers on license plates of cars in the parking lot. However, it could not see deep beneath the facility, where the Israelis had built an entire nuclear weapons operation hidden from prying eyes. The Americans didn't learn of this sprawling underground secret until 1986, when a disaffected Israeli nuclear technician publicly revealed it.

Since then, there have been further problems. Smaller nuclear powers have learned to avoid detection of their atomic weapons development programs by hiding them (usually underground) and decentralizing the programs' other components to make them hard to spot. International controls over nuclear weapon materials – especially enriched uranium – have proven ineffective, mainly because intelligence agencies have found it next to impossible to keep track of them all.

The chief reason for the intelligence blindness is a lack of good human sources with insight into the small, tight circles of those who make nuclear decisions in such dark corners of the world as Iran and North Korea; or, to put another way, there is an acute need for another Paul Rosbaud.

RIGHT: Klaus Fuchs, a German physicist who infiltrated the British and American atomic bomb projects and passed detailed information on them to the Soviets.

DEATH IN THE PERFUMED GARDEN

Perhaps sensing some scepticism that he could actually deliver all that he had promised, the old man dressed in the flowing robes of the Nizari Isma'ilis sect decided to address the question directly.

ABOVE: On 11 September 2001 al Qaeda declared war on the United States as two hijacked jetliners smash into the World Trade Center in New York City.

LEFT: The Black Standard has a long history in Islamic heraldry, but it is most recently associated with its adoption by the Taliban and al Qaeda in the 1990s.

Was there any doubt, he asked Count Henry of Champagne, leader of the Frankish knights, that his fida'i could kill the local Arab chieftain Henry wanted eliminated?

As the two men stood before the Nizari fortress that winter day in 1197, the Count did not answer immediately. The hesitation confirmed the suspicion of Rashideddin Sinan that this tall European in chain mail doubted that the supreme leader of the Nizari had the wherewithal to guarantee the death, especially the way he said it would happen. The assassination would occur the Friday hence, Rashideddin had promised, just as evening prayers began at the mosque. His man would approach the leader and plunge a knife into his heart, in full view of hundreds of the faithful – and the leader's bodyguards. He would make no attempt to flee, unhesitatingly accepting his inevitable death for the murder.

"With respect," Henry said, "I must wonder: the deed will be committed in such a way as to make certain your man's death as the bodyguards slay him on the spot? And if they instead decide to capture him…"

There was no need for Henry to finish the sentence, for Rashideddin immediately understood. "No man of the Nizari has ever broken under torture, no matter the torment. I tell you that when one of my men was seized after his slaying of Emir Porsuki of Aleppo and Mosul, for the express purpose of putting him to the torture, he uttered not even a sound as they forced him to watch his member sliced from his body. He still remained silent when they then burned out his eyes with hot irons. Do not doubt our devotion to the cause, even unto the most unspeakable agonies and death."

Henry still seemed not entirely convinced, so Rashideddin decided to arrange a demonstration. Rashideddin caught the attention of a man standing guard in one of the towers of the fortress, then made an elaborate downward motion of his arm. The man in the tower unhesitatingly leaped to his death, smashing into the ground at the feet of a stunned Henry. He was just recovering from the shock of that sight when Rashideddin made the same motion to a man standing in another tower. That man also instantly jumped from the tower to his death.

With that graphic demonstration of Nizari obedience, the deal was struck. Rashideddin's sect would eliminate the local Arab leader, the first in a series of such murders to broaden Crusader control in the Levant, in exchange for Crusader support for the Nizari campaign against other Arab sects. A few days later, just as Rashideddin promised, one of his fida'i walked up to the intended target in the mosque as prayers were about to begin and plunged a dagger into the man's heart, instantly killing him. The fida'i then calmly stood there, the bloody knife in his hand, waiting for the chieftain's bodyguards to hack him to pieces.

To Henry and the Crusaders, the Nizari represented just another sect in the apparently inexhaustible number of warring Arab sects in the Holy Land. It was a profusion the Crusaders found confusing. What counted was that at least one of them was willing to assist the Crusaders. They did not spend much time trying to understand the Nizari, the strangest sect of all – and the scariest. It had hundreds of suicide warriors whose fanaticism made the Crusaders' own religious fervour seem tame by comparison. No Crusader, however devoted to the holy mission that had brought the Europeans to the Middle East, would throw himself from a tower simply because his leader told him to do so. Nor would a Crusader unhesitatingly carry out an order to carry out an assassination in full view of hundreds of witnesses with the certainty of a subsequent death or the agony of torture.

Enlisting the Nizari as allies was, for the Crusaders, simply a marriage of convenience. They did not realize that they had allied themselves with something new and terrible in the history of conflict – the world's first terrorist organization. The Arabs called these terrorists 'Ashishin' or, as the Europeans pronounced it, 'Assassins'.

The Nizari were born in Islam's great schism, the irrevocable divide in 632 CE between Sunnis and Shiites, a divide that continues to have deadly implications to this day. For reasons that remain not entirely clear, somewhere around 1088 one of the Shiite leaders, a Persian named Hasan Sabbah, broke away from the movement and founded his own sect, the Nizari Isma'ilis. Proclaiming his group the only "true faith" of Islam, Hasan set about to destroy rival sects. However, instead of the standard recourse to armed conflict that had plagued the Arab world for so many centuries, Hasan carried out a very different kind of war, one never before seen in that world – pure terrorism.

He began by recruiting a core group of like-minded men. They moved to a remote mountain at Alamut, in present-day Iran, where they built a self-contained town, surrounded by a fortress. Hasan's followers emigrated into this separate world, creating a theocratic state for which Hasan served as supreme spiritual leader and military commander. Below him, he organized a three-tier system. The upper tier was occupied by his chief lieutenants, the 'grand priors', each of

whom was in charge of a particular district. Then came the 'propagandists', whose functions included recruiting new adherents. At the lowest level were the foot soldiers of the movement, the 'fida'i'. These were its real strength, for it was those men who carried out the killings that would terrorize all of Islam.

The recruits for the ranks of the fida'i were drawn from a pool of young men aged 12 to 20 who had demonstrated sufficient religious zeal to enter Hasan's unique training program. They were brought to Hasan's headquarters in the Alamut fortress in small groups. There, they were given an intense, hours-long religious lecture by Hasan that

ABOVE: The aftermath of a suicide bomber in Iraq. It is hard for the intelligence agencies to predict and prevent the death and destruction caused by religious zealots, often working alone or in small cells, who are prepared to die for their beliefs.

amounted to something of a pep talk on their "holy mission", which he left unspecified. At the end of the talk, each recruit was given a potion to drink – at which point they fell into a deep sleep, since the potions were laced with hashish.

In that state, they were carried into the centre of the fortress. When they awoke, the recruits found themselves in a beautiful perfumed garden, one so magnificent they could only believe they were in some sort of dream. Amid pools and lush vegetation, beautiful women appeared. They led them to tables laden with the finest food, wine, and milk and honey, and on to luxurious divans to eat and relax. The recruits spent many hours in this paradise of food, drink and sex until nearly dawn, when they finally fell asleep from still another round of hashish-laced wine. When they awoke, they were no longer in the perfumed garden, having been transported back inside the fortress, where they reencountered Hasan. This time, he told them they had just experienced paradise – the paradise that would be their reward when they successfully completed their still unspecified "holy mission".

Now the real training began. For the next several months, the recruits were subjected to a rigid, 12-hour daily regimen, a combination of intense religious indoctrination and schooling in the espionage arts and techniques of murder. They were taught how to create and maintain disguises, how to infiltrate an enemy city, how to conduct surveillance to learn the habits and movements of a target and how to pose as adherents of other religious sects. They were also taught the art of using a dagger, to the point where they were capable of stabbing a victim in the heart with great force in a split second.

By the time the training regimen was finished, the recruits knew the "holy mission" Hasan had mentioned at the outset meant assassination of those he decreed were "unholy ones" or "defilers of Allah". They also learned that they were the eleventh century equivalent of suicide bombers, for they were trained for just one single mission, from which they would not return. They were to carry out their assigned murder mission using only daggers (to avoid killing any innocent persons) and the assassination was to take place in as public a place as possible, usually a mosque. They were then to die at the hands of bodyguards or infuriated supporters of the victim.

If captured, they were to die in agony in torture, never to utter a word about Alamut, Hasan, the Nizari or anything else that might be of interest to their tormentors. No attempt would be made to rescue them. Their death, they were taught, was a holy martyrdom. It would be rewarded with a permanent afterlife in the paradise of the perfumed garden, there to spend their days of eternity in indolent luxury, with an inexhaustible supply of food, drink and beautiful women under the favour of Allah. Above all, they were to give absolute, unquestioned loyalty, willing to die on command from Hasan, the man they regarded as God's messenger.

In the spring of 1092, the Assassins struck for the first time. The vizir of the Saljuq sultanate, Nizam al-Mulk, one of the most distinguished figures in the Arab world, was stabbed to death as he emerged from his palace one morning. His attacker made no attempt to flee and was cut down by the vizir's bodyguard. That was followed by a string of similar assassinations of rulers, religious leaders, generals and ministers all over the Middle East, plunging the Arab world into panic. Not even beefed up details of bodyguards and an intensive effort to track down the killers before they could strike made any difference. Everyone soon understood there was a connection between Hasan's furious denunciations of other sects as heretical enemies of Allah and the assassinations of the very men he specifically singled out for criticism. However, no one had any conclusive proof. This was not surprising, given the fact that not a single Assassin ever revealed anything about the sect.

Despite Hasan's death in 1124, his sect continued to grow under new leadership and, by 1140, the Nizari had established a virtual separate state in northern Syria, plus branches scattered throughout present-day Iran and Iraq. An expanded training program was turning out hundreds of suicide terrorists and no one seemed able to stop them. To make matters worse, when the Crusaders invaded the Holy Land, the new Nizari leader, Rashideddin, saw an opportunity to enlist an ally in the sect's drive to eliminate the leadership of competing sects – all the while intending to turn on his allies once they had outlived their usefulness.

Rashideddin's Assassins eliminated a number of Arab leaders under this arrangement. However, they failed to kill the one man the Crusaders wanted to see dead – Saladin, the charismatic Arab leader who was their most dangerous opponent. There were two assassination attempts on Saladin's life, one of which badly wounded him. He survived further murder attempts by extraordinary security precautions, including wearing armour under his clothes and sleeping in a tower accessible only by a narrow staircase controlled by bodyguards.

In 1272, the Assassins' reign of terror was finally brought to an end, not by their enemies in the Arab world, but by a threat they never saw coming – the Mongols. A Mongol army swept into Alamut and other Assassin strongholds, slaughtering everything in its path. The few survivors scattered and the Nizari sect died, never to revive. However, the bloody deeds of that terrorist organization would echo nearly 1,000 years later, when a successor generation of terrorists would borrow the philosophy and techniques of the Nizari to conduct a new campaign of terror. Tragically, a collective intelligence failure made that new wave of terror all the more bloody.

LEFT: Johann Most, the German anarchist, on trial in Great Britain for incitement to riot.

TERROR TAKES CONTROL

For hundreds of years after the scattering of the Assassins, terrorism as an instrument of war and statecraft fell into disuse, mainly because war itself became formalized, with elaborate rules to regulate its conduct. That began to change when the revolution of 1848 swept across Europe, a revolution suppressed by the ruling oligarchies of the day. An entire generation of political radicals spawned by the revolution, including Karl Marx, came to the conclusion that the only way the politically oppressed could achieve the sweeping changes they wanted was a direct assault against those oligarchies to destroy them. As they argued, millions of people were in the grip of predatory capitalism linked to ruling monarchies that were not accountable to the people, who in any event had little or no political power.

In Europe and Asia, ruled mostly by royal dynasties, and India, ruled by an absentee queen, there seemed to be no hope that the people could effect change against monoliths supported by large armies and repressive internal security apparatuses. Marx and other theorists had come up with their own solutions to the problem, but to the more radical factions of the disaffected, they all amounted to long, evolutionary change that probably would not work. What was needed, the radicals argued, was direct, violent action to crumble ruling monoliths from within. Once they collapsed, the people could move into the vacuum and take power.

That view was summarized by the German radical Karl Heinzen, who criticized the revolutionaries of 1848 for failing to demonstrate sufficient resolution and ruthlessness. What they needed, he argued, was an equalizer between the oppressed and the oppressor. That equalizer he said, would be terror. It would be created by using the weapons produced by modern technology, especially explosives. Looking far ahead, he predicted the day when terrorists could overthrow a repressive regime using rockets, poison gas and most ominously, biological weapons (which he said could be used in the poisoning of food supplies).

Heinzen's theory became the guiding vision of the chief terrorist organization of the late nineteenth century and early twentieth century, the Anarchists. The Anarchists basically believed that political change could not be effected until the existing political and social order was completely destroyed. However, since they lacked the kind of weapons Heinzen advocated, they resorted to a method within their modest means – assassination.

Their preferred method was killing rulers as they appeared in public in the belief that such violent actions would destabilize a regime and hasten its collapse. A wave of assassinations broke out across Europe: French President Marie-Francois Carnot (1894); Spanish Premier Canovas del Castillo (1897); Empress Elisabeth of Austria (1898); King Humbert of Italy (1900); U.S. President William McKinley (1901); and King Carlos of Portugal and his crown prince (1908). The assassins who carried out these deeds with pistol or knife were that era's suicide bombers, since they had to be within close range of their targets and had no chance of escaping.

However spectacular, the assassinations did not achieve what the Anarchists wanted, the dissolution of the existing political establishments. The failure was severely criticized by one of the more striking figures in the Anarchist movement, a German radical to whom can be accorded the dubious distinction of being the father of modern terrorism. It was said that no human being ever combined a hideous outer appearance with an equally hideous inner being as did Johann Most.

As a boy, an operation to repair a severely infected jaw was botched, turning his lower face into some sort of grotesque mask that he hid later in life with a luxuriant beard. Born into a broken family mired in poverty, he was apprenticed to a bookbinder whose employees worked 12-hour days in appalling working conditions for a few cents a day. Already enraged at a world that laughed at his disfigurement, Most was further infuriated by the misery of his workday world, experiences that radicalized his politics. He became a Socialist, but impatient with the movement's advocacy of evolutionary change, joined the Anarchists.

With a gift for oratory and fiery prose, Most quickly became one of the movement's most striking and admired figures. He vented his hatred for the prevailing political system in a series of speeches and writings that revealed a man fairly aflame with rage. "Long live vengeance!" he fulminated in one editorial for an Anarchist newspaper in his native Germany. "Let us all work for the day when attacks will multiply against all those who bear responsibility for the servitude, exploitation and misery of the people!"

Most began to evolve an entirely new theory of terrorism he summarized as "propaganda by deed". The basic idea

behind all so-called reformist political movements, Most argued, was patient organizational propaganda work to mobilize the masses against an oppressor. However, the oppressed people were already prepared for revolution; all that was needed was a small, dedicated minority of activists who could lead. Those activists would lead with terror, since the present system, essentially barbaric, could only be destroyed by barbaric means. It was not enough, Most said, for the rulers to be killed; the regime itself had to be attacked from all sides by attacks of terror using "dynamite and poison, fire and the sword". This "propaganda by deed" was designed to sow confusion among the oppressors, inspiring the masses to seize power. An important part of the terror campaign, Most argued, was the media. Terrorist actions – the more spectacular, the better – had to be publicized as widely as possible to help foment unrest.

Among other devices Most advocated for terrorist acts was the letter bomb or package, designed to explode when opened. Such a device, Most pointed out, would cause the maximum terror for the least cost, since an entire postal system would be totally disrupted as the authorities were forced to search thousands of letters and packages to find and defuse ones containing explosives. More chillingly, Most advocated indiscriminate bombing aimed at what he called "the ten thousand", the aristocracy, the very wealthy and top government officials. Terrorists could not be bothered with such notions as innocent victims, since only the most drastic means would succeed against an oppressive and powerful enemy. The best approach was to set off powerful bombs where "the ten thousand" congregated in large numbers – major public events, church services and social occasions. If those bombs also killed many innocent people, it was the price that had to be paid in the name of a higher goal.

That kind of thinking made Most the most notorious Anarchist in the world (he was the model for the Anarchist Yundt in Joseph Conrad's classic novel, *The Secret Agent*). The newspaper he began publishing, *Freiheit (Freedom)* became the most widely-read Anarchist publication. It was full of exhortations to terrorist violence, using the methods and means Most advocated. He summarized it all in one of the most influential pamphlets ever written – *The Science of Revolutionary War: A Manual of Instruction in the Use of Nitroglycerine and Dynamite, Gun Cotton, Fulminating Mercury, Bomb Fuses, Poisons, etc.* It was published in 1885 and sold for ten cents per copy. Many years later, during the 1960s, far-left radicals in the American student anti-war movement borrowed huge chunks of it for their own terror manual – The Anarchist Cookbook – which has sold nearly a million copies.

Most published his pamphlet after emigrating to the United States in 1882. He had been briefly imprisoned in both Germany and Great Britain for his advocacy of violence, but in America, protected by the First Amendment, his inflammatory pamphlet was considered free speech and he continued publishing his newspaper, the equally inflammatory *Freiheit*. Although popular cartoonists caricatured him as the typical Anarchist, a wild-eyed bearded figure, complete with bomb in one hand and knife in the other, the authorities left him alone, since he had not committed any overt act that violated the law.

That abruptly changed on 3 May 1886, when some 80,000 people gathered on Haymarket Square in Chicago to protest the killing of two strikers by police 48 hours earlier. Although the city's Anarchists had organized the protest, it was peaceful – until a force of 200 police showed up and demanded that the protestors disperse. Just then, a bomb was thrown into the ranks of police, killing seven of them and injuring 70 others. The police fired into the crowd, killing seven protestors and wounding 60 others. Although it was never proven exactly who threw the bomb, eventually eight of the city's most notorious Anarchists were charged with the murder of the seven policemen; four were hanged, a fifth committed suicide in prison and the others received lengthy prison terms. Most, whose pamphlet was alleged to have served as inspiration for the Anarchist attack, learned that American tolerance for free speech suddenly had its limits. In the wake of the Haymarket incident, he was clapped into prison for 'disturbing the peace' after publishing articles in *Freiheit* praising Anarchists for killing policemen.

The strong political reaction to the Haymarket incident – states rushed to pass new laws restricting labour unions and freedom of expression – proved how badly Most had misread the American psyche. The public associated violence with the ideals of the Anarchists, which meant they found it impossible to relate to someone they regarded as a murderous fanatic. Americans do not like extremism from either end of the spectrum, a fundamental truth about U.S. politics that Most, as a European, never quite grasped.

The majority of the American Anarchists were also

ABOVE: U.S. President William McKinley assassinated by an Anarchist during the Buffalo Exposition in 1901.

European-born, and like Most, they also misread the U.S. political culture. They persisted in "dynamite by deed" – assassinating President McKinley, bombing Wall Street, blowing up a newspaper office – which succeeded only in alienating public opinion and giving the government license to introduce oppressive laws intended to destroy the movement altogether. New York State, for example, among the more politically liberal states in the union, passed the 1902 Criminal Anarchy Law, which flatly declared any expression or action in support of Anarchism illegal. By 1914, the Anarchists as a political movement of any consequence in the United States of America was dead.

LESSONS LEARNED

Although the Anarchists failed to heed the lesson about misreading a political context, elsewhere there were others in the small kingdom of Serbia who had understood it. That understanding led them to a key conclusion. Terrorism was an important weapon of covert political warfare, but it could not be left in the hands of freelance Anarchists or anybody like them. It would have to be brought under control of an intelligence agency, which would wield terrorism as the equalizer in the struggle between unequals. In their case, little Serbia and its chief rival, the mighty Austro-Hungarian Empire. What resulted was something new and terrible in world history, state-sponsored terrorism. The Serbians had no idea that it would set off a world war.

On 9 May 1911, a small group of Serbian ministers and military officers met secretly in Belgrade and formed the Ujedinfenje ili Smrt (Union or Death) – a terrorist organization. The purpose was simply to cause as much damage as possible to Austria-Hungary, which a few months before had annexed the adjoining Balkan province of Bosnia and Herzegovina – to the fury of Bosnian nationalists who were seeking independence. At the meeting, plans were hatched to recruit the most rabid Bosnian nationalists that could be found and organize them into terrorist cells to carry out a subterranean war against the Austro-Hungarian occupation. Methods would include propaganda, murder of Bosnian collaborators, disruption of the occupation government and assassinations of Austro-Hungarian officials.

In charge of the clandestine organization was Colonel Dragutin Dimitrijevic, chief of intelligence for the Serbian Army General Staff. A devoted Serbian nationalist who hated Austrians, Dimitrijevic had cut his teeth in covert warfare during the Balkan Wars of 1912–1913, when he organized terrorist squads to operate against the Turks. The experience had taught him that terrorism, covertly directed and supported by an intelligence agency, could be a valuable weapon against an opponent with superior resources, provided certain conditions were met. These included avoiding hurting innocent civilians, never carrying out an act of terror that would undermine popular support and carefully hiding any connection between the terrorists and their official sponsors.

Essentially, the Union or Death organization amounted to an undeclared war by Serbia against Austria-Hungary.

BELOW: Violence at the 1886 Haymarket riot in Chicago was ignited by a bomb which killed seven police officers. The police retaliated and shot seven protesters.

As Bosnia began to be wracked by a series of sabotage operations, shootings and general unrest, the Austrians suspected that war was indeed being made upon them and the natural suspect was Serbia. The Serbians blandly denied increasingly angry Austrian diplomatic protests, asserting that acts of terrorism in Bosnia were the work of indigenous Bosnian nationalists reacting to a brutal Austrian occupation. At least part of that denial was true. In a classic mistake committed so often by occupation authorities, the Austrians reacted to an internal security threat by increasing repressive measures that simply incited more popular support for the insurgents.

By 1914, Bosnia and Herzegovina was in a state of ferment. To end it, the Austrians decided on a dramatic move. Archduke Ferdinand, heir to the Austro-Hungarian throne, would be dispatched sometime in late spring on a state visit to the restless province. He would assure the Bosnians of a 'new approach' of conciliation and reform to end the troubles. Ferdinand, known to be relatively liberal and opposed to Austria's harsh occupation policies, would be the symbol of the new policy. He would also serve as a subtle warning to Serbia that Austria-Hungary would do whatever it took to maintain its grip on to the province.

In response, Dimitrijevic conceived a plan that represented a significant escalation in the covert war: Ferdinand would be assassinated. That dramatic action, Dimitrijevic believed, would compel the Austrians to undertake a sharp escalation in its repressive operations in Bosnia. This in turn would ignite a full-fledged uprising. He sent one of his best agents to prowl the steamy coffee shops of Belgrade, looking for willing recruits among the many Bosnian exiles living in the Serbian capital. He found three young high school students – Gavrilo Princip, Nedjilko Cabrinovic and Trifko Grabez. They all shared the requisite fanaticism suitable for the operation, namely a willingness to die in the attempt. If arrested, they would swallow cyanide capsules to balk any interrogation. One reason for their willingness to die for the cause was the fact that all three suffered from tuberculosis, in those days a terminal disease. They were told that Serbia would deny all knowledge of them; officially they were independent zealots who had decided to carry out the assassination on their own. Thus, there would be no attempt to rescue them if they were captured.

The three men were taken to a secret training base in Serbia run by Serbian military intelligence, where they were schooled in the art of throwing bombs and pistol marksmanship. In early June, they were smuggled across the border into Bosnia via an underground railroad of contacts Dimitrijevic had set up. They settled in Sarajevo under cover as students, waiting for their quarry to appear.

The assassination plan was simple. As the newspapers openly reported, Ferdinand and his wife Sophie would arrive in Sarajevo on 28 June. They would then immediately ride in an open car – in order to be seen by the anticipated crowds of citizens eager to cheer the Archduke – among a motorcade to inspect army manoeuvres outside the city. They would then return for a reception at city hall. The motorcade route would be along a wide avenue called Appel Quay, which paralleled the Miljacka River. Members of the assassination team were to be strung out at separate points all along the route, each with a bomb and a pistol. When Ferdinand's car appeared, the man closest to it would heave a bomb. If the bomb failed for any reason, he would shoot the Archduke, then commit suicide.

Just after 10 a.m., Ferdinand's open car proceeded slowly up the Appel Quay. As the car neared Cabrinovic, he pulled a bomb from his coat pocket and threw it. At the last second, Ferdinand spotted the bomb sailing toward him. He deflected it with his arm and the bomb exploded in the street, injuring a dozen spectators. Cabrinovic immediately swallowed his cyanide capsule and jumped into the river – only to discover that the river was only about a foot deep at that point. Worse, the cyanide he had been given apparently was from a weak batch, for it only caused him to vomit as he was seized by the crowd.

Meanwhile, Ferdinand sped on past Grabez – who unaccountably failed to do anything – and on to the city hall, where welcoming ceremonies took place, just as though nothing had happened. Although his aides begged him to cancel the rest of the day's schedule, Ferdinand insisted he would proceed to the next event, a visit to a museum. He and Sophie climbed back into the car, intending to proceed back down Appel Quay. However, fate now took a strange turn. Ferdinand's driver mistakenly drove into Franz Josef Street. Suddenly realizing his mistake, he jammed on the brakes, intending to back up. The car stopped directly in front of a food store – which just happened to be where Princip was at that very moment eating a sandwich.

Assuming the mission had failed when he saw what happened to Cabrinovic's bomb, Princip had walked to the food store to get a bite to eat while he considered what to do next. Now, he could hardly believe his luck: the target was sitting in a car no more than several feet from him. He pulled the pistol from his pocket, took one step toward the car and fired two shots. One struck Ferdinand in the neck; the other struck Sophie in the abdomen. Princip then turned the gun on himself, but before he could pull the trigger, he was subdued by a crowd of people. The Archduke and his wife, rushed to a hospital, bled to death en route.

True to their word, Princip and Cabrinovic went off to prison insisting that the assassination was strictly their own idea, an assertion they maintained in the face of marathon interrogations. They did admit there was a third

LEFT: Gavrilo
Princip was found
guilty of the 1914
murder of Archduke
Ferdinand, which
sparked World War
I. He escaped the
death penalty, but
received a lengthy
prison sentence.

co-conspirator, Grabez, who had already been detained near the border as a 'suspicious person'. It hardly mattered though; Austria-Hungary, eager to settle scores with the Serbians, decided to use Ferdinand's murder as justification for a showdown. Flatly accusing Serbia of arranging the assassination, although they had no proof, the Austrians took a hard line. They demanded that the Serbians turn over Dimitrijevic and other Serbian officials whom the Austrians claimed were the 'instigators' of the plot to assassinate the Archduke and who were further the 'puppet masters' behind the Union or Death terrorist organization (popularly known as the 'Black Hand' from the symbol it painted on walls in Bosnia). The ultimatum ignited the tinderbox that was Europe's delicate system of alliances and just a few weeks after the death of Ferdinand, Europe was plunged into the most terrible war in its history. Both the Kingdom of Serbia and the Austro-Hungarian Empire were consumed in the conflagration.

The cataclysm set off by two gunshots in Sarajevo represented not only a failure of state-sponsored terrorism, but an even greater intelligence failure as well. Most importantly, the Serbians had never bothered to consider what the reaction of Austria-Hungary would be to the assassination of the heir to the throne, a very significant escalation over the murders of Bosnian collaborators and

local officials in the occupied province. As for the Austrians, they were completely unaware that sending the Archduke to Bosnia on 28 June represented a colossal insult to the Serbians, certain to raise the temperature in an already volatile situation. That day was known as 'Vidounan' among Serbians, the date when the old Kingdom of Serbia was conquered by the Turks in 1389. Serbians considered it a solemn day of remembrance.

Another Austrian intelligence failure involved security for the Archduke's visit. Austrian intelligence had received some vague indications that there was probably a plot underway to murder the Archduke during his visit, but they were not specific enough for him to be concerned. Ferdinand was notoriously indifferent to security, the kind of man who had little concern for his own safety. Given that indifference, Austrian intelligence shrugged off all the reports about a possible assassination attempt and took no security measures whatsoever. Only a grand total of 120 policemen were on duty in the entire city of Sarajevo on 28 June 1914, none of whom were told to be on the alert for any assassination attempt.

For those directly involved in the assassination, history exacted an extreme penalty. All three assassins escaped death sentences, because Austrian law forbade executions of anyone under the age of 20, but they received long

prison terms. As Europe was plunged into war, their names and deed were forgotten; when all three died in prison years later of tuberculosis, hardly anyone noticed. Colonel Dimitrijevic, the Serbian intelligence chief who set the fateful assassination plan in motion, came to be widely regarded as the man most responsible for the disastrous war that destroyed the Kingdom of Serbia. A convenient scapegoat, he was arrested in 1917 on vague charges of plotting against the government and shot by a firing squad. Like the three assassins he sent to Sarajevo, his fate also passed with hardly any notice in a world preoccupied with weightier matters.

Whatever its unanticipated effects on world history, the state-sponsored terrorism of Serbia proved that the concept worked. It was a conclusion that took firmest root in an area of the world where it would cause the greatest havoc – the Middle East.

DESPERATE MEASURES

In the spring of 1942, a group of Egyptian army officers met secretly in a Cairo apartment to discuss the unthinkable: the defeat of the British empire in the Middle East; a free and independent Egypt; control of the Suez Canal in Egyptian hands and a triumph of Arab nationalism throughout the region, restoring Arab glory to a height not seen since the fourteenth century. This grand vision was inspired by military events taking place hundreds of miles to the west, where the German Afrika Korps under General Erwin Rommel was achieving spectacular victories over British forces. Rommel's forces had crossed the Egyptian border and all over Cairo Egyptians were secretly stashing swastika flags to be flown the day the Germans marched down the city's streets in triumph.

As things turned out, Rommel's grand vision of sweeping through Egypt and taking the Suez Canal did not come to pass as his forces were defeated by the British at a small railroad junction named El Alamein. With Germany's defeat, Egypt returned to the status quo, a quasi-independent kingdom under British suzerainty, ruled by a fat, sybarite monarch, King Farouk. The Suez Canal bisected the country like a great gash, its revenues from shipping tolls seldom trickling down to the vast numbers of Egypt's impoverished. However, a seed had been planted by wartime events: the mighty British could be defeated and there was a genuine chance that Egypt could be wrested from their grasp.

But how? The group of ten Egyptian officers who met in 1942 realized that to take on the British military was foolhardy. The British had large forces in Egypt, complete control of the air and sea, and there were dozens of large military bases in the country. The Egyptian army, such as it was, functioned largely as an adjunct to the British military and was in no position to challenge what still was one of the world's leading military powers. Besides, as the Egyptians were acutely aware, the British were prepared to do anything to maintain control of the strategically vital Suez Canal.

The Egyptian officers, who christened their movement the Free Officers, were led by a charismatic and highly intelligent colonel named Gamal Abdel Nassser, whose key subordinate was another bright officer, Anwar Sadat. They decided that the best route to complete Egyptian independence was a covert war to destabilize, and then collapse, the Egyptian monarchy. Nasser recruited an important resource for this underground war: Egypt's Islamic fundamentalists, who bitterly hated King Farouk and his corrupt government as 'unholy'. They wanted to establish an Islamic theocracy in Egypt, an objective Nasser did not share, but he found it convenient to use the Islamic radicals as allies – for the moment.

The radicals, organized into a loose confederation called the Muslim Brotherhood, played an important role in Nasser's triumph in 1952, achieved with every tool of covert war – strikes, riots, selective assassinations, disruption of the government and terror. However, if the Brotherhood believed that a new Egypt under Nasser's leadership would bring them any closer to their dream of an Islamic state, they would be disappointed. Nasser was a secular Arab who paid lip service to fundamentalism, so

long as it was useful in his drive to overthrow the existing order. Now that the Muslim Brotherhood had outlived its usefulness, he was no longer interested in the group's goals. To their fury, he refused to give the Brotherhood any role in the government. The group struck back, attempting an assassination of Nasser. It failed and the result was a crackdown on a political-religious entity that Nasser now believed was a danger to his own rule. Thousands of Brotherhood members were thrown into prison, where they were brutalized and tortured by Nasser's secret police. Those who managed to escape the crackdown fled to other Arab countries to begin new Muslim Brotherhood organizations.

What emerged was a split in the Muslim Brotherhood. One faction, radicalized by its ordeal at the hands of Nasser, passed into the hands of firebrands who believed that nothing less than a holy war had to be waged against everything they believed was thwarting their goal of a 'pure' Islamic republic – Western influence, secular Arabs like Nasser, and 'accommodationists' who believed that the Islamic and non-Islamic worlds could coexist. In that latter category they placed the other faction of the Brotherhood, relative moderates who responded to peace overtures by Nasser's successor, Anwar Sadat. They had reached an arrangement of sorts, where the Brotherhood could continue to function in Egypt with full privileges, including control over religious schools, provided it played no role in Egyptian politics. That kind of accommodation was anathema to the radical faction, now calling itself Islamic Jihad, a dislike they underscored by assassinating Sadat in 1981.

By that time, Islamic Jihad had come to dominate the entire Islamic rejectionist movement. Its core was among the Brotherhood members who had suffered in Egyptian prisons, survivors of an ordeal that had hardened them into committed radicals determined to impose their will. Among them were Sheik Rahman, who would go on to direct the terror bombing of the World Trade Center in 1993, and Ayman al-Zawahari, who would become the number two man to Osama bin Laden. Their vision was fixated on the total destruction of what they perceived as the impediments to Islamic purity: the influence of Western nations, especially their culture; 'Zionist interlopers' in Palestine; modernist corruption of the Islamic religion; and the corrupt rulers of Arab nations who accommodated themselves to the lure of the West's money.

How was this total destruction to be achieved? The answer was terror, the traditional weapon of David versus Goliath. The Islamic fundamentalists turned to history, searching for terror campaigns they could emulate, especially those that had succeeded in achieving political change in the face of great odds. There were a number of examples that fit the category. One was the Black Dragon Society of Japan, the far-right organization that in the decades before World War II terrorized moderate Japanese politicians by assassinations, paving the way for militarists to take over the government. Another was the Croatian separatist movement that conducted a 70-year-long campaign of terror against Yugoslavia, including the assassination of King Alexander in 1934. However, the most instructive examples involved, ironically enough, terrorist operations in the United States and Israel – the fundamentalists' greatest villains.

A GLOBAL AFFAIR

In the spring of 1865, following the final collapse of the Confederacy, six Confederate soldiers made their way back to their homes in Tennessee. As required, their first act was to "swallow the dog" as southerners put it, the oath of allegiance to the United States. That was only the first shock in a world turned upside down: federal troops patrolling the countryside to enforce Reconstruction; newly-freed slaves registering to vote; plantations carved up to distribute land to ex-slaves; a state government of carpetbaggers (Northerners assigned to government posts in the occupied South), blacks and 'scalawags' (southern collaborators) running the government.

Disgusted and infuriated by what they saw, the six southerners met one night and created the Ku Klux Klan (KKK), America's first terrorist organization dedicated to a simple proposition: destroy Reconstruction by terror. It began with what they called "night rides", harassment of blacks by men on horseback whose faces were concealed by hoods made of flour sacks. The next step was outright violence. They broke up meetings of blacks, burnt schools and churches, and killed local sheriffs and Unionists. By 1867, the original group of six charter Klan members

RIGHT: King Alexander of Yugoslavia was murdered by a Croatian terrorist in 1934 in Marseille, while on a state visit to France. His assassin was killed on the spot by police.

had grown to several hundred, operating in 'dens' throughout the state. In April of that year, all the KKK branches met secretly in Nashville and named the famed ex-Confederate cavalry general Nathan Bedford Forrest (who had made a fortune before the war as a dealer in slaves) as head of a united Klan that would organize Klan branches throughout the South. The enlarged organization would then focus its efforts on the upcoming 1868 election.

That election was crucial to the KKK, since it would mark the first time that emancipated slaves would vote in a state and national election. The objective was to terrorize blacks and the carpetbaggers from voting in the election in favour of native southerners who would enact local laws to balk Reconstruction. A wave of terror broke out all over the South as the KKK made life a living hell for blacks, carpetbaggers, Unionists and a thin force of federal troops trying to enforce the Fourteenth

RIGHT: In the present-day United States Ku Klux Klan membership has dwindled, but historically its 'success' has shown other organizations that terrorism works.

Amendment. The campaign of terror proved to be a spectacular success. Although Ulysses S. Grant, a man the southerners despised, was elected President, the Klan succeeded in driving 100,000 newly-registered black voters away from the polls. Virtually all state and local offices in the southern states were won by Klan supporters. They immediately began writing laws whose practical effect was to deny blacks their civil rights. It would take 86 years and a crusade by Martin Luther King to reverse those laws.

In the next century, the Klan would fragment into warring factions and finally crumble in the face of a strong federal assault. However, before then, it had retaught other terrorists an important lesson – terrorism works. A relatively small group of terrorists, armed with nothing more than rifles, had managed to defeat a government, despite that government's mighty power, and to forcibly change the course of history.

The same lesson was provided by events in pre-1948 Palestine. Although all Zionists shared a common dream of a Jewish homeland in Palestine, a radical faction insisted that the only way the movement could achieve that dream was by force. Like all Zionists, the radicals were especially upset that the British government, in the name of its overall foreign policy objectives in the Middle East, had cut off all Jewish emigration to Palestine. The radicals argued that so long as the British were more concerned about their relations with the Arabs (meaning Arab oil), there was no hope they would ever allow Jewish emigration to Palestine – or the creation of a Jewish state.

However, removing the British by force was a goal far beyond the capabilities of the ragtag forces of armed settlers the Zionists controlled in Palestine. The British presence in Palestine had a central weakness – it existed in a democratic system, which meant it was there at the sufferance of British public opinion. If the people of Britain arrived at the conclusion that the cost of maintaining that presence was no longer worth it, then the presence would be at an end. Therefore the solution, the radicals concluded, was to raise the price so that the cost became prohibitive. The price would be exacted by terror.

That terror was carried out by two tight-knit terrorist groups. The larger of the two was the Irgun Zvai Leumi, headed by Menachem Begin (later a prime minister of Israel), a band of violent extremists largely made up of veterans of

the long underground struggle of the Jewish settlers against the Arabs in Palestine. The second group, also composed of underground veterans, was the Stern Gang, whose leaders included Yitzhak Shamir (also later a prime minister of Israel).

Some members of both groups were veterans of the long underground struggle by European Jews, including the most radical underground group, Nakam. After World War II it had sought to avenge the deaths of six million European Jews by mass killings of German SS men in Allied prison camps. In one operation, Nakam agents put poison in the bread of several thousand SS prisoners, killing dozens. In another, unsuccessful, operation, they tried to poison the water supply of the city of Nuremberg in an effort to kill all the defendants at the war crimes trials. A subsidiary operation by several former members of the Jewish Brigade that fought with the British during World War II targeted former SS men for murder, ultimately killing more than 200 of them.

The terror war began on 9 September 1946, when an Irgun operative threw a grenade onto the balcony of a house in Tel Aviv, killing Desmond Doran, the senior MI6

officer in Palestine. The assassination was meant as a clear message to British intelligence. Doran was involved in MI6 operations against the Zionist underground and that was something both the Irgun and the Stern Gang would not tolerate. Six weeks later, the Irgun delivered another message. Two suitcase bombs were placed against the front door of the British embassy in Rome; the MI6 chief of station there narrowly escaped death as the resulting explosion demolished the entire front of the building. The Rome embassy had been especially active in British efforts to block Jewish emigration to Palestine.

SERIOUS SOURCE OF PROBLEMS

Despite their best efforts, the British were unable either to stem the flood of illegal immigration (more than 73,000 Jews were smuggled into Palestine during 1945–46 alone) or to make much of a dent in the Zionist terrorist movement. Both the Irgun and the Stern Gang were well versed in such tradecraft as countersurveillance and combating penetration attempts. Moreover, they operated with a very strict cellular structure, which made penetration virtually impossible. Above all, although the Zionist movement officially disavowed the terrorists, they enjoyed at least tacit support at the upper levels of the movement for the simple reason that the Irgun and the Stern Gang were helping to achieve the Zionists' chief goal: driving the British out of Palestine.

The two groups concluded that the best way to achieve the goal was to raise the price in blood and treasure to the point where the British finally decided Palestine was not worth the cost. That is precisely what happened. British popular opinion was appalled by such terrorist acts of the Irgun and the Stern Gang as the murder of two British soldiers in retaliation for the execution of a convicted Irgun terrorist; the murder of over 200 Palestinian Arabs at a village called Deir Yassin; the assassination of Count Folke Bernadotte, (the United Nations mediator in Palestine) and the blowing-up of the King David Hotel in Jerusalem, killing several hundred. However, they also came to realize that the price of keeping the Mandate was simply too high. On 14 May 1948, the British threw in the towel: Great Britain announced that it would withdraw from the Palestine Mandate.

The success of the Irgun and the Stern Gang illustrated a central truth that would govern all terrorism for the rest of the century. Terror was the perfect – and sometimes the only –

weapon for the have-nots in their struggle against the haves. However, it was not a weapon to be used indiscriminately, an important caveat that not everyone grasped. Among those who learned the lesson imperfectly were the Palestinians.

The Palestinians represented the classic formula for terror as a solution to an intractable political problem: a people displaced from their homeland, their national destiny thwarted; a general worldwide indifference to their plight and a powerful and implacable enemy in the form of Israel. The Palestinians concluded there was no military solution to the problem, as proven by the Arab failure to defeat Israel militarily in three wars. Confronting Israel's superior military power was suicidal, which left terror as the alternative. Terror would gain world attention for the Palestinians' plight and, as the Zionists had done years before during the time of the British Mandate, raise the price of Israel's policy to the point where it would be forced to accept the legitimacy of Palestinian national aspirations.

However, from the first moment, the Palestinians were divided over what their terror campaign was supposed to achieve. Yasser Arafat and other Palestinian leaders had a limited objective in mind – gain international recognition and force Israel into accepting the reality of a Palestinian

BELOW: A pair of West German policeman traverse the roof of the building where Israeli Olympic athletes are being held hostage in Munich.

LEFT: U.S. government office building in Oklahoma City, Oklahoma, destroyed by a right-wing terrorist bomb in 1995.

RIGHT: A commuter train in Madrid ripped apart by an Islamic terrorist bomb in March 2004.

national state in occupied territory. However, another, more radical, faction believed that the whole point was to destroy Israel utterly, driving all the Jews from Palestine, and replace the state of Israel with a Palestinian nation.

This split would cause the Palestinians no end of problems because they began to carry out terrorist operations using both approaches. Those sympathetic to Palestinian aspirations might accept the idea of terrorist operations directed strictly against Israeli targets. However, it was difficult to see the connection between those aspirations and such terrorist spectaculars as the hijacking and destruction of airliners with no discernible connection to Israel, the seizure of an Italian cruise ship Achille Lauro (including the murder of an elderly Jewish man confined to a wheelchair) or the kidnapping of Israeli athletes at the 1972 Olympic games in Munich. Such operations portrayed the Palestinians as international outlaws, not a movement of genuine national liberation.

Few believed assertions by the Palestinian leadership that the more odious terror operations carried out in the name of Palestinian aspirations were the "unauthorized" work of radical factions. Overall, Palestinian terror operations must be judged a failure, for they were never to achieve the goal of an independent Palestinian state. Progress toward that goal was achieved not by terror, but by an event that no one

anticipated – the intifada – a spontaneous popular uprising that made Israel's position on the West Bank untenable.

Among the more avid students of Palestinian terror was an entirely new generation of Arab radicals with roots deep in the Muslim Brotherhood, the Iranian fundamentalist movement and the fundamentalist Muslim movement in Saudi Arabia. They were driven by an apocalyptic vision of a world that had become hopelessly corrupt, contaminated by secularism and the pervasive influence of Western culture. The existence of Israel was only part of the problem, defined as the evil of modernism. The solution they devised involved nothing less than destruction of that world, to be replaced by an Islamic fundamentalist hyper-civilization of 'purity', uncontaminated by the evil of Western ideas. It would be a civilization based on what they perceived as Islamic civilization's last golden period, somewhere around the fourteenth century.

This vision took hold in a number of new Islamic fundamentalist groups that suddenly arose in the Arab world, including Hezbollah in Lebanon, Hamas in the occupied West Bank, the Taliban in Afghanistan and Islamic Jihad in Iran and several other countries. They all understood that a total Islamic revolution could not be achieved by any kind of military confrontation with the West, a battle that would be fought on the West's terms and against its overwhelming scientific and technical superiority. The answer was terror on a scale never seen before – total, indiscriminate terror aimed at destroying the existing order. It rested on two key assumptions. Firstly, the victims of terror will surrender their beliefs to save themselves from further terror. Secondly, terror on a grand scale, applied indiscriminately, will result in a collapse of will.

The new fundamentalists carefully studied other terrorist movements and concluded there was nothing to learn from them. For one thing, the scope of their operations was too narrow. Organizations such as the Irish Republican Army (IRA) in Northern Ireland or the ETA Basque separatist movement in Spain were never sufficiently indiscriminate to threaten collapse of the existing order. Even as shocking a terrorist act as the Oklahoma City bombing struck them as pointless; the federal government of the United States was not about to collapse simply because one of its office buildings had been the target of a terrorist attack. The perpetrators of the bombing had repeated the Anarchists' mistake, believing that a 'propaganda by deed' would inspire the masses to rise up and overthrow the government.

They also believed that many terrorist movements had made the error of seeking help from foreign governments. It was help that could be withdrawn when those governments decided it was no longer in their interest to be involved – such as Libya's Muammar el-Qaddafi, who decided to get out of the terrorism business altogether. It was also help that came with strings attached as experience with the Russians and East Germans – who always wanted to control whatever they were supporting – had demonstrated. There was also an understanding that most terrorist organizations eventually become vulnerable to the anti-terror efforts of intelligence organizations willing to be as ruthless as their terrorist opponents (witness the assassinations of Palestinian terrorist leaders by Israeli intelligence).

THREAT FROM THE EAST
What emerged was a loose confederation of Islamic fundamentalist terror groups united in a common goal of purifying Islam and destroying all Western influence. They were led by the best financed and organized of the groups, al Qaeda ('the base'), brought to life by Osama bin Laden, the son of a wealthy Saudi Arabian construction contractor, who had drifted into radical Islamic politics as a result of his service in Afghanistan fighting the Russians during the Soviet invasion. A large training camp in the country used to train foreign Islamic militants for combat in the war was called, simply, "the base" – a name that came to be used for all the militants who trained there and the umbrella organization that evolved from that base.

Bin Laden invested his millions and considerable energies building a new jihad (holy war) movement among the radical

RIGHT: Wreckage of a Russian school destroyed by a Chechen separatist terrorist bomb in 2004.

RIGHT: One of the IRA's most spectacular terrorist attacks, the bombing of the Grand Hotel in Brighton during a 1984 Conservative Party conference.

Islamic warriors who had flocked to Afghanistan to fight the Russian infidels. At its core, al Qaeda is basically a militant Sunni organization that subscribes to Wahhab, the radical doctrine that proclaims all non-believers in fundamentalist interpretations of Islam as 'infidels' who must be destroyed. It aims to establish radical Islamist states wherever there are Muslim populations throughout the world, overthrow all regimes that do not subscribe to the Wahhabism doctrine, remove all Western influence from the Arab world and take control of Jerusalem and make it an exclusively Muslim city.

The first group of Islamic militants to achieve any kind of political power were native Afghans called the Taliban (literally 'students'). The group formed a potent political faction in a factionalized Afghanistan after the Soviet withdrawal, ultimately emerging as the victor in that country's civil war. The Islamic fundamentalist state they created provided a preview of what kind of Islamic state bin Laden meant – strict adherence to religious laws, women reduced to no more than chattels, a ban on all Western influences and an end to all education except religious schools. In 1996, when bin Laden was driven out of Sudan under American pressure, he and his al Qaeda were invited to set up shop in Afghanistan. There, bin Laden set up a number of training camps to which Islamic militants from all over the world migrated for a course in terror.

On 23 February 1998, bin Laden and Ayman al-µ, along with three other Islamic militant groups, issued what amounted to a declaration of war against the United States and the rest of the Western world. It took the form of a fatwa (binding religious edict) calling on all Muslims in the world to "kill the Americans and their allies, civilians and military". Later that year, al Qaeda carried out its first major terror attack, the bombings of U.S. embassies in East Africa, killing more than 300 people. In response, the U.S. bombed one of the al Qaeda training bases in Afghanistan, an attack that not only failed to kill any militants, but convinced bin Laden and his allies that the Americans had been intimidated. Not unreasonably, they concluded that if all the Americans had done in response to a terror attack was to bomb some empty buildings, then they clearly were afraid of antagonizing the terrorists further.

At that moment, one of the greatest intelligence failures in history began to unfold. Without any sources within the militants and lacking any real understanding of what the new terror offensive was all about, the CIA and other Western intelligence agencies tended to underestimate bin Laden and the al Qaeda threat. The common perception was that al Qaeda was simply another Islamic terror group whose danger lay almost entirely in attacks on American installations overseas. The American intelligence establishment, oriented to gather data on large formal organizations with bureaucratic structures and communications systems vulnerable to interception, was ill-suited to deal with low-tech terrorist organizations of small, independent cells that communicated with cell phones and messengers.

The intelligence blindness was responsible for the next terrorist spectacular of al Qaeda – the bombing attack on the *U.S.S. Cole* in Yemen. The U.S. had no clue about a flourishing terrorist network operating in Yemen, nor did it have any insight into a large-scale recruiting drive all over the Muslim world for suicide bombers (although everybody in the Arab world seemed to know about it).

Most significantly, the Americans had no idea of al Qaeda's next fateful step – an attack on the United States itself, the first such terrorist attack in history. On 11 September 2001, four commercial jetliners were hijacked in midair. Two were flown by suicide bombers into the twin towers of the World Trade Center, killing more than 3,000 people and collapsing the buildings. A third, also flown by a suicide bomber, ploughed into the Pentagon. The fourth jetliner, apparently aimed to fly into either the White House or the Capitol, crashed into the ground in Pennsylvania after passengers tried to overcome the hijackers.

The shock of what would become known simply as 9/11 finally moved the U.S. and its allies to drastic action – a military invasion of Afghanistan to destroy the Taliban, the world's only terrorist regime, which provided sanctuary and support to bin Laden and al Qaeda. The terrorist organization was also a target for destruction. Those objectives were largely accomplished, including a severe crippling of bin Laden's organization, but events have since proven that al Qaeda is far from being totally defeated. Indeed, its assorted components and affiliated groups have shown a remarkable ability to conduct large-scale terrorist attacks, most spectacularly the bombing of transportation facilities in London in July 2006.

One striking example of al Qaeda's resilience has occurred in Iraq. During the 2003 invasion of Iraq by the U.S. and Great Britain, al Qaeda organized and aided the local resistance fighting coalition forces and the emerging government. The group advertised its presence with two spectacular terrorist actions: the blowing up the United Nations headquarters in Baghdad, followed by the destruction, also by suicide bomber, of the Red Cross headquarters. Then al Qaeda took over the town of Fallujah as its main headquarters and were driven out in 2004 only after a large-scale attack by the U.S. military, suffering heavy casualties. The organization was no sooner removed from Fallujah when it suddenly revived, aided by the terrorist organization of Abu Musab al-Zarqawi, a Jordanian Islamic terrorist who declared his loyalty to bin Laden and his intention to drive the Americans and the British out of Iraq. Zarqawi was killed in a U.S. air strike in

ABOVE: Osama Bin
Laden, leader of al
Quaeda, the Islamic
fundamentalist terror
organization that
carried out the World
Trade Center attack and
other major attacks
around the world.

against the Iranians during the Iran-Iraq war and against the Kurdish minority. A lack of sources inside Iraq and over-reliance on the questionable assertions of Iraqi exiles meant there was no way to verify the exiles' reports. It led to a fateful decision that only a full-scale military invasion of Iraq would solve the problem, in the mistaken assumption that the dictatorial government could be overturned, then replaced by Iraq's educated middle class to form an enlightened, moderate leadership.

However, both American and British intelligence failed to understand that, by 2003, Iraq had largely fallen apart as a cohesive society. Decades of oppression had taught Iraqis to take care of their own families and give their loyalty only to whichever tribe or sub-tribe they belonged to. Intelligence analysts, trained to deal with technical hard data that could be quantified, disregarded the variables of culture and society. As a result, they missed the fact that the enlightened, moderate segments of Iraqi society had been destroyed by a brutal dictatorship. There was no enlightened middle class waiting to emerge, like some phoenix arising from the ashes, into the power vacuum – especially after the U.S. committed a major blunder in disbanding the Iraqi army.

That meant the American and British soldiers were now occupiers, not liberators. The power vacuum was filled by the imans, who proclaimed the Western soldiers 'infidels' – whom all Muslims must resist.

Although intelligence failure has been a consistent theme in the rise of modern Islamist terror, there is another aspect that has proven even more troubling. It involves a fundamental question: to what lengths should a democratic society, governed by rules and laws, go to combat a ruthless, deadly threat that has no rules or laws? How far should a democratic society deviate from its own values to protect itself?

There is no easy answer. Western countries have come to accept a degree of state control and tightening of civil liberties in the name of the 'war on terrorism', although there is a great deal of unease over assertions that to fight the terrorists effectively governments must be given sweeping,

June 2006, but his forces largely succeeded in fomenting the sectarian conflict between Sunni and Shiite that has convulsed much of the country.

FUTURE THREAT

The constant morphing of al Qaeda into still newer guises and forms has proven a huge threat to Western intelligence, one they have largely failed to meet. The greatest failures occurred in Iraq, the graveyard of a number of intelligence errors. It began with a shared perception that Iraq had weapons of mass destruction, a threat of the first order, since Saddam Hussein had already used chemical warfare

ABOVE: The twisted remains of a London double-decker bus, ripped apart by an Islamic terrorist bomb, one of four targeted at the city's transportation system in 2005.

unprecedented powers to monitor and investigate its citizens. There is also a great deal of unease over the powers given to security establishments to fight the war, including torture, 'rendition flights' to hide terrorist suspects from due process and imprisonment of presumed terrorists without any proof or charges.

At some point, these dilemmas will have to be resolved, for how a democracy conducts the business of intelligence reveals a great deal about that democracy.

The central dilemma for Western democracies is that freedom without security is useless, but nobody wants security without freedom. The dilemma has become even more intractable as the governments of democratic states insist that the only really viable weapon against terrorism is preemption – uncovering potential sources of terrorism, keeping close watch on the areas where terrorists are bred and profiling potential terrorists. Accomplishing preemption, however, requires intelligence in the form of pervasive surveillance, the kind of snooping into the lives

of private citizens that democracies most detest (and the most dangerous threat to civil liberties).

The price of enhanced security is always diminished liberty, since there is no other way to achieve the kind of immunization against terror that societies want. Governments justify such diminution by arguing that law-abiding citizens have nothing to fear from increased surveillance – the traditional argument against tyranny. However, it is a weak argument to justify a departure from the traditional standard of 'clear and present danger' as a basis for pervasive surveillance of a nation's private citizens. It is an even weaker argument to justify some of the more disturbing aspects of contemporary anti-terror operations, including 'renditions' (holding suspected terrorists without charges) and torture as a means of gathering information on terrorist cells.

As the High Court of Israel concluded, in striking down official regulations that permitted the mistreatment of terrorist suspects, accepted legal norms are "how we distinguish ourselves from the terrorists themselves".

THE AGE OF SURVEILLANCE

IN 2004, AFTER EX-PRESIDENT CLINTON SUFFERED A HEART ATTACK AND WAS RUSHED TO NEW YORK-PRESBYTERIAN HOSPITAL IN NEW YORK CITY, HIS SECRET SERVICE DETAIL WENT TO THE HOSPITAL'S ADMINISTRATION OFFICE AND TOOK WHAT THEY CONSIDERED TO BE A VITAL SECURITY PRECAUTION.

They admitted him under a false name. It might have seemed to be an odd action. After all, Clinton is an instantly recognizable figure and there was virtually no danger of assassination in his private suite. However, the Secret Service agents were not so much concerned about his personal safety as they were about something of equal importance in the Information Age, his identity. As they were aware, hackers by the thousands were already attacking the hospital's computers, trying to gain access to Clinton's medical records. So were several hospital employees, aware that getting those records would earn them six-figure payments from supermarket tabloids.

The ruse was successful. Clinton's records remained safe from prying eyes. However, at the same time there were plenty of non-hackers who had legitimate access to the most intimate medical details of the former President's life. These included cardiac specialists from all over the country, consulted on how best to proceed with Clinton's heart operation, downloading the information to their computers to provide long-distance diagnoses. They also included clerks at his health insurance company downloading information to underwrite whatever payments they would make to the hospital, pharmacists filling his prescriptions and hospital officials updating his records with the details of his latest medical treatment.

The incident is instructive. It illustrates the double-edged sword that modern information technology has become. Technology has made daily life much more convenient, but it has also provided the means to keep track of and control people. It is an unprecedented tool with momentous implications for espionage.

It all began quietly enough during the 1960s with the development of the microchip, the technological innovation that few could have guessed would be so revolutionary. The tiny chip permitted the development of very powerful computers of small size with the capability to store large amounts of data that could be retrieved instantly. It was a godsend for such governmental tasks as collection of taxes and preparing millions of old age pension checks every month. However, it had a dangerous implication. All that data stored in computer memories – school records, military records, criminal records, credit information, employment records – is retrievable. What the government collects in the name of greater efficiency is available to the government for other purposes. With just a single identification marker (in the United States of America most commonly a Social Security number), the government can create an instant dossier on anyone with a stroke on a computer keyboard.

The simple truth is that individual privacy is now largely a thing of the past. We live in a surveillance society, in which even ordinary transactions subject people to intrusion into their lives. The use of a bank card will result in a computer check of the user's bank account to determine if the account has sufficient funds. Tiny chips in credit cards will tell a computer the user's basic identity information (address, etc.) and credit rating. Shopping in an upscale store will result in constant monitoring by video surveillance cameras, as will all ordinary transactions in a bank. Gambling in a casino, even at a 25-cent slot machine, will be surveilled by hidden cameras. A gambler's 'rewards card' issued by the casino will contain computer chips that tell the casino how much money he gambles, his creditworthiness and which games he plays, information used to determine the level of 'comps' (complimentary amenities such as free hotel rooms) the casino needs to extend to lure the gambler into returning. Many cities, particularly London, have TV surveillance cameras to monitor high-crime areas on behalf of the police.

YOU ARE BEING WATCHED

Almost all modern surveillance technology was born as a tool of espionage, especially the high-speed computers first developed with government funding to process the huge amount of communications intelligence collected by the U.S. National Security Agency (NSA) and its chief partner, the British Government Communications Headquarters (GCHQ). Both organizations grew out of the cryptanalytical successes of World War II. However, the postwar communications explosion –

LEFT: Modern airport security is a prime example of the array of intelligence governments maintain on their citizens.

teletypes, fax machines, microwave-relayed telephone systems, computer-to-computer data transfers – soon overwhelmed the capacity to process it all. Thus, the birth of high-speed computers, an instrument that presented the opportunity to gather even more intelligence. That potential reached full flowering one morning in the spring of 1971, when the Russians noticed a new American spy satellite overflying the Soviet Union. Code-named HEXAGON, the satellite (nicknamed 'Big Bird' by the Americans) was a 55-foot-long monster weighing 15 tons. Given its relatively low operating altitude, around 90 miles, and geosynchronous orbit, the Russians assumed it was designed to photograph ground targets.

Indeed it was, with two advanced cameras that could distinguish objects as small as eight inches in diameter from 100 miles up, but the Russians didn't know Big Bird also had advanced electronic detection gear aboard, capable of sucking up every electronic transmission within its reach, even including local telephone calls. Two years later, when a CIA agent approached the KGB and offered to sell the secrets of U.S. spy satellites, the Russians were astounded to learn that Big Bird had been peeking into the full spectrum of their communications.

The take from Big Bird, and an even more advanced successor generation of sigint satellites, was downlinked into vast arrays of satellite tracking dishes and radomes at the GCHQ station at Menwith Hill, near Harrogate, England, and to an equivalent NSA site at Fort Meade, Maryland. To process the mountain of electronic data such satellites as Big Bird collected, high-speed computers were indispensable, especially when equipped with still another innovation, so-called 'discrimination capability'. More familiar as the 'search' feature on home computers, the technology allowed a computer to be programmed to search a very large amount of data for a specific piece of information – a word, a phrase, a name – and retrieve it in a matter of seconds. For example, assume American intelligence was interested in the development of new nuclear warheads at the nuclear testing site in Petrovsk. The comint collected in the Soviet Union would be fed through a computer programmed to select any message

that mentioned the term 'Petrovsk', references that might reveal evidence of shipments of particular technology to the site, as well as any potential orders dispatching specialists there, etc.

These developments revolutionized signals intelligence, but they also carried two serious implications that remain problematical to this day. One involved the inability of nations with such capability, especially the United States and Great Britain, to resist temptation: technology that swept up every electronic transmission within reach meant collecting a lot of chaff with the wheat. However, that chaff included the communications of ordinary citizens and political dissidents. Examples include the NSA's tapping into overseas phone calls made by American anti-war activists visiting North Vietnam during the 1960s.

The second, and more serious, implication came about after 9/11. The war on terror put a premium on signals intelligence, since the prime target was the communication network among terrorist cells. Unlike the days of the Cold War, however, there were very few fixed targets; instead, there were layers of multiple communications, including cellphones. To get at it, comint collection was broadened to sweep through the entire electronics spectrum, gathering great mountains of data for the computers to search.

Other, subsidiary, operations prowled among electronic bank records and international money transfers, searching for the movement of terrorist funds. Known as 'data mining', this kind of wide net has no end of legal complications. This is especially true in the United States, because it gives the government untrammeled power to pore through the private communications and records of all its citizens and to decide, arbitrarily and without warrant, how many of those citizens will be targeted.

How many of their individual freedoms ordinary people will be willing to sacrifice in the name of security against terrorism remains to be seen. Already they have consented to a drastic curtailment of their civil rights for the privilege of flying in an airplane – searches of their luggage, metal detectors, X-ray 'virtual strip searches', probes by infrared detectors to spot certain kinds of explosive material. However, the real test will come when they will be asked to accept what many security experts regard as inevitable – tamper-proof national identity cards with chips that would include the holder's medical records, personal information, driving record and police record, if any. Even Orwell, in his darkest moments, had not thought of that one.

THE AGE OF THE CYBERSPIES

As night fell on January 17, 1991, electronic circuits in computers all over Iraq came alive, readying the radar networks, missile batteries, and command centers for the blow certain to come.

ABOVE: The humble computer chip has changed espionage in ways that would have been inconceivable in the years preceding its introduction.

LEFT: The seal of
the United States'
National Security
Agency: the most
potent force in
the world of
cyberespionage.

The deadline pronounced by President George H. W. Bush for Iraq to end its occupation of Kuwait had arrived, and in the face of defiance by Saddam Hussein, there was now no doubt that the full military might of the United States and its allies was about to be unleashed against the Iraqi president's regime.

The prospect of an assault by the world's greatest military power caused the Iraqi dictator little concern. "The mother of all battles," as he put it, was certain to result in an Iraqi victory – or, at least, a bloody stalemate in which his enemies would suffer such grievous casualties, they would settle for some sort of compromise peace.

Saddam can be forgiven for such optimism, for decades of relentless militarization – fueled by a vast arsenal of Soviet-supplied weapons, the aid of hundreds of Soviet military advisers, and the latest in Soviet military technology – had resulted in the creation of the world's fourth largest army and advanced military technology the equal of any other nation. Moreover, the regime's military operated in a cloak of absolute secrecy, enshrouded in a vast internal security apparatus that liked to boast that not even a stray cockroach escaped its attention.

But Hussein was unaware that there were actually hundreds of American spies in Iraq busily at work that February night. The result was one of the more stunning triumphs in the history of intelligence.

It began along the border of Iraq and Saudi Arabia, where a line of state-of-the-art radar pickets guarded by batteries of anti-aircraft missiles and anti-aircraft guns was poised to warn Baghdad of the approach of coalition warplanes. Suddenly, eight American Ah-64 Apache helicopters swooped in undetected, firing Hellfire missiles with a precision that destroyed all the radar stations. That was followed by further precise missile strikes that eliminated the missile batteries, then 30-cal. cannon fire that wiped out the anti-aircraft batteries and their crews. In a matter of four minutes, a 20-mile-wide gap was ripped in the Iraqi air defense system. Through that gap would pour some 900 coalition warplanes that, in 38 days, smashed the Iraqi military machine to pieces. To the dismay of the Iraqis,

the attacking planes seemed to have perfect knowledge of just which targets to hit. Even worse, the Iraqi military communication system's computers seemed to be open books to the coalition; coded operational orders were checkmated by countermoves the moment they were transmitted.

It was all the work of the American spies. Not people, but tiny microcircuits lurking inside the computers of Iraq's military communications system. How did they get there? That story begins with a close friendship some years before between William Friedman, America's premier codebreaker, and senior executives of Crypto AG, a Swiss manufacturer of the most advanced cryptographic machines available on the open market. After Friedman's death, several officials of the National Security Agency (NSA) continued the relationship. By the 1980s, the customers for Crypto AG's very strong cryptographic systems used in military communications included Iraq. The company was in the business of making money, but continuing to sell its technology to the increasingly odious Saddam regime was making the company's executives uneasy. Their sympathetic American friends at NSA had a solution: we'll keep track of how those machines are being used by the Iraqis by allowing us to implant so-called "trapdoor" computer chips in them. Crypto AG agreed, and machines shipped to Baghdad had hidden spies inside: microcircuits programmed to reveal all the machines' signals the moment they were turned on. In February, 1991, the NSA tapped into those electronic spies to make the Iraqi military an open book.

The brilliant success of this operation marked still another revolution in espionage, for it revealed the tremendous advantage an intelligence organization would gain if it could achieve access into an adversary's computer systems. With the advent of the Information Age, the computer had become ubiquitous, the essential tool used by governments for everything from monitoring water supply systems to ballistic missile command and control. In other words, a great treasure chest of secrets to be ferreted out by a new breed of intelligence operatives, the cyberspies.

It also marked a watershed in the decades-long debate between "techies" and "humanoids," the argument whether

ABOVE: George Blake was eventually discovered and imprisoned in the UK, but managed to escape and fled to the Soviet Union.

contain ambiguity. Is it possible that an important asset has been doubled by the other side? Are the secret documents he is handing over actually carefully cooked frauds?

In the event of treason for cash, is it possible a traitor is simply making things up to keep the money machine going? Intelligence agencies spend much time and personnel sifting and resifting their human sources to determine the answers to such questions, a process that can lead into the labyrinth counterintelligence agents like to call the "wilderness of mirrors," the often dizzying forays into suspected deception and counter-deception. That labyrinth occasionally takes some odd byways, such as the careful study by the KGB in 1963 of its star British asset, Kim Philby, that concluded he was unquestionably a double agent for MI6, and the conviction by some MI5 officers that Prime Minister Harold Wilson and the director of MI5, Roger Hollis, were Soviet agents.

Human intelligence operations often are plagued with unforeseen complexities. Consider, for example, the dilemma faced in 1960 by Sergei Kondrashev, among the KGB's premier agent handlers. Kondrashev was control agent for the KGB's prize asset in Great Britain, an MI6 officer named George Blake. One day, Blake informed Kondrashev that he had been assigned to keep notes during meetings of a joint MI6–CIA task force planning intelligence-gathering operations against the Soviet military nerve center in East Berlin. That was sensational enough, but Blake had even more stunning intelligence to impart: the British and Americans were digging a tunnel under the city's east-west border to tap into the underground communications lines used by the Soviet military to transmit its most sensitive messages – lines the Soviets believed were absolutely secure.

Kondrashev now faced a knotty problem. If the KGB acted on Blake's intelligence and aborted the tunnel operation, that would tip off MI6 and the CIA that someone in the small circle of intelligence officers aware of the operation had betrayed it to the Russians. Inevitably, a molehunt would probably uncover Blake. On the other hand, if the KGB let the tunnel operation go forward, the British and Americans would garner a treasure trove of intelligence on

either human or machine was the best way to collect intelligence. For the moment, technical intelligence has the upper hand. Sparked by the American success In the Persian Gulf war, all intelligence agencies now have extensive programs to spy on other nations' computers, while trying to devise systems to protect their own. But as the adherents of what the CIA calls HUMINT (human intelligence) point out, technical intelligence (and especially computer intelligence) has its limits. For example, in a closed society like North Korea, technical intelligence – satellite reconnaissance, communications intercepts, penetration of command computer systems – can reveal with some precision the current state of its nuclear weapons program. But all that technology cannot reveal what everybody really wants to know: just what are North Korea's intentions for its nuclear weapons? That's inside the heads of Kim Jong Un and his minions, and only a human source with access to their thinking has the answer.

True enough, the technical adherents admit, but the fact is that all human intelligence operations invariably the Soviet military. Kondrashev opted for the lesser evil: let the tunnel operation alone to protect a prized asset, a decision not shared with the Soviet military. For a year, the Berlin tunnel collected a small ocean of valuable military intelligence until the KGB decided the game had gone on long enough; East German border guards "accidentally" discovered the tunnel and closed it down. Furious Soviet military leaders berated the KGB for allowing their secrets to flow westward, arguing that the high price of protecting an intelligence asset wasn't worth it.

The more serious problem with human intelligence is its misuse by policymakers to buttress preconceptions in the absence of unambiguous technical intelligence. The most glaring modern example is the case of CURVEBALL, code name for an Iraqi refugee who approached western intelligence agencies in 2004 and offered an intelligence blockbuster. He claimed to have worked at a super-secret facility in Iraq that produced large amounts of biological warfare agents. Further, the Saddam regime had developed mobile biological warfare trucks, in which biowar weapons could be produced for immediate battlefield use. He even drew detailed sketches of such trucks. Obviously, the implications of such weapons in Saddam's hands were momentous.

All music to the ears of U.S. Vice President Dick Cheney, who was pressing President George W. Bush to invade Iraq and eliminate the grave threat of what he called "weapons of mass destruction." Although American technical intelligence could find no sign that Saddam had any such weapons, Cheney was convinced they existed, arguing that intelligence's failure to find any evidence simply meant the Iraqis had hidden their weapons so well, they were nearly impossible to spot. CURVEBALL was clinching proof, Cheney argued, that those weapons indeed existed.

In turn, he convinced President Bush, and the ultimate result was a military invasion that got rid of Saddam Hussein and his regime, but created a mess the Americans are still trying to clean up. To America's eternal embarrassment, no weapons of mass destruction were found – for the simple reason that they didn't exist. That led to a reappraisal of CURVEBALL and the disturbing discovery he had made it all up. As he admitted, he actually had worked in a fertilizer factory near Baghdad, a circumstance he converted into a biological warfare complex. And those mobile biological warfare trucks? He made that up, too. His motive: get intelligence agencies to pay him a lot of money for his "revelations."

To the techies, it was all further proof, if needed, that the days of classic cloak and dagger spy were over. They could point to an entire Aladdin's Cave of technological wonders capable of performing all the tasks of espionage quickly and efficiently – and with little risk to humans. Further,

technically gathered intelligence is scientifically neutral; if a spy satellite or a drone spots a deployment of dozens of tanks on a tense border, that's an incontrovertible fact not subject to doubt. There's little reason, it was argued, to go through all the trouble of trying to infiltrate spies into a hostile environment when such marvels as American spy satellites can do the job from 100 miles up with no risk. And with superior precision: modern high-resolution color photography can be transmitted in real time, thanks to the digital revolution.

Just how good that resolution is remains highly classified, but some sense of quality can be divined from just one photograph snapped by the American Corona satellite some years ago over Leningrad (now St. Petersburg). That photograph includes a man sitting in the back of

ABOVE: U.S. Vice President Dick Cheney was one of the high-ranking American officials notably duped by the CURVEBALL incident.

his house reading a newspaper – whose headlines are clearly readable.

But the real superweapon of modern espionage is the computer, a wondrous technology that is an essential part of modern life. Each day, trillions upon trillions of electronic signals from computers fly through the ether, and as intelligence agencies learned very quickly, what can be transmitted can be intercepted. And they also realized that a computer's greatest utility – its ability to store mountains of data in electronic form – is also vulnerable to espionage if access can be gained to a computer's innards. As governments and military organizations shifted communications and data storage to computers, their adversaries also shifted, reorienting their technical intelligence resources to gain access to computer-to-computer transmissions and the banks of data storage. By the beginning of the modern era, there was hardly a nation anywhere in the world that had not developed at least some ability to spy on another nation's computers.

Even a small nation like North Korea, however bereft of resources, managed to create a flourishing cyberespionage capability. In 1995, the North Koreans created Unit 121, an adjunct of the General Bureau of Reconnaissance (GBR), which oversees foreign intelligence and clandestine operations. Unit 121, devoted solely to cyberespionage, recruited students directly out of elementary schools; they were chosen on the basis of their aptitude for mathematics, computer science, and chess. Given military ranks, they were provided with a privileged existence and 12-hour days of relentless training in computer espionage on the most up to date computers.

By 2014, North Korea had a full-fledged cyberespionage capability, with nearly 6,000 personnel working in Unit 121. Very little was known about that capability until November of that year, when the Sony Pictures Corporation released the *The Interview*, a comic movie about two feckless Americans who visit North Korea. The movie included scenes that mocked North Korean dictator Kim Jong Un. Infuriated, Kim ordered Unit 121 into action. On November 24, computers at Sony's New York headquarters suddenly came under attack by an entity calling itself "Guardians of Peace" (actually Unit 121 cyberspies). In short order, over 100 terabytes of data were wrenched out of those computers, ten times the data contained in the U.S. Library of Congress. The data included the emails and sensitive personnel files of senior Sony executives, actors, and producers – much to Sony's embarrassment when the contents were leaked to media outlets. An FBI forensics team discovered unmistakable digital "fingerprints" indicating the attack came from North Korea.

Judged one way, the North Korean attack was not regarded as an especially great achievement. Like most private businesses, Sony's computers have the conventional anti-virus protection software common to home and commercial machines, a minimal roadblock useless against a sophisticated cyber attack from without. But it can be safely assumed that North Korea has not spent 19 years and all those resources merely to be able to hack into a movie studio's computers.

North Korea is rapidly moving into the first rank of cyberespionage, long dominated by the more elaborate and extensive cyberespionage operations run by the major intelligence behemoths – the United States, China, and Russia – that have created huge, sprawling operations to target computers worldwide. Virtually all important government or private industry computer systems have come under attack at some point, seeking the vast array of secrets they contain. In response, governments have devised ever more complex encryption systems to balk such attacks, creating an ever-evolving digital arms race between attack and defense.

As some governments have discovered, to their cost, even the most advanced encryption systems are vulnerable to increasingly sophisticated attacks. One striking example involved an encryption program, Acid Cryptofiler. First developed by the French military to protect their most highly classified traffic, the French in 2017 became aware the program had been compromised by a virus known as Rocra, which introduced malware into the French computers and stripped away the encryption. French computer experts were shocked to discover the malware had first infected their computers in 2011, which meant whoever carried out the attack had been reading France's most sensitive secrets for six years.

The "whoever" almost certainly was Russia, known to have an extensive cyberespionage operation, with one section targeted specifically against the computer systems of European military organizations. Officially, Russia claims that any cyberspying that originates in their country is strictly the work of local, independent hackers who have no connection whatsoever with the government. But no one believes that a group of young hackers in 2017, armed only with laptops, were capable of such feats as penetrating the computers of the Czech Republic's Ministry of Defense, Ministry of Foreign Affairs and the headquarters of the country's armed forces in a sophisticated assault that not only stole classified information, but also the personnel records of all the country's government employees. Nor is it susceptible to belief that these hackers alone were responsible for a major cyberespionage operation in 2018, which attacked government computers in the Ukraine, stealing all the data in the machines (for good measure, the same operation hacked into social media with "fake news" reporting that the Ukrainian government had infected the Black Sea with bacteria to cause cholera). In fact, the hackers worked for the Russian military and government, having been enlisted years before. In effect, the Russian hackers work as something like independent contractors, supported and paid by a government that doesn't officially recognize their existence.

As the Russians are aware, all users of home and business computers know the dangers from so-called Trojans (malware), viruses, and spam to their machines. These threats are easily blocked by conventional anti-virus software, but in the major leagues of cyberespionage, malware and other offensive weapons are thousands of times more sophisticated and require equally sophisticated defenses. One notorious example involves a complex Russian malware known as Flame that, in the mid-2000s, was launched against carefully targeted and vetted computers used by government agencies, diplomatic missions, and aerospace agencies in North America and Western Europe. Nearly 300 computers were found to be infected by what computer experts regard as the most sophisticated malware ever devised. Flame is a mammoth program of over 20 megabytes in size and 650,000 lines of code that usually enters a computer via infected email – but that's just the beginning. Once into the computer, Flame is programmed to extract specific information that is sent back to the cyberspies who dispatched the malware. Like Rocra, Flame was discovered to be a Russian cyberespionage operation, since its forensics match known Russian methods. Those methods involve a patient effort to find vulnerabilities in a computer, then slowly introduce the malware. At first, the malware extracts small bits of information as a test, to determine if the invasion has been detected. If there are no indications, then the malware runs at full blast, emptying the computer of whatever data it contains.

Although Russian cyberespionage operations are very extensive and advanced, Chinese cyberespionage is now ranked as nearly its equal. Like Russia, China has formed a huge cyberesopionage operation that targets government computers around the world, with special emphasis on the United States. Beginning in 2000, the Americans became aware of a full court press by the Chinese against the computers of U.S. defense contractors, with the goal of extracting classified technical data to aid its own military. Before the Americans could harden those computers against the Chinese cyberspying, the Chinese had managed to extract the technical data for the American F-35 jet fighter plane, the most advanced in the world. Less than two years after that attack, the Chinese flew their own advanced fighter plane that was very nearly an exact copy of the F-35, complete with its advanced electronics.

The Chinese cyberspies also carried out an even more sophisticated attack, this one aimed at something called COREU, the European Union's Telex-based communications network used to send classified diplomatic messages. Although the network is protected by encryption, the Chinese were able to infiltrate it and crack the codes in the process of extracting thousands of diplomatic cables. Of particular value to the Chinese were cables that reflected the growing tension between the European Union and U.S. President Donald Trump, a man for whom the Chinese have a special animus. Chinese officials were delighted to learn that the Europeans were so exasperated with Trump, they seriously considered the idea of bypassing him and working directly with the U.S. Congress. The Chinese then arranged for a leak about those cables to major news organizations, a leak that especially irritated Trump, much to their satisfaction. At the same time, the Chinese cyberspies, with some hesitation, showed one intercepted cable to China's President Xi Jinping that reported Xi privately telling the Europeans that he had become totally frustrated by Trump, who he described as "A bully engaged in a no-rules freestyle boxing match." Xi was not happy to see his presumed private conversation bandied about in a diplomatic cable.

At the apex of contemporary cyberespionage stands the giant NSA (currently staffed by more than 30,000 employees and with a $10 billion annual budget), which was first off the mark in recognizing the key role the computer revolution would play in intelligence. In 1987, the agency created an entirely new division known as Tailored Access Operations, which concentrated on developing specific tools to target various types of computers, ranging from ordinary home desktops to big mainframe computers. To staff it, the NSA went recruiting among the new generation of young computer nerds and hackers. NSA wisely did not try to fit many of these free spirits and rebels into the standard bureaucratic mold. Instead, the new employees were given lavish salaries and the kind of free rein they preferred (the typical working conditions at places like Google and Microsoft) – such as the young man who rode a unicycle around the office while practicing his juggling and another who commuted to work on his skateboard. They were encouraged in independent thought, to "think outside the box" in devising original solutions to the challenge of penetrating other people's computers.

By 2000, NSA had 215 of these busy minds working in a new 400,000 square foot building listed on NSA's organization chart as the Remote Operations Center. The bland title concealed a busy beehive of cyberespionage that included hacking into computers worldwide, collecting "voice cuts" from terrorists' cell phones, and infecting the email of terrorist organizations with Trojans. They operated under the office motto, "Your data is our data, your equipment is our equipment – any time, any place by any legal means." As the motto indicated, NSA's young cyberspies believe that no computer system exists they cannot hack – or destroy, if necessary.

How successful NSA's cyberspies have been is highly classified, although several clues occasionally emerge. One 2000 operation that became publicly known, code-named WINTER LIGHT, was a joint effort with Britain's GCHQ and the FRA, the cyberespionage arm of Sweden, through which much Russian cyber traffic moves. The operation aimed at secretly implanting malware on a Russian computer or a computer network that diverted signals between computers and the internet via "rogue" high-speed surveillance servers, known in NSA parlance as "FoxAcid." This amazing technology gave NSA access to a target's computer data, and even the means to tamper with that data as it moved from one computer to another. Other technology, known as "tipping," set up implants on targeted computers that redirected their signals to surveillance servers, which allowed NSA and GCHQ to access all the data on those computers. WINTER LIGHT was supplemented by a GCHQ operation code-named TEMPORA that tapped into the transatlantic fiber optic cables that carry vast amounts of computer and other data between Europe and North America.

Along with Great Britain, America's key ally in its cyberespionage efforts is Israel, which has a growing ability in that area, a capability hinted at by Israel's Vice Prime Minister and Minister of Strategic Affairs Moshe Ya'alon – the man apparently in charge of his country's cyberespionage efforts – during a speech on the subject of cyberspying in which he said, "Israel is blessed to be a nation possessing superior technology, which opens up all kinds of possibilities." That has been interpreted as an underscore to reports of the increasing numbers of personnel and facilities Israel is devoting to cyberespionage. The Israelis are already the premier cyberspies in the Middle East, although not much is known publicly about any successes they may have carried out. There is one exception, a cyberespionage operation about which a great deal is known. That operation marked still another watershed in the history of cyberespionage, for it not only sought to penetrate an adversary's computers, but also to destroy them – a possible forecast of the future of cyberespionage transformed into actual cyberwar.

It was called STUXNET, a joint operation of the NSA and Israeli intelligence. The target was Iran's nuclear weapons program, a matter of paramount concern to both the Americans and the Israelis. The initial objective was to penetrate the computers used by the Iranian program to determine just how far the Iranians had managed to progress in their efforts to develop and deploy nuclear weapons. STUXNET was only 500 kilobytes in size, but was astonishingly sophisticated, the probable result of years of work by computer programmers. In 2010, infiltrated into the computers used by the Iranian nuclear program, STUXNET paid immediate dividends in terms of intelligence, and in the process detected a major weakness in the Iranian system that could be exploited to actually sabotage the entire program. The vulnerability lay in the industrial software systems the Iranians were using, bought from Siemens in the world market. That meant the software's code was publicly known, and the Americans and Israelis got the idea of using STUXNET for cyberwar. The Siemens software was used to run the Iranian nuclear program's expensive nuclear centrifuges that spin around the clock to produce the enriched weapons-grade plutonium for nuclear weapons. STUXNET was ordered to sabotage those centrifuges by infiltrating the Siemens software. Horrified Iranian technicians watched as their expensive centrifuges spun out of control from some mysterious malfunction they could not stop; hundreds of centrifuges became just so much junk. Meanwhile, other STUXNET-produced viruses infected the computers of the Iranian National Oil Company and Iran's Ministry of Petroleum, seriously disrupting Iran's vital oil industry.

Ultimately, the Iranians discovered their computers had been violated and they exerted major efforts to ensure nothing like STUXNET ever occurred again. But the damage had been done; Iran's nuclear program had been set back by at least several years. The setback played no small role in the Iranian decision later to reach an accommodation with the U.S. and the Europeans to at least delay any further nuclear weapons development.

Lurking in all this cyberespionage is an aspect of growing importance: the ability of continually advancing interception and hacking technology to suck up all computer and wireless communications. It is a question of some urgency in democracies, where there are legal barriers to a government snooping on its citizens without warrant. Nothing better illustrates that problem than a controversial NSA program code-named PRISM.

Simply, PRISM is a huge vacuum cleaner that sucks up every electronic signal it can reach, much like a miner panning a stream to find gold nuggets among sand and rocks. PRISM was born in new anti-terror legislation after 9/11 that greatly expanded NSA's mandate to include just about any target considered useful in the "war on terror." Significantly, that very wide net included the electronic signals of major internet companies and social media. Reduced to its basic form, the idea behind PRISM is to collect mountains of electronic impulses to be fed into giant mainframe computers programmed to filter out anything of intelligence interest. The problem, of course, is that PRISM is in effect looking over everyone's shoulder, reading their email, looking at what pictures they're posting on Facebook, and what they're researching on Google, all in the name of trying to determine who's working with terrorists or in contact with a hostile power. Additionally, PRISM spies on internet metadata, cloud-stored files, and geolocation data (IP addresses). It can also request, without warrant, access to cell phone companies by the simple expedient of claiming such intrusion is necessary in the name of national security. The implications are obvious:

BELOW: The Predator drone encapsulates the current era of cyberespionage and remotely conducted warfare.

a government intelligence agency with the capacity to spy on all its citizens – the perfect tool for tyranny.

PRISM was NSA's darkest secret, and would have remained so were it not for one of its hackers, a 29-year-old NSA employee named Edward Snowden. Since he had worked on PRISM, Snowden was perfectly aware of what NSA was doing, especially its widespread spying on ordinary Americans. One day in 2013, he watched a televised congressional hearing on the subject of NSA's operations against terrorists and heard Director of National Intelligence James Clapper assure the committee that the NSA operations did not include domestic spying on innocent Americans. A flat-out lie, and Snowden apparently was instantly radicalized. "I don't want to live in a society that does these sorts of things," he said later by way of explaining why he decided then to approach a journalist from the *Guardian* and reveal everything he knew about PRISM.

His revelations created a firestorm, and an angry U.S. government vowed to have Snowden charged with a lengthy list of violations, treason among them. Before the government could get its hands on him, however, Snowden fled the U.S. to Hong Kong, then to Russia, where he has been living ever since at a Moscow airport, awaiting a decision whether the Russians will grant him political asylum. The Russians have ignored U.S. requests for his extradition, but at the same time they have done nothing about Snowden's request for asylum. (It is unknown whether he has provided any sensitive information to Russian intelligence).

The practical effect of Snowden's revelations remains to be seen. There are ongoing efforts in the U.S. Congress to rein in NSA's pervasive "dragnet surveillance," and cell phone giants Verizon, AT&T and Sprint are fighting NSA's scooping up of all their telephone records. Additionally, Apple has defied a NSA request to turn over the keys to its encryption software, while Microsoft, Google, and Yahoo! have asked Congress to end the legal compulsion under the 2001 Patriot

Act to hand over user data to the government. Ultimately, the probability is that the entire controversy will wind up in the U.S. Supreme Court, which will have to address a question it has faced a number of times before in its long history: to what extent can the government intrude on Fourth Amendment protections in the name of national security?

While all this has been going on, what of the traditional cloak and dagger spies? To a certain extent, they've been downgraded in favor of technology. But rampant technology is not the sole reason. For one thing, there is a paucity of the master agent handlers who once spent years of patiently nurturing a source, protecting him, and reassuring him in times of greatest danger. Agent-handling is an art, and requires an investment of years of effort to hone the fine skills of supervising human beings in an activity that means their death if caught. A close look at the major assets recruited by intelligence services during the past few decades reveals that almost all of them were not patiently recruited and developed, but "walk-ins," people who simply contacted an intelligence service to volunteer as spies for one reason or another.

Even Russian intelligence, renowned for years for an entire pantheon of brilliant agent recruiters and handlers who enlisted a long list of valuable assets, no longer seems to be developing that kind of talent. Several years ago, Oleg Gordievsky, a KGB official recruited by MI6, revealed to his surprised MI6 debriefers that his fellow officers in the current generation were universally lazy careerists who spent their time inventing false intelligence reports and pocketing the money supposedly used to pay assets they recruited.

What, then, have the cloak and dagger types been doing? Largely they've gotten into the murder business. Assassination – or "executive action," to use the prim CIA term – has been a tool used by governments for many years to solve certain intractable political problems, such as political exiles who threaten a government from without. The dirty work is assigned to intelligence agencies so as to avoid the government's fingerprints; as a general role of statecraft, governments are not supposed to murder people they don't like.

There is a long and bloody record of such killing – murders by Soviet intelligence of White Russian exile activists, killings by Nazi Germany of anti-Nazi exiles, assassinations of prominent Chinese Communists by Nationalists, and so on. But by the end of World War II, assassination as a weapon fell into disfavor – until the modern era, when it was suddenly revived. The main proponent (and master) of such operations was Israel, whose Mossad intelligence service developed an unparalleled talent for carrying out Israel's policy of murder to defeat the myriad threats it faced. It began in 1972, when Mossad was ordered to track down and kill the Palestinian perpetrators of the massacre of Israeli athletes during the Olympics in Munich. Mossad perfected the art of assassination to a degree never seen before. Hit teams of Mossad agents composed of specialists that ranged from agents adept in the use of commercial cover to surveillance experts and the actual killers who often used unconventional means (such as planting a bomb in a target's telephone that blew up when he dialed a particular number).

Mossad also carried out assassinations designed to nip incipient threats in the bud – such as murdering the key leaders of Syria's development of nuclear weapons, killing leading nuclear scientists assigned to Iran's nuclear weapons program, assassinating Hamas militants. The brilliant success of these operations convinced other nations that they, too, could solve certain political problems the same way. But lacking Mossad's expertise and experience, the results were decidedly mixed. The CIA's comic opera attempts to kill Fidel Castro led to new U.S. laws banning any such future "executive action" by the agency. Vladimir Putin ordered his spies to murder several dissidents living overseas, but the agents who conducted the assassinations left a trail a mile wide that led right back to Moscow. Of particular note was the botched attempt on former GRU officer Sergei Skripal's life in Salisbury, England. Not only did the attempted poisoning via a nerve agent fail, it resulted in the unintentional death of a British civilian, and subsequently the expulsion of more than 150 Russian diplomats from the UK and its allies.

Perhaps the most botched operation of all involved the murder by Saudi Arabian intelligence of an exiled dissident in the Saudi consulate in Istanbul, Turkey, a tragic farce in which Saudi agents somehow overlooked the fact that the fiancée of the dissident, Jamal Khashoggi, was waiting outside the consulate for him to return. Also overlooked was the fact that Turkey, as a bitter rival of Saudi Arabia, undoubtedly had the consulate under close surveillance; indeed, they had planted bugs in the very room where Khashoggi was killed.

Given such "blowback," as the CIA likes to call it, there is now a general trend for intelligence agencies only to provide the necessary intelligence for such operations, which are carried out by the military. The CIA and NSA provided the necessary intelligence to track down Osama bin Laden, but his murder was carried out by U.S. SEALs. In the war on terror, the U.S. military, does the actual killing of radical Islamist leaders. Often, the weapon of choice is the Predator drone, a technical marvel with television cameras that track targets; live pictures are dispatched many miles away to a controller, who orders the drone to fire its Hellfire missiles.

Yet another innovation in the ever-changing world of intelligence. Which raises the question: where does espionage go from here? One clue can be found in the rare public speech of MI6 Direction Alex Younger in December, 2018. Younger outlined a future of intelligence as the "fourth generation of espionage," which he said will be a fusion of traditional human skills with "accelerated technological innovation." Technological change, he said, as well as the degree of interconnectedness, has made the world dramatically more complicated, and that will profoundly change espionage's operating environment.

True enough, as a general statement, but the real essence of espionage was best summarized by General Samuel Wilson of the U.S. Defense Intelligence Agency several years ago when he was asked what intelligence was supposed to accomplish. "We can't tell you what God is going to do next week," he replied, "but I like to think we can tell you when He is getting mad."

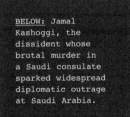

BELOW: Jamal Kashoggi, the dissident whose brutal murder in a Saudi consulate sparked widespread diplomatic outrage at Saudi Arabia.

SCORPION TONGUES

ON MARCH 14, 1967, THE ROME DAILY NEWSPAPER *PAESE SERA*, A RABIDLY ANTI-AMERICAN FAR-LEFT TABLOID, REPORTED THAT A THEN-DEFUNCT COMMERCIAL ENTERPRISE KNOWN AS CENTRO MONDIALE COMMERCIALE (CMC) HAD, IN FACT, BEEN A CIA FRONT TO FUNNEL FUNDS INTO ITALY FOR "ESPIONAGE ACTIVITIES" AGAINST THE ITALIAN GOVERNMENT.

It was only the latest in a long string of *Paese Sera* articles alleging assorted CIA plots in Italy. At least some Italians regarded the CMC "expose" as fact, although Italian authorities and mainstream newspapers derided it as nonsense. CMC, they noted, was hardly nefarious: created in the early 1960s by American and Italian businessmen as an initial step toward a European Common Market, it failed in its goal of making Rome the centre of that market and ended operations in 1962. However, lurking in the article was a ticking time bomb, and when it exploded, something new and odious in modern espionage had been born – with consequences that resonate to this day.

The time bomb was an assertion in the article that the CIA's point man in the alleged CMC espionage operation was Clay Shaw, a prominent New Orleans businessman who had been the head of the New Orleans Trade Mart. A copy of the *Paese Sera* article somehow found its way into the hands of New Orleans District Attorney Jim Garrison. Here was confirmation, Garrison decided, of his belief that Shaw was a covert CIA agent – and, even worse, the "evil genius" behind a CIA plot that assassinated President John F. Kennedy.

Garrison had no real evidence for this sensational claim, yet in a glare of worldwide publicity he indicted Shaw for conspiring to murder the President of the United States. A jury laughed the case out of court in less than an hour, but the damage had been done. The Shaw case stirred further doubt among many Americans about the Warren Commission's version of the assassination and some years later, the popular Oliver Stone film JFK presented Garrison as a hero whose "truth" about the Kennedy assassination had been suppressed by a CIA cover up. That, in turn, ignited a furious public controversy in which the government found itself trying to convince millions of Americans that it was not an evil spider that murdered presidents. The controversy became so intense that Congress felt compelled to impanel a new investigation of the assassination. It found nothing to substantiate Garrison's claim, but

discussed the various doubts about the official version that spurred further public skepticism. As a result, today public opinion polls reveal that most Americans believe Kennedy was assassinated by some sort of conspiracy, probably carried out by the CIA.

All of which was of immense satisfaction to the real progenitors of the *Paese Sera* article, Service A of the Soviet KGB, which had fed it into the newspaper via Communist contacts. The Russians had fired the opening shot of a new weapon in modern espionage – infect the minds of adversaries by sowing confusion, suspicion, and distrust of a government, the better to weaken it.

The KGB called this technique "active measures," modeled on the successful British "black propaganda" operation of World War II that the Russians had carefully studied. The keys to the success of such operations, the KGB concluded, was the appearance of credibility and the careful use of intelligence. That involved taking a kernel of intelligence and enlarging and twisting it into a harmful virus, shaping a credible-sounding story for an audience prepared to believe it. The Shaw incident illustrated how that worked: the KGB was aware Shaw was among thousands of American businessmen who

LEFT: Clay Shaw, the New Orleans businessman who was falsely implicated in the assassination of John F. Kennedy.

RUSSIA CALLING!

routinely shared whatever they had managed to learn during their overseas business trips with the Domestic Contacts Division of the CIA. Enough to work up a tale of Shaw as CIA master spy, heading CIA espionage in Italy.

The mastermind of Service A was one of the KGB's legendary operatives, Yuri Modin, who had been control agent for the agency's prize assets in Great Britain, the "Ring of Five" – H.A.R. Philby, Anthony Blunt, Donald Maclean, Guy Burgess, and John Cairncross. Modin recruited some of the brightest graduates of KGB training schools and set them to work. By the early 1960s, Service A was churning out viruses planted in media outlets all over the world. The U.S. State Department found itself preoccupied with trying to refute dozens of stories planted in foreign newspapers and magazines. Some did significant damage, such as a widely-believed story that Gestapo chief Heinrich Mueller, who had disappeared in Berlin in 1945, in fact had been rescued and recruited by the CIA. Another, planted in African newspapers, claimed to have evidence that Martin Luther King Jr. worked for the CIA to discredit leftist African political leaders.

With the collapse of the Soviet Union, Service A went out of business. But its experts were still around, and they finally found new jobs when Vladimir Putin rose to power. An ex-KGB official, Putin put Service A

back to work, but this time with a new twist: the computer revolution offered unprecedented vistas for "active measures." Service A rounded up every hacker in Russia it could find and set them up in a nondescript St. Petersburg office building with the organizational title of Internet Research Agency. Their target was social media, soon infected with what the Russians called "fake news," bogus sites designed to sow discord. By 2006, the operation reached 126 million computer users, with the U.S. as the prime target.

Ten years later, the Russians took a significant step by widening the operation to include an attempt to influence the outcome of the U.S. presidential election by planting "fake news" blogs and posts by fictional groups to support the candidacy of Donald Trump, favored by Putin over Hillary Clinton. How effective that operation was in terms of influencing voters remains to be determined, but the important point is that a very ominous precedent had been set: even a presidential election is vulnerable to the machinations of modern espionage.

ABOVE: The rise to power of Vladimir Putin in Russia has coincided with a resurgence in the country's "active measures", notably with the advent of "fake news".

GLOSSARY

AGENT: A spy in the pay of a nation's intelligence service on a regular, salaried basis, with the status of government employee.

AGENT OF INFLUENCE: An asset enlisted for the purpose of influencing government policy, rather than collecting intelligence.

ASSET: A foreigner enlisted – either for pay or political conviction – to serve as an intelligence source.

BIGOT LIST: British intelligence term for a list of personnel (usually very restricted) authorized to have full knowledge of a highly compartmentalized operation.

BLACK BAG JOB: FBI term for a break-in or burglary to gain access to secret papers which are then photographed and returned, usually in the same operation. Also used to denote a break-in or burglary to plant electronic surveillance devices.

BLOWN: Arrest of an agent or asset by counterintelligence.

BLOWBACK: CIA parlance for unintended consequences (usually bad) of a failed intelligence operation. Also known as 'flap'.

BOX: Polygraph machine. A polygraph examination is called a 'flutter'.

BRUSH CONTACT: Rapid, apparently accidental, physical contact between an agent or asset and a case officer or control agent during which material is handed over, usually in a crowded public place to balk surveillance.

BUG: Electronic surveillance device.

BURN: Break contact with a suspected double agent. An official notice by an intelligence agency to cease any contact with such a suspected source is called a 'burn notice'.

CASE OFFICER: CIA term for an intelligence agency official assigned supervisory duties for an agent or asset.

CELL: Small unit of spies, part of a larger spy ring.

CHICKEN FEED: Low-level intelligence given to double agents or assets to boost their credibility.

CIPHONY: Use of electronic scrambler devices to protect sensitive telephone conversations.

COBBLER: Russian intelligence term for a skilled forger of passports and other identification documents.

CODE NAME: One-word term used in communications within an intelligence agency to conceal the real identity of an agent or asset (e.g. FARMER or ANTENNA).

COMINT: Acronym for communications intelligence.

COMPARTMENTALIZATION: Restricting knowledge of an intelligence operation to as few people as possible as a security measure.

CONTROL: British intelligence term for a senior intelligence official supervising an agent or a group of agents.

COOKED: False intelligence concocted by an intelligence agency to mislead an enemy.

COUNTRY TEAM: CIA term for a team of agents assigned to operate in a particular country.

COVER: Commercial or other type of employment behind which spies operate to conceal their intelligence collection activities. A well-established cover that offers strong protection to an agent is called 'deep cover'.

COVERT OPERATION: CIA term for an intelligence operation aimed at destabilizing or overthrowing a government.

CRYPTANALYSIS: The process of solving codes and ciphers.

CUTOUT: Use of a middleman between agent and control as a security measure.

DANGLE: Agent or asset falsely offered to an enemy intelligence organization.

DEAD DROP: Site where agents and assets leave and exchange messages with their controls, most often nooks and crannies in public areas.

DISCARD: Agent or asset deliberately sacrificed, usually to deflect attention from a more valuable agent.

DOUBLE AGENT: Agent or asset who professes allegiance to one intelligence agency while secretly working for a competing agency.

ELINT: Acronym for electronic intelligence.

EXECUTIVE ACTION: CIA euphemism for assassination.

EXFILTRATION: Operation to covertly withdraw an endangered agent from enemy territory.

FALSE FLAG: Recruitment of an asset by claiming to represent one agency while in fact actually working for another agency.

FERRET: Seaborne or airborne platform with detection gear to collect electronic signals.

FIST: Distinctive 'touch' of a clandestine radio operator on his keypad.

HARD TARGET: Country difficult to penetrate by an intelligence agency.

HONEYPOT: Blackmail operation using sex.

ILLEGAL: Russian intelligence term for an agent operating under non-diplomatic cover and thus subject to arrest if caught. An agent operating under diplomatic cover is a 'legal'.

LEGEND: Faked biography of an agent to conceal real identity.

LETTERBOX: Asset serving as communications link between agent and control.

MOLE: Agent or asset embedded deep inside an enemy's government or intelligence apparatus.

MUSIC BOX: Clandestine spy radio. An operator of such a radio is a 'musician'.

ONE-TIME PAD: Cipher device that utilizes a pad with sheets of random numbers used to encrypt messages once, then discarded.

PLAYBACK: Use of a captured enemy radio to feed false intelligence.

RAVEN: Male agent trained specifically for honeypot operations.

RING: Group of assets or agents, usually divided into cells. Also called a network.

SAFE HOUSE: Location, usually a house or apartment under an intelligence agency's control, where spies and controls in enemy territory can meet without fear of detection.

SHOE: Forged passport.

SIGINT: Acronym for signals intelligence.

SLEEPER: Agent planted in another country under orders to carry out a normal life and conduct no spying until 'switched on' – usually in the case of hostilities.

STATION: CIA term for an overseas post, usually located in an embassy. In Russian intelligence parlance, it is known as a rezidentura and the agent in charge is known as a rezident.

SWALLOW: Female agent trained specifically for honeypot operations.

TRADECRAFT: Intelligence-gathering methods and security procedures.

TURN: Convince an enemy agent to work for the other side.

WALK-IN: Asset who contacts a foreign intelligence agency and volunteers information or work as a spy in his own country.

WET AFFAIRS: Russian intelligence parlance for assassinations.

PICTURE CREDITS

INDEX